# LAND REFORMS IN INDIA
# VOLUME 10

# LAND REFORMS IN INDIA

This is the tenth volume in a series of studies conducted under the aegis of the Lal Bahadur Shastri National Academy of Administration (LBSNAA), Mussoorie. These studies are an outcome of a research programme entrusted to the LBSNAA by the Ministry of Rural Development, Government of India. The primary aim of this series is to assess the current status of land reforms in India.

The collection of basic data was entrusted to successive batches of probationers of the Indian Administrative Service (IAS). The field of study component was divided into four major sections covering respectively the implementation of land ceiling laws, the status of tenant-cultivators, the progress in allotment of government lands to the poor and landless and the position concerning tribal lands and forest rights. In the process the probationers collected village-level primary data by interviewing landowners, tenants, allottees of surplus lands and tribals, and supplemented this data by consulting land records and other official documents.

This material was processed by the LBSNAA's project core group on land reforms comprising scholars from diverse disciplines. The findings were analysed, refined and integrated into comprehensive all-India and state-level reports which form the bulk of the volumes in the series. In addition, the LBSNAA conducted state-level workshops bringing together administrators, academics, activists and legal experts to explore the various dimensions of land reforms in India.

The series will comprise about 14 volumes in all.

# LAND REFORMS IN INDIA
# VOLUME 10

# Computerisation of Land Records

*Edited by*

## Wajahat Habibullah
## Manoj Ahuja

**Sage Publications**
New Delhi/Thousand Oaks/London

*First published in 2005 by*

**Sage Publications India Pvt Ltd**
B-42, Panchsheel Enclave
New Delhi 110 017
*www.indiasage.com*

**Sage Publications Inc**
2455 Teller Road
Thousand Oaks, California 91320

**Sage Publications Ltd**
1 Oliver's Yard, 55 City Road
London EC1Y 1SP

Published by Tejeshwar Singh for Sage Publications India Pvt Ltd, phototypeset in 10/12 Times by Star Compugraphics Private Limited, Delhi and printed at Chaman Enterprises, New Delhi.


**Library of Congress Cataloging-in-Publication Data**

Computerisation of land records/edited by Wajahat Habibullah, Manoj Ahuja.
     p. cm.—(Land reforms in India; v. 10)
  Includes bibliographical references and index.
    1. Land tenure—India—Data processing. 2. Land titles—India—Data processing. I. Habibullah, Wajahat, 1945–. II. Ahuja, Manoj, 1964–.
III. Title: Computerisation of land records. IV. Series.
    HD876.C66     333.3'0285—dc22     2005     2005007840


**ISBN:**  0-7619-3347-6 (Hb)       81-7829-496-6 (India-Hb)


**Sage Production Team:**  Malathi K. Ramamoorthy, Anamika Mukharji, Neeru Handa and Santosh Rawat

# Contents

## Part II: Digitisation of Cadastral Maps 225

## Part III: Land Information System 297

# List of Tables and Figures

## Tables

# Figures

# Acknowledgements

We take this opportunity to express our gratitude to all those who helped us in conducting the national workshop on 'Computerisation of Land Records', held at the Academy on 23 and 24 November 2001. We are grateful to the Ministry of Rural Development, Government of India for extending moral and material support in undertaking the workshop.

We wish to express our sincere thanks to all the contributors. Without their support, this volume would not have been possible. Our sincere thanks to Sage Publications for bringing out this volume in the form of the Land Reforms Series.

We must also express gratitude to Shri D.S. Mathur, Director, Lal Bahadur Shastri National Academy of Administration, who has provided the support and impetus necessary to carry out this work, and to Shri Binod Kumar, the then Chairman of the Centre for Rural Studies and former Director of the Lal Bahadur Shastri National Academy of Administration for his encouragement and guidance. We also thank all the faculty and staff of the Academy for their cooperation.

We cannot forget the help extended by Dr A.P. Singh, Researcher, Centre for Rural Studies, LBSNAA, in the preparation of this volume and in various other fields at the final stages of publication. No words can adequately acknowledge his debts.

Last but not least we would like to express special thanks to all the members of the Centre for Rural Studies, LBSNAA, for sharing innumerable responsibilities in conducting the workshop and for putting up a team effort in bringing out this volume.

# Editors' Introduction

The basic system of land records in India was developed during the British rule and it has not yet been modified according to the needs and characteristics of present-day requirements. Land records are of great importance to contemporary socio-economic imperatives and their revision and updation are necessary for capturing the changes in social dynamics. The poor nature of land records has also to some extent defeated the land reforms programme.

The Government of India and the state governments have been grappling with the recurring problem of an inadequately maintained land records system. A weak land records system has also been viewed as a systematic weakness. As a result, the Government of India started the centrally sponsored scheme of Computerisation of Land Records (CoLR) in 1988–89 with the main objectives of: (a) creating a database of basic records; (b) facilitating the issue of copies of records; (c) reducing work load by elimination of drudgery of paper work; (d) minimising the possibilities of manipulation of land records; and (e) creating a land management information system. The scheme was 100 per cent funded by the Government of India. The CoLR scheme has involved three agencies: the National Informatics Centre (NIC); Ministry of Rural Development (MoRD); and the state governments. NIC is responsible for upgrading its district centres with the latest hardware, software, terminals and printers to expedite the work of data entry. It is also responsible for creating the software packages and providing training on the software to revenue officials. MoRD provides financial support to the states for site preparation, data-entry work, purchase of capital equipment, and miscellaneous expenditures. The state governments are responsible for data collection, data verification and validation, and distribution of the new records of rights to landowners. It is a fact that after 15 years (1988 to 2003) of efforts, the progress across the country has been highly skewed. Some states have made good progress while other states have lagged behind. This book is an outcome of a National Workshop on 'Computerisation of Land Records' organised by the Centre for Rural Studies of the Lal Bahadur Shastri National Academy of Administration, Mussoorie on 23–24 November 2001. It is divided into three sections (*a*) Computerisation of Land Records; (*b*) Digitisation of Cadastral Maps; and (*c*) Land Information System.

Chapters 1 to 13 constitute Part I. Chapter 1 is jointly authored by S.D. Meena, Vinay Thakur, D.R. Shukla, O.P. Sisodia and S.K. Narula. According to them, the centrally sponsored scheme on Computerisation of Land Records (CoLR) was started in 1988–89 with 100 per cent financial assistance as a pilot project in eight districts/states with a view to removing the problems inherent in the manual system of maintenance and updating of land records and to meet the requirements of various group of users. Later, the scheme was extended to more districts. NIC has conducted the system study and prepared the system requirement, specifications and flow. The design was standardised and implemented in all the states with local variations. The software has been made for generation of updated records of rights (RoR), mutation updating, query support system for DSS (decision support system) at district and *taluk* level, security mechanism, menu-driven backup and recovery procedure and report generation, etc. The latest security tools, namely biometric scanner and smart card, etc., have been used for adding an extra layer of login authenticity and non-repudiation. The Ministry of Rural Development has sanctioned 32 pilot projects on Digitisation of Cadastral Survey Maps covering 21 states. This spatial data will be used for integration with attribute data and other datasets. States like West Bengal, Andhra Pradesh, Karnataka, Tamil Nadu, Sikkim, Orissa, Kerala, Madhya Pradesh, Gujarat, Rajasthan, Goa and Maharashtra have done satisfactory work under the scheme of Computerisation of Land Records. Overall 473 *tehsils*/taluks/blocks have been operational with the distribution of computerised copies of RoR to landowners.

In the second chapter entitled 'Computerisation of Land Records: Inter-state Variations' Manoj Ahuja and A.P. Singh indicate that the states can be categorised into advanced states which have forged ahead of others in e-governance in computerisation of land records. Then, there are the middle-stage states which are close at their heels. In the third category, there are the beginners who are yet to take significant steps in this field.

The issue is: what has made some of the states advanced while others are still struggling. The beginner states have an advantage in that while they are trying to catch up they need not make the same mistakes which the advanced states have made. The beginner states can adopt any successful model suited to their local conditions and infrastructure. Therefore, it is necessary that advanced states should play an important role in computer- isation of land records across the country.

There is considerable diversity between states in the matter of land records they maintain and the details contained in various registers. It is necessary to bring about standardisation in the field. Any system, which is uniform throughout the country, will have its own inherent advantages. Therefore, the advanced states should be involved in developing common land records across the country. Formulating and implementing a National Policy on Land Records is now due.

The third chapter entitled 'Bhoomi: Online Delivery of Record of Rights, Tenancy and Cultivation to Farmers in Karnataka' is written by Subhash Bhatnagar and Rajeev Chawla. The authors discuss the imple- mentation challenges, benefits accrued due to Bhoomi and cost of the project. According to them the revenue department in Karnataka has computerised 20 million records of land ownership of 6.7 million farmers in the state. Previously, farmers had to seek out the village accountant to get a copy of the Record of Rights, Tenancy and Cultivation (RTC)—a document needed for many tasks such as obtaining bank loans. There were delays and harassment. Bribes had to be paid. Today, a printed copy of the RTC can be obtained online at computerised land records kiosks (Bhoomi centres) for a fee of Rs 15 in all taluk offices. In the next phase, all the taluk data-bases are to be uploaded to a web-enabled central database. RTC would then be available online at Internet kiosks, which are likely to be set up in rural areas.

In the fourth chapter entitled 'Bhoomi: A Case Study', A. Rama Mohan Rao and P.V. Bhat present a success story of Karnataka in computerisation of land records. This case study is presented as an overview of computer- isation of land records, widely known as Bhoomi (land), implemented by NIC, Karnataka state unit for the Revenue Department, Government of Karnataka, India. Bhoomi is an online system to carry out mutation on the live data. It has a built-in workflow automation, which moves trans- actions from one officer to another on the system. It has also been integrated with Fingerprint (Bio-metrics) Technology to ensure a foolproof authenti- cation system, instead of the traditional password system. This enforces the concept of non-repudiation.

The fifth chapter entitled 'Evaluation of Computerisation of Land Records in Karnataka: A Study from Gulbarga District' by Manoj Ahuja and A.P. Singh, presents the evaluation of CoLR programme in Karnataka. According to the authors, CoLR in Karnataka has adequately dealt with some of the deficiencies of the old manual records system. Now the land records are more transparent and open for public scrutiny. It has also made the land records less prone to manipulations by making land records freely available to public. The village accountants have very little scope to manipulate or cause harassment to the public.

The Government of Karnataka is in the process of tackling teething problems of power backup for the computer kiosk, additional computer kiosks and additional computer operators. It will be essential to monitor farmers' satisfaction with the CoLR and ask for their suggestions for improvement. In the end, the authors indicate that CoLR in Gulbarga provides solutions for the multiple problems of Indian land records system. CoLR has certainly improved land records systems in Karnataka.

Maha Singh in his chapter 'Computerisation of Land Records in Haryana' indicates that registration of a deed is the beginning point that triggers the process of updating of the land records. This is the crucial stage and offers an opportunity for online updating of land records.

S. Suresh Kumar in his chapter entitled 'Centrally Sponsored Scheme of Computerisation of Land Records in West Bengal' attempts to present the status in West Bengal, reasons for the success, technical spin-offs from the data for computerisation of land records, and gaps/deficiencies in the CoLR scheme. The entry of textual data and its generation as a printout is a very limited exercise being undertaken at the moment. There are a host of other activities related to the maintenance of record of rights which can be derived from the existing database created. In addition, other administrative routines can also be computerised to make the utilisation of computers more pervasive and widespread. The database needs to be connected at the sub-divisional, district and state levels to make a more meaningful use of the database.

The eighth chapter, by R.M. Vardhan, presents the status of computerisation of land records in Goa. According to Vardhan Goa was declared to be the first state in the country to have completed the computerisation of RoRs of all 11 taluks of the state in December 2001. Tiswadi taluk has become the first taluk in the state to have a complete Land Records Information System (LRIS). A notable step taken by the Government of Goa in the direction of delivering the benefits of information technology to the common man is the opening of Electronic Information Centres in the cities of Panaji and Margao. The centres are being run by a private agency with the support of the government. At these centres the land records are available across the counter on demand by the public, in addition to other services. It is proposed to extend this service to other places in the state in the long run. In the near future it is planned to set up intra-net connecting all the 11 taluks so that any person from any taluk office will be in the position to get records of any part of state. Besides this, it is also planned to computerise the entire mutation process so that long delays are eliminated and online updation is available. In conclusion, it may be said that the state of Goa has reached a milestone. It is also hoped that the achievements of Goa add impetus to the mission of computerisation of land records at the national level.

Chapter 9: 'Appraisal of Computerisation of Land Records in West Bengal: A Micro Study' by Manoj Ahuja and A.P. Singh gives an idea about the benefits accruing to landowners due to the implementation of computerisation of land records programme in the state. According to the authors, though a lot of work has been done towards CoLR in West Bengal, there are still deficiencies in the system, which need to be addressed to make this programme useful and beneficial to the citizens. Unless the database of land records-related information is updated concurrently with a mutation order, the database loses relevance as it does not reflect the current reality. Therefore, the mutation process has to be made online along with imparting training to the concerned staff, ensuring proper security mechanisms and providing the necessary infrastructure.

Chapter 10 by Rajesh Kumar examines several propositions in the context of restructuring the existing system, especially with respect to the ongoing programme of computerisation of land records in Bhojpur district of Bihar. The computerisation programme in this district is still in the initial stages.

In Chapter 11 Sunil Kumar indicates that IT has been used in land records maintenance since the Government of India introduced a centrally sponsored scheme for computerisation of land records in 1987–88. Haryana also implemented a pioneer project at Rewari with technical assistance of NIC. The scope of the project was to automate *jamabandis* (records of rights), mutations, *khasra girdawari* (crop inspection), *shajra nasb* (pedigree table) and their integration. Since all the documents are maintained by a *patwari* in a bag, the software was named as Patwari Information System (PATIS). The major objective was to help the public by giving them updated copies of land records through computer in time and in a hassle-free manner. With considerable success of the pilot, the project was replicated in all districts of Haryana in a phased manner. Now, 98 per cent data entry is complete for record of right and *nakal* services to the public have started. Technology, which is changing at a very fast rate, also played a crucial role (Unix to Windows, FoxBASE+ to SQL, maturing of Hindi solutions). The state government initiated another project on computerisation of registration of deeds with technical support by NIC. Haryana Registration Information System (HARIS) has been in place in all the 67 tehsils of Haryana. Since both the projects are to be implemented at tehsil level and interrelated, the integration of PATIS and HARIS becomes the obvious choice. Haryana also took the lead in the execution of 'Digitisation of Cadastral Map (*musavis*)' in six tehsils covering two districts of Haryana. The technical progress of the said project has been considerable, but the matching of area calculated automatically with the one available in the books, and the matching of digital boundaries with ground realities still remain issues to be resolved. Efforts are being made to make the project a success on the ground. Success on integration of spatial data (digital maps) with non-spatial (record of rights) has also been achieved. NIC, Haryana has always associated with revenue department as technical consultant, developer, and implement supporter at state, district and tehsil levels. According to the author, Haryana has a clear vision to achieve the objective of online land records management system (E-HARLAND). It will facilitate access to the land record of Haryana anytime, anywhere.

In Chapter 12, Manoj Ahuja and A.P. Singh specify the ways for the implementation of computerisation of land records in a systematic manner in Punjab. According to them, the progress of computerisation of land records in the state is highly disappointing.

Indu Gupta discusses the details of the software used for the computerisation of land records in Rajasthan. According to her, the success of computerisation of land records depends on online mutation, which would work only in a workflow automation system. The real process of online mutation may not be possible without amendment in the present mutation procedure, which has given powers to the *panchayat* to approve mutation in some cases.

Chapter 14, in Part II, is by N.K. Agrawal. According to him the survey of land, preparation of cadastral maps and land records on paper and/ or in digital form, in a comprehensive land information/management system, involve a number of processes. A number of difficulties/problems exist in the whole process. In this chapter, an attempt has been made to detail and discuss these and suggest possible solutions from a technical point of view.

Chapter 15, 'Digitisation of Cadastral Maps in Madhya Pradesh', highlights the status of the pilot project sanctioned by the Ministry of Rural Development for Madhya Pradesh. M.K. Agarwal indicates that in continuation of the centrally-sponsored drive for the computerisation of land records, in 1999, pilot projects were sanctioned by the Ministry of Rural Development, Government of India for digitisation of village-level cadastral maps on an experimental basis in Raghogarh tehsil of Guna district and Shivpuri tehsil of Shivpuri district. Although a computerised RoR system was implemented a long time back in MP, the copy of map was still being distributed by making a manual copy of the selected area/ plot. After the digitisation of maps in these two tehsils, any selected *khasra* (plot) map can be printed at random along with the adjoining khasras. Government of Madhya Pradesh has given legal sanctity to it by amending the copying rules in the year 2000. The generation of the base map and attachment of attribute data not only help revenue administration but also the landholder and other government organisations, providing multiple usage of one-time effort.

In Chapter 16 S. Suresh Kumar highlights the core issues relating to cadastral maps. According to him the present-day land records have hardly undergone much change so far and are under severe strain to serve the planning and developmental requirements of the present economy. The programme of digitisation of cadastral maps was started in 1998–99 through the pilot projects in the states of Andhra Pradesh, Kerala, Orissa, Bihar, Tamil Nadu, West Bengal, Maharashtra, UP, Gujarat, Madhya Pradesh, Pondicherry, Karnataka, Goa, Punjab, Jammu & Kashmir, Manipur, Mizoram, Nagaland and Haryana for generating cadastral maps through various modern technologies. In India, all the projects have been treated as infrastructure projects and have been totally funded by the government. In the USA it has been totally federally funded and in the UK partly by the Ordnance Survey and some private participation. In other countries such as Singapore, Malaysia, New Zealand and other European countries it has been a mixture of federal and state involvement. The funding model for India should be a centre-state equal sharing model which is already in operation under the Strengthening of Revenue Administration and Updating of Land Records (SRAULR) scheme. Efforts to create a digital cadastral database (DCDB) had been pioneered in many countries but India, in this respect, has remained totally aloof from all developments and is yet to reach a position of competence.

In Chapter 17 entitled 'Modern Technology in Survey and Settlement Operations in West Bengal' C.R. Das, discusses the methodology adopted in West Bengal for cadastral mapping.

In Chapter 18 entitled 'Computerisation and Digitisation of Survey and Land Records in Andhra Pradesh', T. Radha discusses different systems of survey which were adopted in Andhra region. The author describes the types of land records maintained in Andhra Pradesh and their physical condition, as well as the experimental projects on digitisation of survey and land records in Kuppam assembly constituency of Chittoor district in Andhra Pradesh. The author also points out the practical problems in computerisation and re-survey of survey and land records.

Chapter 19, which is the last chapter of Part II, deals with 'Updation of Land Records, Computerisation and Digitisation of Cadastral Survey Maps with Reference to J&K'. Mohd. Afzal and Ishfaq A. Khan discuss the technology involved in digitisation of cadastral maps in Jammu & Kashmir. They have also written about the process involved in strengthening revenue administration in the state.

Finally in Chapter 20, in Part III, Alok Sharma and Lokesh Shrivastav write that India's present land management system is far from being efficient and thus recommend that we should be looking for alternatives in order to evolve a fair, user-friendly, robust and efficient land management system. Land information system or LIS is a powerful tool that can provide an alternative to the existing cadastre-based land management system. An LIS is a digital database essentially having the same two components, that is maps or the graphical/spatial inter-phase and the aspatial record attributes created in an RDBMS for each landholding. In order to create the LIS, the first and foremost task is to assess all that needs to be included in the database. A consensus needs to be arrived at on the platforms of generating the database and attributes to be attached to the land parcels by the concerned authorities looking at the final objective to be achieved. To reap all the rewards of an LIS and to generate maximum gains out of it, the database structure will have to be defined in the national context. At present different databases are available in different places. There is no single coherent source where the entire data is available as a single cohesive database. A national level database can fill this vacuum.

We sincerely thank all the participants of the workshop who spared their valuable time and made it a success by their distinctive contribution and critical comments. This volume would never have been possible without their valuable and active association. We deeply appreciate the efforts of Dr A.P. Singh, Centre for Rural Studies, Lal Bahadur Shastri National Academy of Administration, Mussoorie whose role in organising the workshop was not only pivotal but also helped us in the preparation of this book. The shortcomings and errors in this book which remain are ours alone.

**Wajahat Habibullah**
**Manoj Ahuja**

# Part I: Computerisation of Land Records

# 1

# Computerisation of Land Records:
# National Perspective

S.D. MEENA, VINAY THAKUR, D.R. SHUKLA,
O.P. SISODIA AND S.K. NARULA

## INTRODUCTION

In India, land ownership lies in the name of individuals and not with the state. It has been a universally accepted principle that the rulers of the state are entitled to a portion of the produce of the land from those who utilise it, as a price for the protection of their life and property, and also to meet the common expenses of the community. Consequently, the system of land records was also organised to serve that purpose. After Independence, the necessity for reliable statistics related to crops, irrigation and land use was considerable, so that they could form the basis of land development of the country. This, in turn, helped in strengthening the land records development process. All these situations helped in development of the present-day land records system. In any land record, a number of records

---

For all figures in lakhs and crores, please note that 1 lakh = 100,000 and 1 crore = 10,000,000.

are prescribed to be maintained at the village, *tehsil* and district levels, such as statements of landholdings, land revenue, rental cropped areas and land-use pattern. There are more than 20 registers that are being maintained by the revenue department. The number of registers again varies from state to state.

The principal records being maintained are (*a*) village map: a pictorial form showing the village and field boundaries; (*b*) field book or *khasra* which is an index to the map, in which changes in the field boundaries, their area , particulars of tenure-holders, methods of irrigation, cropped area, other uses of land, etc., are shown; and (*c*) records of rights (RoRs) also known as *khatouni*, in which the names and classes of tenure of all occupants of land are recorded.

To remove the inherent flaws in the existing land records maintenance and to bring about efficiency, transparency and easy accessibility of land records, Ministry of Rural Development (MoRD), Government of India, initiated a centrally sponsored scheme in 1988–89 to computerise land records with 100 per cent financial scheme to states for utilising IT as a tool to build a Land Information System. The centrally sponsored scheme on Computerisation of Land Records (CoLR) was started as a pilot project in eight districts/states namely; Rangareddy (Andhra Pradesh), Sonitpur (Assam), Singhbhum (Bihar), Gandhinagar (Gujarat), Morena (Madhya Pradesh), Wardha (Maharashtra), Mayurbhanj (Orissa), and Dungarpur (Rajasthan) with a view to removing the problems inherent in the manual system of maintenance and updating of land records and to meet the requirements of various groups of users. It was decided that efforts should be made to computerise Core Data contained in land records, so as to assist development planning and to make records accessible to people, planners and administrators. Under this scheme, financial assistance is provided for completion of basic data entry of land records, setting up of computer centres at tehsil/*taluk*/block level, sub-division and district, setting up a Land Records Data Centre and imparting computer training to revenue personnel for regular updation and distribution of land records through computers. Further, the scheme was extended to more districts. But when the scheme was reviewed in 1993–94, it was seen that states were finding it difficult to sustain the project on account of non-availability of skilled manpower and hardware maintenance, etc. So, it was decided to use National Informatics Centres' (NIC) infrastructure and network. NIC upgraded its district centres with latest hardware and software, and states were requested to allocate one room near the NIC district centre to start data-entry operation.

NIC has conducted the system study by visiting 17 states and prepared the system requirement specifications and flow. The design was standardised and implemented in all the states with local variations. The software has been made for generation of updated RoR, mutation updation, query support system for decision support system (DSS) at district and taluk level, security mechanism, menu-driven back-up and recovery procedure and report generation, etc. The latest security tools namely biometric scanner and smart card, etc., have been used for adding an extra layer of login authenticity and non-repudiation.

# OBJECTIVES

The main objectives of the scheme are:

1. to provide computerised copies of ownership, crop details and updation of RoRs to landowners on demand;
2. to provide legal sanctity to computer-generated certificates of land records after authentication by authorised revenue officials;
3. to ensure accuracy, transparency and speedy dispute resolution;
4. to provide fast and efficient retrieval of information for decision making;
5. to realise low costs and easily reproducible basic land record data through reliable and durable preservation of old records;
6. implementation of a comprehensive land information system for better land-based planning and utilisation of land resources; and
7. to focus on citizen-centric services related to land and revenue information.

Since inception of the scheme (1988–89), MoRD has released Rs 300.51 crore up to 31 March 2004. The utilisation of funds reported by the states/UTs is Rs 203.01 crore which is approximately 68 per cent of the total funds released. At present the scheme is being implemented in 582 districts of the country.

# ROLE OF AGENCIES

The roles of different agencies are:

### National Informatics Centre

The scheme is being implemented in joint collaboration with the National Informatics Centre (NIC) which is responsible for upgrading its district centres with the latest hardware, software, terminals and printers to expedite the work of data entry. NIC is also responsible for providing training on application software to the revenue officials and technical support for implementation of the scheme.

### MoRD

The Ministry of Rural Development is providing funds to the state governments for site preparation, data-entry work and purchase of furniture and other miscellaneous expenditure, and financial support for tehsil-taluk level set-ups, training, etc.

### States

States are responsible for data collection, verification and validation, distribution of RoR to landowners at nominal rates, on demand, and automating the entire workflow in land administration process and report back the quarterly physical and financial progress to MoRD.

### Operationalisation of the Scheme at Tehsil/Taluk Level

During 1997–98, the decision for operationalisation of the scheme at the tehsil/taluk level was taken for facilitating delivery of computerised land records to users and the public at large. Under this programme, funds to the tune of Rs 3.80 lakh per tehsil/taluk are released to state government for purchase of hardware, software and other peripherals (printer, touch screen kiosk, scanner, etc). Up to 31 March 2004, 3,142 tehsils/taluks have been covered under the programme. In 2,172 tehsils/taluks, computer centres have been set up and in 1,553 tehsils/taluks computerised copies of RoRs are being issued to the landowners on demand. MoRD is proposing to enhance this amount as requested by many states.

## Mapping

Village maps were prepared by using the individual survey field data. Such maps tended to be slightly inaccurate due to error in individual fields being accumulated across the village. Errors generally crept in due to measurement resolution being rounded off and also due to undulating nature of the ground. Field sketches assume the ground to be flat; however, the same data when mosaiced across a village result in sizeable differences.

The boundary of the village was traverse-surveyed and was used to control the accumulated error in the mosaiced village map. In traverse survey, the entire village was divided into more than one block and known boundary points (called traverse stations). The method involved starting from first station and recording the distance and the angle to the next station and so on till the circuit was closed. In many northern states, the individual field records were either lost or abandoned after preparation of accurate village map and this map became a basis for obtaining individual survey boundaries.

## Issues

Though many states have digitised their records, it will take time to achieve a 'sync' between data entered and transactions, so the manual system of issuing of RoRs is prevalent in most of the states. The main issues are:

- Data entry and verification of legacy data.
- Regular updation of the records because of mutations.
- Unstructured data.
- Language issues.
- Land records maintained on paper/cloth are in a very bad shape.
- Duplication on similar media is cumbersome and will result in similar problems of maintenance after a few years.
- Updation to boundaries or title information by manual process is highly time consuming and any error will get propagated to the village maps.
- Cross-verification is required over records for a large period of time to ensure absence of inconsistencies after updation.
- Retrieval for redressal of any dispute is time consuming due to the large bulk of information.
- Every retrieval/use has an associated risk of further physical damage to the old records.

- Legal sanctity to computer generated RoR.
- Accuracy of maps and different scales of available maps.

# IT TOOLS AND TECHNOLOGIES

## GIS

GIS is a tool that can be effectively used for better visualisation and spatial analysis applications. Maps are a powerful medium for planning, analysis and monitoring. It integrates non-spatial and spatial datasets for query and better display. Cadastral maps can be used on a day-to-day basis by decision makers at the grassroots level. The data of cadastral survey forms the basis for generation of any accurate high-level map.

### Data Warehousing

Information is one of the valuable assets to any government. When used properly, it can help planners and decision makers in making informed decisions leading to positive impact on targeted group of citizens. An information warehouse can deliver strategic intelligence to the decision makers and provide an insight into the overall situation. This greatly facilitates decision makers in taking micro-level decisions in a timely manner. By organising land-related data into a meaningful information warehouse, the government decision makers can be empowered with a flexible tool that enables them to make informed policy decisions for citizen facilitation and accessing their impact over the intended section of the population. Hence, a data warehouse built on land data containing history of property transfer, division of land parcels, yield trends, crop pattern and revenue details can be beneficial to the government decision makers and citizens.

At present most of the states have captured their data in computers and copies of records of rights are being distributed from computer centres. But the need of the hour is to have a uniform system and storage format for land records maintenance where national-level data warehousing will ensure better micro- and macro-level planning of land resources. This will ensure that:

- Decision makers who at present have to deal with the heterogenous and sporadic information generated by various state-level computerisation projects can access current data with high regularity from the information warehouse.
- Decision makers' micro-level decisions can be made in a timely manner without the need to depend on their IT staff.
- Decision makers can obtain easily decipherable and comprehensive information without the need to use sophisticated tools.
- Decision makers can perform extensive analysis of stored data to provide answers to the exhaustive queries to the administrative cadre. This helps them to formulate more effective strategies and policies for citizen facilitation.
- The citizen is the ultimate beneficiary of the new policies formulated by the decision makers and policy planners' extensive analysis on person- and land-related data.
- Citizens can view frequently asked queries, results for which will already exist in the database and be immediately visible to the user, saving the time required for processing.
- Citizens can have easy access to the government policies of the state.
- Citizens' web access to information warehouse enables them to access the public domain data from anywhere.

### Web-based Data Dissemination

The World Wide Web at its present level of development makes it possible to process and disseminate all the land record on the GIS platform along with the attached data. It is so structured that anyone and everyone can interact on the website in a query-based structuring. Even all applications and requests for mutations can be accepted online. The access is provided all around the state through kiosks that are self-financed and pay a certain fee to the state for the right to provide the authenticated records. 'View free, pay for the signed record' includes free downloading of records. It is for the legal document that the person will have to pay a charge, which would be much less than the informal charge that he has to pay to the revenue official.

The web-based technology has given great scope for integration and dissemination of map and multi-lingual attribute data. Any one on the Internet can access the information. The data updation and authentication has to be done at server with proper password protection.

### Use of Hand-held Device (Simputer)

Simputer is a low cost, simple hand-held computer developed by a team of scientists from the Indian Institute of Science and the Bangalore-based Encore Software and can be used for data collection directly from field. This is being done in Karnataka state where village-level revenue functionaries have been given Simputers for data collections.

### Data Security

Security should be of paramount consideration while developing software and processing data. Apart from this, a full set of security policies has to be worked out so that this vital data can't be tampered with. The importance of security policies has to be clearly conveyed to the officers working in the tehsils and they should be directed to adhere to these policies. For local authentication purpose and for non-repudiation, state-of-the-art biometric fingerprint readers should be used, thus obviating the need to remember passwords and the dangers of weak passwords being cracked by unscrupulous elements. Transactions on database must generate entry into hidden log files, which can help the administrator to identify transactions done by various officials.

A full set of guidelines for recovering the crashed system should be formulated in the system and regular backup of the system has to be taken at the end of the day. If backup is not taken at the end of the day, system should not boot next day without taking backup of the data.

### Online Connectivity

As to the future, one hears of extensive broadbanding of rural communications and the advent of wireless technologies for local linkages and horizontal and vertical integration. A basket of satellite-based technologies is waiting to be used. Those pursuing the vision of a land records information system are fired up with ideas and dreams. But then the final goal, clearly, is just to render clean, efficient, updated and quick yet economical land records information and services to the rural population.

### Kiosk and Smart Card

The public delivery needs to be further strengthened to provide certified copies of RoR to the landowners at their doorsteps through village-level kiosks. These kiosks can be set up by private entrepreneurs. The landowners can also be given smart cards in order to provide them the access to their land records data on 'when and where' basis.

### Open Software

The open source community has significantly enhanced the open source databases such as MYSpl, Postgress SQL and front-end development tools like Java. These will provide cost-effective enterprise solutions for implementing land records information system.

So, why not try a judicious mix of a minority of strategically placed electronic competencies with a majority of well-managed manual work. The technologies available will not only allow integration of various spatial and non-spatial datasets, but will enable online gathering, recording, warehousing, retrieving, disseminating and employing the data, which will lead to improved effectiveness and efficiency of land management both from the perspective of the common man as well as that of decision makers implementing land-based development activities at the grassroots level.


## PILOT PROJECTS ON DIGITISATION OF CADASTRAL MAPS


The MoRD had also requested all the state governments to submit proposals for pilot projects for digitisation of cadastral survey maps in two or three tehsils of any district in their state. So far 32 pilot projects on digitisation of cadastral survey maps covering 21 states namely Andhra Pradesh, Madhya Pradesh, Maharashtra, Manipur, Meghalaya, Mizoram, Gujarat, Goa, Haryana, Jammu & Kashmir, Bihar, Kerala, Karnataka, Tamil Nadu, Tripura, Nagaland, Orissa, Punjab, Uttar Pradesh, West Bengal and Pondicherry have been sanctioned by the ministry. These projects are at various stages of implementation and expected to be completed soon. This spatial data will be used for integration with Land Records Centre attribute data and other datasets.

### Physical Progress

States like West Bengal, Andhra Pradesh, Karnataka, Tamil Nadu, Sikkim, Orissa, Kerala, Madhya Pradesh, Gujarat, Rajasthan, Goa and Maharashtra have done satisfactory work under the scheme of computerisation of land records. Overall 1,553 tehsils/taluks/blocks have been fully operationalised with the distribution of computerised copies of RoRs to landowners.

### Monitoring of the Scheme

The progress of implementation of the scheme is periodically reviewed at the level of Joint Secretary as well as through annual conferences of revenue secretaries and revenue ministers of the states/UTs. The officers of the ministry also visit various states in order to assess the progress of the scheme and to have a first-hand information regarding bottlenecks in the implementation of the scheme. The progress of the scheme is also being monitored through video conferencing interaction with the states/ UTs. The following are the details of the monitoring and review of the scheme:

1. strengthening district-level committees by including elected representatives for effective implementation and qualitative monitoring;
2. reconstitution of state-level review and steering committee under mission leader with specific role of undertaking business process re-engineering, fixing milestones, change management, finalisation of proposals, certification of project completion, wide publicity and acceptability by public, and undertaking concurrent audits;
3. setting up national-level Steering and Monitoring Committee to resolve implementation issues, framing guidelines for security and technology upgradation and effective monitoring of the scheme;
4. evaluation studies by reputed organisations for getting feedback to facilitate remedial measures;
5. participation of elected representatives and *panchayati raj* institutions to give impetus to the scheme at the grassroots level; and
6. complete documentation and multimedia presentations of case studies.

### Evaluation Studies

Since the feedback from the states regarding implementation of the scheme has not been forthcoming and progress of utilisation of funds has also been very low, it was decided in 1998 to conduct comprehensive evaluation studies in eight districts of different states namely Andhra Pradesh

(Rangareddy), Madhya Pradesh (Hoshangabad), Maharashtra (Amravati), Karnataka (Mysore), Orissa (Mayurbhanj), Rajasthan (Jaipur), Uttar Pradesh (Aligarh) and West Bengal (Haora).

These studies have since been completed and the main findings of these studies are:

1. the monitoring mechanism needs to be strengthened, as this is a crucial component for the success of the scheme;
2. there is a need to develop more awareness about the implementation of the scheme;
3. training under the programme is inadequate; it should be conducted at different levels—district, tehsil and village;
4. computerisation of land records and setting up a Land Information System (LIS) is incomplete without a vectorised database of land-holdings through digitisation of cadastral survey maps; and
5. there is a need for networking of the scheme at different levels so that data move from district to state and then to centre through NICNET.

## BOTTLENECKS IN IMPLEMENTATION OF THE SCHEME BY THE STATE GOVERNMENTS

There are some bottlenecks in the implementation of the scheme by the state governments. The bottlenecks, as the well as remedial measures required to be taken for effective implementation of the scheme are indicated as follows:

1. delay in transfer of funds to implementing authority by the state governments;
2. delay in construction of airconditioned rooms for installation of computers and other equipments;
3. delay in development of appropriate software due to non-freezing of requirements, changes in operating environment, etc;
4. lack of adequate training facilities to revenue staff to handle computers; and
5. non-availability of private vendors for taking up the job of data-entry work.

*Ways and Means to Make the Scheme More Effective*

These include:

1. to gear up monitoring mechanism for review of implementation of the scheme, as the physical and financial progress reports are not being received regularly from the state governments;
2. direct release of funds to the state-level implementing authorities;
3. organisation of regular training programme for revenue staff; and
4. entrusting the task of further evaluation of the scheme by the states, to reputed research organisations.

# FUTURE APPROACH

Once data entry is over and data verified, states are requested to start RoR distribution at the tehsil office. Software as developed by NIC can be implemented at the tehsils and installation and configuration support can even be taken from some external agency. Distribution of RoR on demand, online lodging of demand for various certificates, complaint through the system should be started at the tehsil computer centre in order to bring e-governance to the grassroots. States are requested to give legal sanctity to computer-generated certificates. Proper care must be taken to provide data security and devices such as biometric scanner, smart card, setting up of virtual private network may be used, etc.

Training of the revenue staff at various levels must be undertaken on a continuing basis to make them conversant with the use of modern technology in the maintenance of land records. MoRD has prepared an identical syllabi for revenue staff and it will be circulated to the states. The states are also required to upgrade the existing training schools with IT infrastructure.

In case of re-survey, uniform methodology to generate graphic records of land parcels, villages, towns and cities in prescribed scales must be evolved for adoption by all states. Digital cadastral survey methods need to be considered for adoption by the states.

It is important to evolve a national policy for generating cadastral maps by scanning or digitisation, as per their suitability for storage, accuracy standards and legal sanctity through a cost-sharing pattern between states and the central government.

For usage at national-level planning, core data fields common to all the states shall be identified. These may include plot number and its extent, landholders, occupants and enjoyers, land classification, source of irrigation, assessment, land use, crop-statistics, abstract of all government and communal lands in the village, particulars of encroachments and details of waterbodies. This can be compiled by the states and sent to MoRD, which can then be used by different agencies at state and national level for land-based planning.

MoRD has proposed to set up a monitoring centre in the office of implementing agencies where states are to feed the online monthly physical and financial progress. This monitoring centre will be equipped with video-conferencing facilities and can work as a centre of excellence.

Integration of map and attribute data will enable the system to distribute copies of RoRs with their map details. Once we have the core map cadastral data available village-wise, the same can be integrated with other datasets for a comprehensive land information system.

Public delivery mechanism has to be strengthened. We need to set up touch screen kiosks at village level for better dissemination of data. Unemployed youths may be encouraged to own these kiosks for distribution of basic land record data to the people at nominal cost. Based on need, general land records data may be made available to the people through Internet.

# 2

# *Computerisation of Land Records: Inter-state Variations*

## MANOJ AHUJA AND A.P. SINGH

## INTRODUCTION

Land records give landholders the fullest security of tenure and minimise the possibility of disputes and litigation. They enable landholders to obtain credit more easily and to transact in land more quickly, safely and cheaply. They secure the rights of absentees and of those enjoying restrictive rights of any kind. They prevent the growth of unwanted prescriptive land rights and assist in proving the existence of such rights wherever this is desired.

Before Independence all provinces, other than the permanently settled ones, had a reasonably adequate system of preparation and maintenance of land records and it subserved the main objectives of the revenue administration in that period. The records showed who owned the different plots of land in the village, the area and boundaries of each plot and who cultivated it, what crops were grown and how much was payable to the government as land revenue. It was the duty of the village accountant to update

For all figures in lakhs and crores, please note that 1 lakh = 100,000 and 1 crore = 10,000,000.

the entries every year. The superiors in the hierarchy supervised the work of the village accountant. Since the mid-1950s when the measures of land reform were initiated this work has been badly neglected. In the opinion of P.S. Appu,

the neglect was in some cases deliberate and it was done within the knowledge and often with the blessings of the state governments. For example in the wake of enactment of tenancy laws to protect the interests of tenants, the practice of recording the names of the tenants in the register was given up in several states. Furthermore in several states, the record of rights is invariably out of date because mutations are not updated promptly. The rules require that as soon as inheritance, partitions or transfers take place, the names of the new owners should be entered in the registers. But the work of mutations in most of the states is in arrears and hence the land records need to be updated (Appu 1995).

In the permanently settled areas, there was no need for the British administration to have records other than those prepared at the time of survey/re-survey. There was no practice of annual updating of records. The position of land records in the native states was also unsatisfactory. Even after Independence no serious effort was made to bring about an improvement in the situation. In the late 1980s, it was realised that application of information technology could help maintain and update land records. As a result, the Government of India started the centrally sponsored scheme of Computerisation of Land Records (CoLR) in 1988–89 in eight districts in different states of the country. The main objectives of the scheme were: (*a*) create database of basic records; (*b*) facilitate issuing copies of records; (*c*) reduce work load by elimination drudgery of paper work; (*d*) minimise the possibilities of manipulation of land records; and (*e*) create a land management information system. The scheme was 100 per cent funded by the central government. This was a result of emphasis laid by the Planning Commission on proper maintenance of land records as the basis of good administration. The Conference of Revenue Ministers in 1985 advocated the pilot project approach for CoLR data. Therefore, pilot projects were taken up in many states. After nearly a decade of the ongoing projects, it was envisaged that the cadastral map or spatial data should also be digitised. In 1998–99 funds were allotted for digitisation of maps and 32 pilot projects were sanctioned in 21 states. Evaluation studies were carried out in different districts during 1999 and after that the government issued out a comprehensive policy document called the

Vision Document. Some of the important policy issues were covered in this document. However, there is a lot more to be done. What we have mentioned so far is to highlight the fact that after 16 years (1988 to 2004) of efforts, the progress across the country has been highly skewed. Some states have made far-reaching progress whereas other states have lagged behind. States like Karnataka, Goa ,West Bengal, Madhya Pradesh, Gujarat, Tamil Nadu and Rajasthan have done satisfactory work under the CoLR scheme. In this chapter we will discuss the variations in the status of different states after the implementation of CoLR scheme.

## CURRENT STATUS OF COMPUTERISATION OF LAND RECORDS IN DIFFERENT STATES

In Karnataka, the progress made in the CoLR project has been remarkable. Karnataka has 67 lakh owners of rural land spread across 177 *taluk*s in nearly 30,000 villages. Together they account for 2 crore records of RTC (Records of rights, tenancy and cultivation). A printed copy of the RTC can be obtained online from a computerised land record kiosk (Bhoomi centres) in 177 taluk offices after paying a fee of Rs 15. In add-ition to this, the farmer can see his land records documents and status of the mutation-in-process without the intervention of the officials on the touch screen kiosk, set up at the entrance of taluk/block office. This brings in total transparency in the maintenance of land records documents. Bio-metrics authentication, a fingerprint scanning device has been introduced by the state government to check manipulation of land records. This has replaced the traditional method of using passwords. With the fingerprint authentication device, only an authorised person will be able to edit re-cords. Of course, the current implementation requires a villager to go (or send someone) to the taluk office in order to get the copy of land records. The state government legally abolished all handwritten records after the implementation of this project. Karnataka's CoLR programme has at-tracted widespread recognition in the country as well as internationally. Recently, this programme was one of six award winners among 150 global entries in a competition on innovation in governance, instituted by the Commonwealth Association of Public Administration and Management. The software for the programme, called 'Bhoomi', has been developed by National Informatics Centre (NIC). Karnataka is in the forefront of all states in the implementation of CoLR. The inclusion of 'online mutation' in the software has been the major factor for success of the programme in Karnataka. This 'online mutation' module has ensured that the database is always updated. The present system has been developed through the dedication and cohesion of those who worked on the variety of technologies employed in it, and through cooperation between the state and central governments.

Goa has become the first state in the country to have completed the computerisation of RORs of all villages for all 11 taluks of the state. The reason for the success are: (*a*) cooperation and coordination between all departments and people involved in this exercise; (*b*) positive attitude of officers and officials involved in the task of computerisation; (*c*) regular monitoring and periodical review of the scheme at the field as well as at the state secretariat level; (*d*) determination and commitment of all directorate staff, NIC staff, *mamlatdar* staff and the personnel of the private agencies; (*e*) motivation and leadership factors; and (*f*) availability of power and other infrastructure.

Goa still needs to computerise the mutation process so that online mutation is possible. In the field of computerisation of cadastral maps, the department undertook pilot project for the digitisation of cadastral survey maps in technical collaboration with the private agency involved in the work of Geographic Information System (GIS).

Madhya Pradesh is a state which also implemented this scheme. In Madhya Pradesh, the computerised copies of RoR are being distributed in 256 *tehsils* on demand. Due to decentralised system of authorising the gram panchayat to certify the mutations, a parallel system of issuance of RoR from the tehsil as well as the *gram panchayat* is in existence. Madhya Pradesh has also successfully implemented pilot project of digitisation of cadastral maps for Raghogarh tehsil of Guna district and Shivpuri tehsil of Shivpuri district. As per output received, these projects had immense utility and benefits for the users. The progress of Madhya Pradesh has also been quite good but some constraints have been felt in speedy execution of the computerisation project. These include: inadequate trained staff, problem in maintenance of hardware, slow speed of input, inadequate number of terminals, lack of enthusiasm for this project and absence of an online workflow based mutation system.

Rajasthan has 0.7 crore land records (RoRs) and 3.4 crore plots in nearly 42,000 villages. A computerised printed copy of RoRs can be obtained from Apna Khata Centre in 235 out of 241 tehsils, after paying

Rs 10 for up to 10 plots, and Rs 5 per 10 plots thereafter. The state government has provided a validity and legality for the computerised RoRs but still there is need to abolish legally handwritten RoRs. The *chausala* (four years) updation process can be accomplished through computer. Unavailability of regular power supply, lack of trained personnel in remote tehsils, the unfamiliarity of revenue officers with computer applications, etc., have been some major teething problems in the computerisation process.

All the 341 blocks 18 districts of West Bengal have been made operational, from which various services like computerised certified copies of RoR and plot information are being provided to the *raiyat*s and other interested citizens within a day. The issue of manual copy of RoR has been prohibited. Rs 98 lakh have been collected from issue of 7.5 lakh certified copies of record of rights. Online mutation that essentially computerises the mutation process has been implemented in three blocks. One Touch Screen Kiosk has been installed for providing information to the raiyat regarding land at Kolkata. Pilot project for digitisation of 900 finally published cadastral maps of about 725 *mauza*s of Hugli district has been taken up. The Map Digitisation Centre has been installed at the Department of Land Records and Surveys at Kolkata with appropriate software and hardware like high-end workstations computers, A0 size scanner and other peripherals, all connected in LAN, for validation and electronic storage of the digitised maps. Research and development work for achieving accuracy in digitisation of the complicated A0/A1 size cadastral maps of this state is continuing with the assistance of the NIC. On experimental basis digitised mauza maps were integrated with the corresponding RoR database, forming a land GIS for the mauza. This has paved the way to integrate all the 725 mauzas with the RoR. Software to update mauza map online at the block has been envisaged using Collabcad, a CAD software from NIC. A mechanism to deliver maps of the plots referred in the RoR along with the computerised RoR has been worked out and would soon be completed.

In Gujarat, all 226 taluks have been made operational with on-demand distribution of RoRs. In the operational taluks, at the click of a button the status of any land is displayed on the screen. All the records pertaining to Form no. 7/12 (which details the location, ownership and other aspects of the land) have been computerised. Since all the taluk-level headquarters are connected through the Gujarat State Wide Area Network (GSWAN), status on any land record can be obtained in any taluk at any moment.

In Tamil Nadu, the data entry and updating of entries of 'A' register and *chitta* of all rural villages has been completed. Out of 206 taluks, all except five urban taluks in Chennai, have online module of distributing computerised RoRs. Tamil Nadu government has notified a ban on issue of manual extracts of land records in the operationalised taluks. Till 31 July 2004, an amount of Rs 3.42 crore has been collected through the issue of computerised land records extracts. To increase the public interface, Touch Screen Kiosks were installed in 29 taluks, one each from every district. Installation of Touch Screen Kiosks in 97 more taluks has also been recently completed.

Sikkim has led an example in implementing IT in different areas of activities in north-eastern states. All the land records of the state have already been fed into computers and the instant updating and querying software which has been developed by the NIC is working very successfully. The present situation in Sikkim is that, data entry of all taluks has been completed. Two sub-divisions has been operationalised and seven sub-divisions are expected to be operational soon. Online mutation is completed in one district.

According to the latest information in Orissa, RoRs are being computerised in 93 tehsils. Land registration activities in the state would be computerised in the second phase. The state government is planning to consolidate all aspects of land records and revenue administration by merging the survey and settlement wings to form a single directorate. However, on the issue of availability of computerised *patta*s to the farmers, there has not been much success.

In Andhra Pradesh, computerised copies of RoR are being distributed in 308 *mandal*s of various districts. Andhra Pradesh still needs to computerise the mutation process so that online mutation is possible. In the field of computerisation of cadastral maps, the Department undertook pilot project for the digitisation of cadastral survey maps in technical collaboration with the private agency involved in the work of GIS.

In Maharashtra, basic data-entry work has been completed in all 35 districts and data verification work is going on. The online operations for computerised distribution will be started shortly in two taluks of each district. The state also happens to be one of the few states in India where pilot project for digitisation of cadastral maps has been initiated. The total cost on computerisation of land records in Maharashtra and establishing a network linking all divisional land record offices is estimated to be over Rs 20 crore.

Latest available reports from Kerala suggest that one taluk has become operational but 61 per cent of the amount was already spent by 31 January 2003. Pilot projects on digitisation of cadastral maps are still under progress.

In Jammu and Kashmir, computer facilities have been provided to all the 59 tehsils of the state and the *patwari*s have been imparted training in data feeding and elementary computer application. The revenue department has so far procured 400 computers for the state. The amount of Rs 230 lakh for the computerisation programme was totally funded by the central government. Jammu and Kashmir was the first state to adopt the latest Electronic Total Stations (ETS) for land measurement. ETS furnishes accurate, error-free and perfect data besides being economical in measuring land. By adopting ETS, the state has bid goodbye to the age-old chain system. ETS has been introduced throughout the state and is working successfully with Swiss and Japanese technology. With ETS method at least 292,000 survey numbers have been measured comprising 234 villages. The field data collected through ETS is being fed into computers and an accurate print out of the village map comes out. The introduction of this technology augurs a revolutionary change in the agricultural history of the state. A landholder can now obtain a copy of his landholdings from the provincial record room and preserve it for posterity. He can also use the same as a ready reference without going to the office of patwari. But the work of computerisation of land records is yet to gain momentum.

In Assam computerisation of land records was first implemented in the Sonitpur district as a pilot project in 1989. The data-entry work pertaining to land records was completed in the district in 1993. At present, the district is ready to supply computerised RoRs to individual owners of land but due to some legal provision, which requires amendment, the matter has been delayed. After Sonitpur, the scheme was extended to Kamrup and Nagaon district. In both the districts data-entry work is going on. In Kamrup district data-entry work has been completed for Guwahati and Rangia sub-divisions. The data-entry work in respect of Pragjyotishpur sub-division is going on. The scheme is also being implemented in Darrang district. Apart from Sonitpur, in all other districts the data-entry work has been entrusted to private firms. In Sonitpur district the data-entry operators were originally recruited by the deputy commissioner and after completion of the data-entry work, they were sent to High Court. Two Civil Rules are pending on the matter of absorbing the data-entry operators in the normal posts in the deputy commissioner's establishment. The Government of India has so far sanctioned 23 projects and the total amount was Rs 335.5 lakh but only 20 per cent of the amount has been utilised. This indicates that the pace of computerisation of land records in the state is very slow.

Arunachal Pradesh has not yet started either aerial survey or computerisation of land records. Land records are yet to be prepared and hence no project for computerisation has been prepared and implemented. The Government of India has included Arunachal Pradesh under the centrally-sponsored computerisation of land records programme and has given Rs 75.30 lakh for this purpose. The amount is yet to be utilised.

In Tripura, a total number of four projects have been sanctioned at an estimated cost of Rs 85 lakh. Latest data shows that about 14 projects of computerisation have been in operation in Tripura and an amount of Rs 1.53 lakh has been released up to 31 January 2003. No appreciable results have been reported as yet on computerisation from Tripura.

The latest report regarding the utilisation of funds in Bihar shows that only 22 per cent of the total amount has been used so far. It has revealed that the low capacity of the computers, lack of sufficient terminals and adequate trained manpower have caused the delay in the computerisation process. Efforts are being made so that the computerisation of land records is accelerated.

A pilot project for computerisation of land records was undertaken in the Kangra district of Himachal Pradesh (HP). The installation of hardware and the preparation of the software was done with the help of NIC. Seven other similar projects have been prepared in HP with a sanction by the Government of India. In March 1996, when an in-depth review was conducted by the financial commissioner (revenue), it was found that the entire approach for computerising the land records in Kangra district on a pilot basis needed to be reworked because the software was aimed at exclusively reproducing the existing records of rights without the associated documents and without anticipating the need for incorporation of changes taking place in the records. This resulted from the lack of interaction between NIC and revenue agency during software designing and development. As a result it was decided in July 1996 to prepare a comprehensive software covering not merely the RoRs but also the genealogical table (*shajra-nasb*), mutation (*intkal*), harvest inspection register (*khasra girdawari*), agricultural statistics, etc. In this regard, 16 tehsils were selected for the implementation of the scheme. The data-entry work for the 1,008 villages has been completed. Final *jamabandi* was generated for 379 villages and final khasra girdawari for 145 villages. The scheme is operational in one tehsil. The Government of India has provided up to Rs 346 lakh as full financial assistance to the state under the scheme of computerisation of land records. But the state government has not been able to utilise the amount in time. The figures published in the Annual Report of the Ministry of Rural Development shows that only Rs 101 lakh, which is 29 per cent of the total amount, have been spent. This is rather a disappointing picture.

In Haryana, computerisation of land records was taken up for the first time in Rewari district on pilot project basis. The scope of the project was to automate jamabandis, mutations, khasra girdawari (crop inspection), shajra-nasb (pedigree table) and their integration. Since all the documents are maintained by patwari in a bag, the software was named as Patwari Information System (PATIS). With considerable success of the pilot, the project was replicated in all districts of Haryana in phased manner. Ninety-eight per cent data entry is complete for RoRs and *nakal* services to the public have started. The latest figures show that the state has utilised Rs 255 lakh which comes to only 45 per cent. The unspent balance is Rs 312 lakh. Evidently the state utilisation of the central grant has been very poor and consequently the computerisation has been suffering. The state government initiated another project on computerisation of registration of deeds with technical support of NIC. Haryana Registration Information System (HARIS) has been in place in all the 67 tehsils of Haryana. Since both the projects are to be implemented at tehsil level and kept interrelated, the integration of PATIS and HARIS becomes the obvious choice. The required software has been developed by the Haryana unit of NIC in consultation with the state revenue department. Such computerisation is expected to achieve spot registration, single window service, scanning of photographs of applicants, printing on the back of registered documents to avoid fraud, identification and proper valuation of property and minimising revenue leakage. It would also provide a database with photographs of authorised witnesses such as *lambardars* to ensure genuine witness, structuring and standardising of deed document language to minimise intermediaries, increased transparency in the system, maintenance of permanent records of deeds on CD-ROM, online queries about registered deeds, generating index registers and other reports and better monitoring of revenue collection.

In Punjab, some progress had been made in the districts of Jalandhar, Fatehgarh Sahib and Kapurthala through private agencies covering only one *kanungo* circle from each district. In terms of utilisation of funds, the state has utilised only 19 per cent of the total funds released by the Ministry of Rural Development, which is highly disappointing.

In Uttar Pradesh, data-entry work is in advanced stage of completion. In five tehsils, data verification work has been completed and efforts are being made to start regular operation of distribution of RoRs in five tehsils.

In northeastern states like Manipur, Nagaland, Arunachal Pradesh and Meghalaya, the progress of the computerisation of land records has not been satisfactory. The utilisation of funds for computerisation has been very poor. The basic reason is the lack of any commitment on the part of state governments regarding the preparation of the record of rights. Unless efforts are made in right earnest, modernisation and computerisation cannot be undertaken.

## SUMMING UP

After studying the status of the computerisation of land records for the major states of the country, we can divide the above states into three distinct groups. There are the advanced states who have forged ahead of others in e-governance in computerisation of land records. These states are Karnataka, Goa, West Bengal, Madhya Pradesh, Gujarat, Tamil Nadu and Rajasthan. Goa becomes the first fully computerised state in terms of land records. The picture in Karnataka seems quite satisfactory, because all taluks would have access to computerised land records with online updating. In Karnataka, when a change of ownership takes place through a sale or inheritance, farmers can file their request for mutation of the land records at the taluks headquarter (Bhoomi centre). The process of mutation is online in Karnataka. A number is assigned by the computer for each request. The number can be used to check the status of the request on a touch screen kiosk. The computer automatically generates notices. This type of facilitation process can be seen only in Karnataka. As far as security and threat of hacking are concern, the Bhoomi software incorporates the bio-logon metrics system, which authenticates all users of the software using their fingerprint. These are the best examples of how information technology can change lives at the grassroots apart from bringing in efficiency and transparency in government administration known for delays. Then there are the middle states which are close at their heels, namely Maharashtra, Himachal Pradesh, Orissa, Haryana and Uttar Pradesh. In the third category, there are the beginners that are yet to take significant steps in the direction. The issue that arises is what has made some of the states advanced while others are still lagging behind. The beginner states have the clear advantage that while they are trying to catch up they need not make the same mistakes which the advanced states made. The beginner can adopt any successful model suited for their local conditions and infrastructure. Even though there were a number of states which had been allotted the project of computerisation of land records, they did not make much headway till 2001. The reason was the periodic updating done by the revenue authorities. This led to an anomaly as the computerised data was not current and did not reflect reality. Only in Karnataka, the 'mutation' process was made online as a result of which the database of land records was updated as soon as a mutation was approved. This has been the crucial factor behind the success of the CoLR project in Karnataka. The other states would do well to follow the Karnataka model for their CoLR programme.

There is a considerable diversity between states in the matter of land records they maintain and the details contained in various registers. As a legacy of the past, every state has some registers that serve no useful purpose. It is very necessary to bring about standardisation in the field. Any system which is uniform throughout the country will have its own inherent potency. The system of land records is no exception. A uniform national system of land records is very much essential because of its vital importance in ensuring better micro- and macro-level planning and in guaranteeing peaceful/productive cultivation by the holder. We are in desperate need for a common national system of land records. The formulation and implementation of a national policy on land records is now due.

Countries with a high level of awareness about the importance of a well-organised system of land records have not only succeeded in bringing a uniform procedure into existence but also put the record in the digital environment for efficient maintenance, notwithstanding the problems initially faced. Indian land records database is one of the best in the world by any reckoning. Through rational and scientific structuring, it is possible to achieve a national spatial data infrastructure that pre-supposes appropriate integration of topographic and cadastral map data. Such data infrastructure will have immense potential not only to make country-level planning an accurate statistical exercise but also to produce a range of value-added data products that can be widely utilised by a host of government, private and voluntary organisations.

# GLOSSARY

| | | |
|---|---|---|
| *Chitta* | : | accounts, old measurement papers |
| *Jamabandi* | : | an inspection and audit of the accounts of land revenue maintained by village officers and a comparison of these accounts with the taluk or tehsil accounts at the time of inspections of villages by collectors, mamlatdars, *mahalkari*s or tehsildars |
| *Jinswar* | : | cropwise survey conducted by statistical and revenue officers |
| *Khasra* | : | field book in Madhya Pradesh is known as khasra or *khasra panchsala* |
| *Khasra Girdawari* | : | statement of crops grown and the respective acreage, arranged in descending order of field numbers given at the time of settlement in Rajasthan |
| *Khatiyan* | : | record of tenants' rights including the identity, extent, quality and possession of land |
| *Khatauni* | : | term which refers to jamabandi in UP and Rajasthan |
| *Kistbandi Khatauni* | : | another name given to jamabandi in Madhya Pradesh |
| *Kanungo* | : | hereditary registrar or village headman; sometimes also referred to as revenue official; in modern times entrusted with the work of realisation of revenue, and measurement and survey of land |
| *Lambardar* | : | chief headman over several headmen of village sections in Haryana |
| *Lekhpal* | : | lowest revenue functionary in UP below the *naib-tehsildar* and the revenue inspector who is responsible for the upkeep and maintenance of land records |
| *Mamlatdar* | : | native land revenue officer in charge of a taluk or division of a district |
| *Milan Khasra* | : | area of statement by class of land (classification of land village by village) |
| *Patwari* | : | village accountant |
| *Shijra* | : | cadastral map of the village |
| Survey Number | : | portion of land of which the area and assessment are separately entered under indicative number in land records |

*Tehsil*         : sub-division of a district consisting of a number of villages

*Tehsildar*     : chief revenue officer for the administration of a tehsil

*Taluk*         : sub-division of a district consisting of a number of villages

*Tippon*        : field measurement book

Village Accountant : village-level revenue functionary in Karnataka who collects revenue, makes crop entries and carries out functions as directed by tehsildars and others

## REFERENCES AND SELECT BIBLIOGRAPHY

**Appu, P.S.** (1995). *Report of the National Committee on Revitalization of Land Revenue Administration*. Government of India: Ministry of Rural Development, pp. 9–10.
————. (1996). *Land Reforms in India*. New Delhi: Vikas Publishing House.
**Centre for Rural Studies.** (2001).'Contributory Papers of National Workshop on Computerisation of Land Records', November. LBSNAA, Mussoorie.
**Government of India, Ministry of Rural Development.** (1985 and 1992). Conference of Revenue Ministers on Land Reforms.
————. *Annual Reports, 1995–1999*.
————. (1999). *Vision Document*.
**Government of India, Planning Commission.** First to Ninth Five Year Plans (chapters on Land Reforms).
**Singh, S.K.** (2001). *Dictionary of Land Revenue Terms in India*. Dehradun: Greenfield Publishers.

# 3

# *Bhoomi: Online Delivery of Record of Rights, Tenancy and Cultivation to Farmers in Karnataka*

SUBHASH BHATNAGAR AND RAJEEV CHAWLA

## APPLICATION CONTEXT

### Importance of Land Records in India

The collection of land revenue and the existence of the institutions of the state have been coterminus. A historical analysis of ancient Indian policy suggests that tax on land played a pivotal part in the evolution and maintenance of the systems of governance.

In ancient times land revenue was possibly the only source from which the entire income of the government was derived. Further, its incidence was on a large section of the population as a major proportion of the people relied on land for their livelihood and existence. Thus, tax on land proved to be the primary source of the state's wealth. The revenue collected varied among regions and also depended upon the regimes.

Broadly speaking it was a share of the produce paid in kind or cash. The mode of assessment and collection underwent a change when the British took over the administration. Lands were measured roughly and village records of lands were gradually built up. Thus, closely linked to the collection of land revenue was the creation of an array of land records wherein collection of revenue could be systematised and recorded.

India's independence ushered in the era of the welfare state and accordingly land revenue or the tax on the agricultural land also witnessed a reduction. Further, other sources of taxation became the primary sources of income for the government. However, the importance of land records cannot be undermined due to the decline in the importance of land revenue. The entire structure of land records management that was associated with revenue collection now had to sustain its relevance suo moto. The plan document of the Seventh Five-Year Plan rightly opined: '*Land records form the base for all land reforms and therefore regular periodic updating of land records is essential in all states*'.

Thus, the concept of collection of revenue necessitated the maintenance of land records, in a rudimentary form in ancient times and a more systematic form during the British administration. Maintenance of land records has now become more vital for administrators and creation of a land information system is one of the key issues facing governance today.

Land records itself is a generic expression and could include, in the state of Karnataka, records like the register of lands of *khetwar patrika*, record of rights, tenancy and crop inspection register—Form 16, *khata* register (Form 24), *khirdi* (Form 25), mutation register (Form 12), disputed cases register (Form 8), etc. However, certain types of information relating to land play a very important role. These may include primary information about land presented in terms of its geological information like the shape, size, land forms, soils; economic information related to land use irrigation and crops; and the information pertaining to the legal rights, registration and taxation. No improvement in land can be made without acquiring rights to the land. These rights cannot be acquired until ownership is established. The rationale for maintenance of land records originates from the following issues:

Land records form the basis for assignment and settlement of land titles. These records must stand the test of legal scrutiny. Land is a very precious source and the land records system must safeguard the rights of the legal owner of the land. Issues of land rights not only raise legal complexities but also have socio-economic dimensions. The state needs to ensure the maintenance of an accurate and genuine land records system to further its policy objectives of land reforms, protection of legal rights over land and efficiency in maintenance and updating of these records. Manual maintenance of land records does hinder effective collation and analysis of the data contained in them.

In Karnataka, land records were earlier maintained through a manual system, involving 9,000 village accountants, each serving a cluster of three to four villages. Eight registers were maintained to record the following types of information:

1. information on current ownership of each parcel of land, its area and cropping pattern, dispute, mutations; and
2. village maps that reflected the boundaries of each parcel.

Requests to alter land records (upon sale or inheritance of a land parcel) had to be filed with the village accountant. However, for various reasons (cases of disputes or to extract speed money) the village accountant could afford to ignore these 'mutation' requests. Upon receiving a request, the village accountant is required to issue notices to the interested parties and also paste the notice at the village office. Often neither of these actions was carried out, and no record of the notices was maintained. Notices were rarely sent through post. An update to the land records was to be carried out by a revenue inspector, if no objections were received within a 30-day period. In practice, however, it could take one to two years for the records to be updated.

Landowners found it difficult to access the village accountant, as his duties entailed travelling. The time taken by village accountants to provide RTCs ranged from three to 30 days, depending upon the importance of the record for the farmer and the size of the bribe. A typical bribe for a certificate could range from Rs 100 to Rs 2,000. If some details were to be written in an ambiguous fashion, out of selfish motives, the bribe could go up to Rs 10,000. Land records in the custody of village accountant were not open for public scrutiny.

Over a period, several inaccuracies crept into the old system through improper manipulation by the village accountant, particularly with respect to government land. Even where accountants were law-abiding, village maps could not remain accurate as the land was parcelled into very small lots over generations. The system of physical verification of records by deputy *tehsildars*[1] (supervisors of village accountants) became weak as the number of records multiplied and these functionaries were burdened with a host of other regulatory and developmental work.

## IMPLEMENTATION PROCESS

The central and state governments have long been aware of the need to reform the land records system. The beginning of computerisation of land records in Karnataka goes back to 1991 when the first pilot was initiated under the Ministry of Rural Development's Computerisation of Land Records (CoLR) project, fully funded by the Government of India. By 1996, projects for computerisation of land records were sanctioned for all dis-tricts in the state of Karnataka. However, no provision was made to install computers at *taluk* level where manual records were actually updated.

The breakthrough came when the state government mandated that project 'Bhoomi—Computerisation of Land Records' would have to be undertaken and finished in all sub-districts by March 2002. It was also decided to fully support development of a citizen-centric land records system even if it meant substantial investment by the state government for those components of the project which were not being funded by the central government. This political mandate was backed by full admin-istration efforts at all levels. The major objectives to be fulfilled by Bhoomi project were:

- Facilitating easy maintenance and prompt updating of land records.
- Making land records tamper-proof.
- Allowing farmers easy access to their records.
- Collating the information to construct database regarding land revenue, cropping pattern, land use, etc.
- Utilising the data for planning and for formulating development programmes.
- Enabling usage of this database by courts, banks, private organisa-tions and companies, ISPs.

The Karnataka government's Department of Revenue planned to set up computerised land record kiosks (Bhoomi centres) across 177 taluk offices. These kiosks were to provide farmers with the Record of Rights, Tenancy and Cultivation (RTC)—a document needed for obtaining bank loans, giving proof of ownership, etc. The Bhoomi project was expected to speed up delivery of RTCs, without delays, harassment or bribery.

## Digitisation of Legacy Data

The first and most important step to kick-start the Bhoomi system was to capture legacy data records in the possession of village accountants, numbering about 20 million. For this purpose, a comprehensive data-entry software 'Bhoomi' was designed after extensive discussions at various workshops at division, district and state level. The feedback from these workshops helped the department in designing this data-entry software.

The manual records were withdrawn from the field in the entire state in a phased manner. A printout of the computerised records was individually signed by village accountants (100 per cent), revenue inspectors (30 per cent), *shirasthedar* (5 per cent), tehsildar (3 per cent), assistant commissioners (2 per cent), and deputy commissioners (1 per cent),[2] after comparing with the manual registers to authenticate the data. They also put their seal with the name and designation along with date of verification. The manual and computerised sets of records on the starting day now serve as original records and are kept in safe custody of taluk office. As and when the process of comparison and certification was over in a taluk, a notification was issued by the deputy commissioner prescribing use of only computerised RTCs for all legal and other purposes.

## Issue of Copies to Farmers

Land records kiosks have been made operational in all 177 taluks. Village accountants can no more issue copies of the manual records, as only computerised records are valid. In every taluk, one village accountant has been designated as the kiosk village accountant. The farmers get the copy of their record on payment of user charges of Rs 15. Records are generated using the Bhoomi software running on kiosk computers and a back-end server holding the database. The records are signed by the village accountant at the kiosk and are provided to the farmers. In case of any small errors on the computerised records, the farmers can lodge a request with the taluk office along with the copy of the record available with him. Correction is made in the computerised Bhoomi database if the error is found to be genuine and the corrected copy is then provided to the farmer free of cost.

## Mutation Process in the Field

When a change of ownership takes place through sale or inheritance, farmers can file an application for a mutation of the land record at the Bhoomi centre at a separate operator assisted counter that handles mutations. Data from the application is entered into the terminal at the counter and a checklist is generated for manual verification of data and documents by a supervisor. Each request is assigned a number. The number can be used by the applicant to check the status of the application on a touch screen provided on a pilot basis in some of the computerised kiosks. Once the manual verification is complete, an entry is made in the back-end server which automatically generates notices that are to be served to affected parties. Notices are collected by village accountants on their visit to the taluk office as per a fixed schedule.

The village accountant serves these notices to interested parties and records their acknowledgement on one of the notice copies. If every thing is in order, the revenue inspector passes appropriate mutation order in the mutation registers after a prescribed period of 30 days from the date the notice is issued to the party. The mutation order is then brought to the Bhoomi centre. Notices with acknowledgement of interested parties and the mutation order passed in the field are then scanned on to the system. The revenue inspector who has passed these orders in the field authenticates this data entry. The deputy tehsildar verifies that everything typed and scanned is as per physical mutation records. The system then automatically updates the particular land record. Physical records are filed in the record room.

## Crop Updation

Crop updation is a batch process. For this purpose Bhoomi data of concerned crop fields are supposed to be provided to private data-entry agency for doing batch updation three times a year. Checklists are to be generated after crop updation and should be validated and signed by village accountants before updated data is merged with Bhoomi main database.

## Legal Framework

The unamended Karnataka Land Revenue Act did not provide for a computerised system. The Act has now been amended and provides for the storage of data on storage devices and use of Bhoomi software to be notified by government from time to time.

## Overcoming Implementation Challenges

Maintenance of equipment at 177 centres, many of which are located in far flung rural areas; dealing with isolated incidences of fraudulent certificates being presented at banks; mitigating problems of farmers that have to travel long distances to reach a Bhoomi kiosk; lack of currency and poor quality of crop survey data; and problems of illiterate farmers in filing mutation forms are some of the challenges that the project team has grappled with.

Many actions have been taken to improve the up time of computers at Bhoomi kiosks. Apart from the 1,000 officials that were trained at the district level, 108 village accountants were trained comprehensively in a two-month residential training course on hardware and networking in Bangalore. Four of these trained VAs are being placed in each district to serve as resource persons for primary diagnostic and repair. Facility managers with service-level agreements carrying stiff penalties have been assigned to each kiosk. The processing of payments to the facility managers has been decentralised so that the facility managers become more responsive to the needs in the field. All these measures have improved the up time to its current level of 98 per cent.

The printing process is being made more secure to deal with the problem of fraudulent certificates. Officers continue to enjoy a large amount of discretion in the process of mutation, even as some measures have been put in place to curb corruption. Illiterate farmers may still face difficulties in filling out mutation applications. A key challenge is to create awareness amongst rural population of all the changes that have taken place in processing RTCs and mutation, so that unscrupulous elements are not able to take advantage of their ignorance. Many of the future plans of Bhoomi are designed to deal with some of the key implementation challenges.

## Future Plans for Bhoomi

The Bhoomi database from all the 177 kiosks are planned to be uploaded on a central database every evening using a VSAT network of another application. Microsoft Corporation and the NIC have developed prototype architecture for the centralised data centre and 15 taluks' data has already been ported on the central platform. Funding support has been sought from the Government of India to establish the central repository in Bangalore. Rural Internet kiosks can access the data after the verification of their password, machine ID and the phone ID. This will provide a robust authentication procedure on the basis of which a rural telecentre will be charged a fee for each transaction.

A government order decentralising Bhoomi to village level has been passed. There are plans for opening a 1,000 kiosks statewide with public–private partnership. In a pilot experiment, 20 telecentres have been established in Mandya district by N-logue[3] using the *corDECT* technology developed by the Indian Institute of Technology, Chennai. These private kiosks can connect to the Mandya database through the N-Logue network, and view, print and distribute the land records. The Internet printing model has been made functional. These telecentres will charge a fee of Rs 25 instead of Rs 15, enabling them to retain Rs 10 per RTC to cover their operational costs and provide a small return on the investment.[4] Other services such as download of 100 important forms for services and beneficiary-oriented schemes could be added to the content. Departments such as forestry, animal husbandry, sericulture, cottage industries may create content in their own domains for delivery to rural areas. A fee of Rs 10 per RTC collected by the owner will make 1,000 rural kiosks viable in rural Karnataka.[5]

In another pilot, around 200 village accountants have been given Simputers (locally developed hand-held computers) costing about Rs 3.5 million. One round of crop updation for 600 villages was done using the Simputers. The second round of crop updation was done in last quarter of 2003. Teething problems such as Simputer maintenance and software bugs have been manageable. However, a further expansion has to wait until the cost of such hand-held devices reduces appreciably. Bhoomi is currently experimenting with hand-held computers designed by Media Lab Asia.

The scope of Bhoomi is limited to maintenance of land records, and issue of RTCs. Departments of Stamps and Registration is responsible for registration of deeds in case a change in ownership takes place through buying/selling or inheritance. The department has recently computerised the registration of such deeds in a project tiled Kaveri (Karnataka Valuation and e-Registration). There are plans to link up the Bhoomi centres with the newly computerised Kaveri centres to provide the cue to Bhoomi to carry out a mutation. Earlier, Kaveri offices sent this information in a paper document. Now it is sent in a digital form using a storage media. Once the statewide area network is established, this information will flow over the wire.

The total land revenue collected by village accountants in Karnataka is Rs 100 million. In future, Bhoomi centres will be asked to collect land revenue. However, the issue of RTC may still not be made contingent on payment of land revenue as such a procedure is deemed coercive by the citizens and is politically unacceptable.

## Impact Analysis

Improving the land record delivery system has a significant social and economic impact in rural areas. Nearly 2,500 bank branches in Karnataka loan approximately Rs 40 billion to farmers as working capital every year. A copy of the RTC is absolutely essential for the farmer to procure the loan. Effective land record management can help banks in recovery. In the long run, Bhoomi will help improve the investment climate of Karnataka by maintaining clean records of land ownership in urban and rural areas.

More than 70 per cent disputes in courts are land-based. Adjudication of disputes can be faster if access to land records is made efficient. Many mutations in land records are challenged in the courts. Such challenges are often upheld on technical counts when defenders fail to produce copies of notice that were served to the affected parties. Since a million notices are served in a year, a manual storage and retrieval system makes it difficult to retrieve old notices for submission to the courts. In the Bhoomi system every notice that is issued is scanned and a copy is easily retrievable from the Bhoomi kiosks. This facility in itself will create a huge impact on the resolution time of disputes. It will also reduce petty corruption for facilitating or hindering the process of retrieval of manual notices. The number of disputes will also come down because of the open access to data and the transparent and traceable mutation process.

Crop insurance has been made compulsory for those who take farm loans in Karnataka. In the year 2000–01 only 0.38 million farmers had insured their crops, paying Rs 112 million as premium and collected Rs 40 million in damages. However, in 2002–03 nearly 1 million farmers (15 per cent of the farming community) insured their crops paying Rs 420 million as premium and collected Rs 2,960 million in damages. There has been a substantial increase in the number of insurers amongst farmers who have not taken a loan. Earlier farmers could obtain falsified crop records from village accountants. Since droughts usually destroy the entire crop, there was no way of verifying such records. Often such favours are done for the rich farmers who can afford to pay bribes. Since insurance is a zero-sum game, the poor would suffer in future as premiums would go up. With the implementation of Bhoomi, crop data on the back of the RTC is the only document that can be used to back a claim. Since efforts are on to make the crop data more current (and accurate) and the VA accountable for the data, corruption in payout of insurance claims is likely to be reduced. At a later stage insurance companies will be able to seek cropping data from a central computerised database. This will make the insurance payout more equitable.

Bhoomi as a transparent land record system is a vast improvement over the manual system that it has replaced. The system is likely to facilitate the land sale and rental markets in Karnataka by reducing a part of the transaction costs. Many researchers have noted that any reallocation of land in favour of landless and small farmers will increase their income as well as overall agricultural productivity (Hanstand 2001).

There is not enough data to isolate and assess the direct impact of the Bhoomi system on reduction in poverty levels. The total annual savings for farmers on the costs of obtaining an RTC are discussed later in the chapter as a part of the cost and benefit analysis. These savings are particularly important for the small and marginal farmers.

For a fee of Rs 15, a printed copy of the RTC is obtained online within 30 minutes at computerised Bhoomi kiosks in 177 taluk offices. The land records are in the public domain. Copies of RTC can be obtained for any land parcel in the taluk by providing the name of the owner or the plot (survey) number and any record can be viewed through a touch screen at a few kiosks.

Farmers can apply for mutation and expedite the process by reviewing the status of their request online, presenting documentary evidence to supervisors in the event that their request is not processed within the stipulated time period. With the computerised system, administrators can quickly determine the number of approved and overdue mutation orders. After computerisation, there is an 85 per cent jump in the number of muta-tion requests. This change would seem to indicate a level of approval of the new system by the population, and willingness to update changes in land ownership that were previously left undocumented.

By the end of April 2004, the total revenue generated through issuance of RTCs was Rs 270 million, and the monthly collection had stabilised to about Rs 8 million. It is estimated that between Rs 90 and Rs 100 million would be collected each year from charges for RTCs. Nearly 78.3 per cent of all Bhoomi users take an RTC whereas 17.2 per cent apply for a modi-fied RTC (involving mutation) and 4.5 per cent collect a copy of the muta-tion order. The users of Bhoomi collect these documents for a variety of reasons. The largest proportion of users (51 per cent) collect the RTCs for applying for loan from a bank. Nearly 14 per cent use an RTC to verify the outcome of a mutation request. About 16 per cent use the documents in courts or to verify details of adjoining property.

Bhoomi is one of the few e-government applications that have been evaluated by an independent agency using a systematic methodology. An evaluation conducted by the Public Affairs Council, Bangalore in July 2002, showed significant impact on efficiency in delivery and corruption:[6]

1. *Ease in use of the Bhoomi kiosks:* Many users (66 per cent) were able to utilise the Bhoomi kiosks with no help, in contrast to 25 per cent in the case of the manual system. Most users of the Bhoomi system (78 per cent) found the system to be very simple. Many of the Bhoomi users (68 per cent) had also made use of the manual system in the past; a majority of users (78 per cent) who had past experience with the manual system found the Bhoomi system simpler.
2. *Complexity of procedures:* Most users (79 per cent) of the Bhoomi kiosks did so without having to meet any official except the counter staff, in contrast to 19 per cent who had to meet one official in the

case of the manual system. The extent of complexity is reflected in the fact that 61per cent of the users of the manual system had to meet two to four officials for their work. Legacies of the manual system have not completely faded away. About 18 per cent of Bhoomi users reported that their document was not signed by the appointed VA operating the kiosk, 6 per cent reported that they filled out an application form for issue of an RTC.

3. *Errors in documents received:* Users indicated that the Bhoomi kiosks provided error-free documents to more users (74 per cent), in contrast to 63 per cent in the case of the manual system. Among those reporting errors, wrongly spelt names were the most frequent error (81 per cent in case of manual system, and 53 per cent in the Bhoomi system). However, major errors in land details were noticed by 31 per cent of those who reported errors in the manual system, in contrast to 4 per cent in case of Bhoomi users.

4. *Rectification of errors:* Given that errors are not unusual at this stage of development of the Bhoomi system, how efficient are the response systems? Almost all users of the Bhoomi system had confidence to complain and sought rectification (93 per cent) as compared to less than half (49 per cent) in the manual system. Half the complainants (58 per cent) got timely response in case of Bhoomi, while such response was reported by only 4 per cent of those using the manual system.

5. *Cost of service:* All users of the Bhoomi facility who wish to receive a hard copy of the RTC pay a fee of Rs 15 each and receive a receipt for the same. A large segment of users (66 per cent) reported that they did not get a receipt for the payment they made.

6. *Hidden costs:* Citizens also incur hidden costs of time and effort to secure these certificates. Most Bhoomi users (79 per cent) reported a minimal waiting time in the queue of 10 minutes or less, in contrast with 27 per cent who could meet the concerned official in such a short time. The bigger issue is the number of times a citizen have to visit these offices to get the certificate. While most users got the RTC (72 per cent) after one visit to the Bhoomi kiosk, only 5 per cent got it that fast in the manual system.

7. *Reduced corruption:* The most serious issue is that of corruption and bribery. Two-thirds of the users of the manual system paid a bribe—66 per cent of them reported having to do so very often. In contrast, only 3 per cent of the users of the Bhoomi system reported paying bribes.

8. *Staff behaviour:* While technical capacity of the system plays an important role in its success, the approach of people who handle the task is of critical significance too. Most Bhoomi users (85 per cent) rated staff behaviour at the Bhoomi kiosks as 'good'; none of the users of the manual system rated staff behaviour as 'good'.

---

**Box 3.1**

**Kudos for Bhoomi**

'I have no complaints [about Bhoomi]', says farmer Basavenappa Angadi, president of about 40 farmer self-help groups in the cotton-growing Dharwad district of Karnataka, 440 km from Bangalore. In Kengeri, a satellite town near Bangalore, farmer Byregowda too likes his new RTC: 'This is now *pukka* [genuine]. The village accountant cannot change names anymore.'

---

Armed with genuine certificates, farmers can raise loans for a variety of purposes and cannot be easily harassed by bank staff. Mutations had become an instrument for rural corruption, exploitation and oppression. Landowners simply bribed the VA to change the titles of poor farmers' lands to their own name. Small farmers, mostly illiterate, could do little to change this state of affairs, either because they did not know of it or because they could not afford the VA's bribes. Media report quoting a farmer makes it evident that after Bhoomi, such practices would become difficult. 'In one district in north Karnataka where feudalism still prevails, land of 32 farmers had been recorded in the VA's name prior to com- puterisation,' says Nagaraj, a prominent left-wing politician of Karnataka. 'The man immediately sold the lot before Bhoomi began. I know of hundreds of such cases'. Many reports in the print media have portrayed Bhoomi very favourably.

However, some early reports (based on small-sample interviews and anecdotal evidence) also pointed to problems and other limitations. For example, Hanstand and Lokesh (2002) interviewed 23 users of the Bhoomi system in January 2001 in one centre and reported that 20 of the 23 farm- ers favoured the old system. Teething problems (the kiosk had been work- ing for six months) like power failure for five to six hours at the kiosk seemed to be the main reason for the dissatisfaction with the new system. Many of these teething problems were overcome subsequently. One inter- esting aspect of Bhoomi is the constant improvements that have been made in the application in response to the feedback received from various stakeholders. For example, the project has already decided to redefine the role of tehsildar and the deputy tehsildar in the process of mutation because the feedback suggests that their intervention causes delay (a problem mentioned by Hanstand and Lokesh [2002]). Some of the reports indicate that there could be a lack of awareness about how the Bhoomi system works. For example, even though there are no forms to be filled in Bhoomi to get an RTC, some reports in media quote complaints in this regard.

**Box 3.2**

**Impediments at the Grassroots**

Ironically, while Bhoomi aims to help the poor, in regions like Bijapur in Karnataka, which has the highest demand for RTCs, it is the poor who appear to be struggling most with the new system. 'We spend Rs 10 ($0.2) as bus fare to reach the town from our villages and pay Rs 15 ($0.3) for an RTC. Sometimes it takes two days because the queue is so long. The VA was better,' complains Mehboob Modi Patel. Another farmer, Amsidda Irrappa Karnal, says, 'I am illiterate. Who will help me fill up the application form [for the RTC] here?'

The project should help address gender inequality. Land ownership has long been a male bastion in India—in Karnataka women own just 12 per cent of the land—and this is reflected in Bhoomi. Women in Dharwad district do not know of the new system. Those from Kalakawatagi village in northern Karnataka say they have not seen their computerised RTC, issued free by the revenue department in 2001 for personal verification. In Kolar district, about 100 km from Bangalore, 42-year-old Pappamma, a feisty leader of some 200 women's groups, says she has visited the local e-kiosk several times to help women obtain RTCs. 'But taluk officials themselves know little of the system and are in no position to even begin helping the women. They need training'. She comments.

(Based on 'Flaws in Bhoomi: India's model e-governance project' by Keya Acharya. Received via e-mail)

# ELEMENTS OF EMPOWERMENT

## Access to Information

Bhoomi empowers the small rural farmer in many ways. Their relationship with lower rungs of civil servants can be on a more equal footing.[7] In the manual system, land records were maintained in registers to which citizens had no access. The records of landownership in Bhoomi can be collected by anyone. Similarly, the status of mutation requests can be tracked online. The process has become transparent to the extent that the clients can observe the stored image of their land records through a second monitor screen facing them. Farmers have access to complete documentation of notices and mutation orders in case of a legal dispute.

Bhoomi will eventually make it possible for a 1,000 rural telecentres to be established and be economically viable in Karnataka. These telecentres will help empower large segments of rural populations by enhancing access to information and services that will be delivered through the telecentres.

## Social Accountability

There are many elements in the system that enhance accountability. The bio-login procedure and the use of encryption and public–private key ensures that the issue of RTCs and changes in data records can be traced back to the operators who were on duty and supervisors that gave the go-ahead. By specifying a first-come-first-served basis for processing mutations and allowing deputy tehsildar to pass mutation orders in case the RI does not pass the orders in 50 days, the power to harass has been taken away. If an application is pushed down in the priority order, reasons need to be assigned for keeping it in abeyance.

## Inclusion and Participation

A number of people, particularly the poor, illiterate and women, may have found it difficult to obtain land records due to corruption, inefficiency and cumbersome procedures in the earlier system. The Bhoomi system does not require an application to be filled in. Data is available to indicate that more people collect RTCs and also come forward to get data corrected when errors are found.

Often, farmers go to bank branches in groups to process crop loans in the hope that corrupt officers will find it harder to demand bribes in the presence of other people. The convenience with which RTCs can be collected, facilitates this group approach.

## COSTS AND BENEFITS

The expenditure on data entry operations for about 2 million RTCs in 27 districts was Rs 80 million. The unit cost of providing hardware, construction of computer rooms and kiosks was of the order of Rs 0.64 million for each taluk. Thus, the total out-of-pocket expenditure on the project was Rs 185 million. This does not include the cost of software development (nearly 100 person-months of effort) done gratis by the National Informatics Centre.[8] The cost of processing an RTC has been roughly estimated at Rs 13, assuming a life of five years for the hardware and an activity level of 2 million RTCs issued from all the kiosks (10 per cent of all holdings). This cost includes an assumed operational expenditure of Rs 2 for stationery, cartridges and electricity. The current user fee of Rs 15 seems sufficient to cover these costs.

The benefit in terms of man-days saved is approximately 1.32 million man-days per annum, leading to savings of Rs 66 million per annum in wages. The weighted average value of bribe paid in the manual system was Rs 152.46 per person, while that in Bhoomi was Rs 3.09. Even if we reduce the saving by the fee that they have to pay that is Rs 15, the net saving is Rs 134.37 and translates to a saving of over Rs 806 million annually.

### Potential Future Benefits

The system generates various types of reports on land ownership by size, type of soil, crops, owner's sex, etc., which would be useful for planning poverty alleviation programmes, and supplying agricultural inputs.

Many other benefits will flow from centralisation of the database. The application has been PKI-enabled so that computer-generated records can be digitally signed. In the future, banks will be persuaded to access land record data of farmers to whom loans are to be issued directly from the central databases. Since authenticated data would be available, there would be no need for farmers to actually collect the RTC and carry it physically to the bank. This would require that the banks change their business processes for providing crop loans to farmers. This will also help the banks in advance planning on the quantum of lending required. Similarly, the high court, district and taluk courts could access the database for resolving legal disputes surrounding land.

The system could also lead to better administration of Land Reforms Act, such as enforcing a ceiling on landholdings, etc. Bhoomi makes it possible to identify and aggregate all land of different types belonging to an individual in a given village. This identification is based on a khata number that links all such records. Bhoomi project is making efforts to clean up the data on khatas. A citizen ID will be needed to link records across taluks and districts. An analysis of ownership by gender has indicated a large divide. Such analysis can be made public and can lead to reforms that will correct the situation.

## DRIVING FACTORS

Computerisation of land records in India has had a checkered history. In 1985, a Conference of Revenue Ministers of States resolved to computerise land records on a pilot basis. In 1988–89 a centrally sponsored scheme on Computerisation of Land Records (CoLR) funded a pilot project in eight districts. The projects were to computerise core data contained in land records, so as to assist development planning and to make records accessible to people/planners/administrators.[9] By 1991–92, the scheme had been extended to 24 districts in different states. However, a review in 1993–94 indicated that states were finding it difficult to sustain the project due to non-availability of skilled manpower, hardware maintenance, etc.[10]

In 1998, a comprehensive evaluation study conducted in eight districts of different states found that not much progress had been accomplished. Some of the bottlenecks were:

- Delay in transfer of funds to implementing authority by the state governments.

- Delay in construction of telecentres and installation of computers and other equipment.
- Delay in development of appropriate software as per the requirement of the state government.
- Delay in supply and installation of the hardware by the National Informatics Centre.
- Lack of adequate training to revenue officials to handle the computers.
- Absence of good vendors for taking up the job of data-entry work.

By 1998 it was realised that a district was not the appropriate administrative level to computerise land records. In 1997–98, a decision was taken to operationalise the scheme at the taluk level for delivery of computerised land records to the public at large. Under this programme, the central government earmarked Rs 0.4 million for the purchase of hardware, software and other peripherals for each taluk. Nearly 2,500 taluks out of a total of 6,000 were to be covered. During the Ninth Five-Year Plan (1997–2002), the central government released a sum of Rs 1,545 million. By the end of 2002, the scheme was under implementation in 569 out of 599 districts in India. Since inception of CoLR, the central government has released Rs 21,894 million (up to 31 December 2001) out of which the states/union territories have utilised around 53 per cent.[11]

In spite of such a large expenditure, there are only a few scattered taluks where computerised land records are being issued. Karnataka is the sole exception where the system is working in the entire state.

Given the variability in the land record systems across India, a single system or software was unlikely to be usable at all places. The central government did not have clarity about the strategy to be adopted for implementation of the scheme. Nor did it insist on a detailed system design and implementation plan from states before funding. This was one project where a thousand flowers should not have been allowed to bloom. Each state should have had a well-coordinated strategy as in the case of Karnataka.

In most projects there was lack of involvement of the revenue department officers and district administration in the project. At most places the quality of manual records was poor and therefore data-entry systems had to be designed with great care. Data entry was done offline by private agencies but due to poor work culture, the process was very slow and error-prone (Islam 2003). Lack of training of field functionaries on data-entry process led to wrong and defective database. The printed records were distributed to the farmers without proper validation. The one-time distribution was itself regarded as computerisation of land records. The pilots in Dungarpur district took 14 years to complete the first stage. There was confusion about roles among the staff, and a lack of institutionalisation of the project by state government. It largely remained a district-level initiative. In a period of rapidly changing technology, the pilot could not emerge as a standard to be followed across other districts (Gupta 2002).

Some of the reasons why the CoLR scheme has succeeded in Karnataka and not in a large number of other states are discussed below.

## Commitment and Political Economy for Change

Unlike the neighbouring Andhra Pradesh where, under Chandrababu Naidu, e-government was seen to be driven by the then chief minister, in Karnataka e-government implementation has largely been bottom-up through departmental initiatives primarily driven by civil servants. Yet it is to the credit of the drivers of Bhoomi that they were able to harness a significant level of political support for Bhoomi. The political executive was completely involved in the computerisation project. The state chief minister and revenue minister highlighted the importance of the project in many public forums. The chief minister wrote regularly to all district deputy commissioners, exhorting them to get fully involved in the computerisation, and inaugurated a large number of land record kiosks.[12] Meanwhile, the revenue minister regularly reviewed the computerisation process and also inaugurated large number of kiosks. A committee of members of the legislative assembly (MLAs) visited the kiosks and deputy commissioners invited MLAs of their districts to witness the functioning of kiosks. All this helped demonstrate that there was a strong political will for computerisation of land records. Perhaps a desire to project a pro-poor image of the government led the politicians to lend full support to the project.

## Institutional Innovation

Resistance from field staff was anticipated and conscious steps were taken to lessen the resistance. To allay the fears of field officials that their job descriptions would change in a major way, 12 state-level information seminars were organised for 1,200 senior and mid-level officers. And four division-level workshops were organised to train 800 officials. These seminars emphasised that maintenance of land records was only one of their many functions and that computerisation will remove the drudgery of maintaining these records manually. Revenue officials would continue to be responsible for field enquiry. Reducing corruption was not a key message at these gatherings.

Selected field-level personnel were invited to participate in the software development process for various Bhoomi modules through a formal state-level Bhoomi committee. Meetings were held with participation from various levels in the department to elicit suggestions for improvement; and decisions taken at these meetings were incorporated into the software design. Nearly 125 man-months were spent on software development. (Bhoomi has already been migrated to Version-3 and all taluks are now using the latest version.)

Field supervision is critical to roll-out of any new system. The project leader-in-charge preferred to appoint four independent consultants who could tour sites randomly in each division and report problems and progress of Bhoomi. Appointing consultants needed special effort, as the central government project did not permit such a line item of expenditure. The expected cost was Rs 1.5 million.

The village accountants who would be in charge of the new kiosks were chosen very carefully. Young persons fresh out of college were recruited and trained at the headquarters. These officials had not experienced the power that a village accountant could exercise over rural farmers. The project leader (additional secretary of the department) personally participated in the training given to every batch of accountants to ensure that they felt complete ownership and a sense of importance in being assigned to this new initiative. Accountants were encouraged to talk to the project leader either at his home or at his office. Nearly 900 officials, including all deputy tehsildars, were trained in the state headquarters, and more than 1,000 officials were trained by the Bhoomi consultants at the district level.

Partnerships were forged with many different agencies. Agencies like the NIC and private data-entry agencies played a pivotal role during various phases of implementation. Since the departmental staff was reluctant to enter data, private data-entry agencies were used. An elaborate mechanism was designed for validating the data to make sure that it mirrored the manual records that had legal sanctity. Every district was provided with a consultant to act as a bridge between the data-entry agency and the district administration. After the system was operational, the consultant trained the taluk staff and helped the district administration in daily work at the Bhoomi kiosk.

Moreover, private operators had been provided for one year to handle online data entry at the Bhoomi kiosks to enable the village accountants to get completely trained. Village accountants took over the work from these operators after a year. A comprehensive training module was designed jointly by the department and NIC to train the accountants. Training lasted seven days, 11 hours each day, followed by a paperless test on the last day.

## Learning and Experimentation

Rollout of the application to 177 locations was a challenge due to the poor quality of manual records and the enormity of the data-entry task. In the first phase, the project was implemented on a pilot basis in a controlled environment at four taluks. After gaining experience in data-entry operations and implementation of the software, the scheme was extended to one pilot taluk in each of the 27 districts. In the third phase the project was rolled out simultaneously to all the remaining 146 taluks.

Based on early feedback on unacceptable levels of downtime at certain kiosks, a facility manager with stiff service-level agreements was appointed to maintain the computer system. This has resulted in the satisfactory working of the centres. The minimum expected configuration (server, kiosk machines, power supply) in every centre is expected to be up and functional all the time. NIC, Bangalore had created the data-entry software for the earlier phase starting in 1992. Even though considerable effort was involved, the software was unable to handle all the variations in land titles. Further, the data entry by a private agency had several errors due to lack of data validation.

In 1998, workshops were organised at both the division and the state level to understand and correct software problems. At the division level, workshops lasted four days and involved about 800 people. At the state level, workshops lasted 12 days and involved about 1,200 mid-level and senior officials. These workshops came up with guidelines and requirements for the new Bhoomi system.

Following the workshops, the state government worked closely with NIC to fix the data-entry software and to develop the back-end Bhoomi software.[13] NIC set up a team of four people to work full-time on Bhoomi. The technical director also devoted about 10–15 per cent of his time towards the management of the team. The end product was a system that has now become a model to be replicated in all states.

Incidence of a forged RTC in one of the taluks prompted experimentation in making the printing process secure so that forging a document would become difficult. Various options such as use of holograms and barcodes were evaluated. More sophisticated solutions that encode and print the key contents of the land title as an image (like barcodes) on the RTC are being tried. Decoders supplied to key users will be able to decode the image to authenticate the RTC.[14]

The system has been responsive to feedback from the clients. The system of charging of mutation fee for every survey number in a farmer's total holding was seen to be hurting farmers with very fragmented small holdings. A new algorithm is now used to calculate the fee on the basis of total holding and the number of parcels.

## External Catalysts

The state government would not have taken up a project of this magnitude involving an upfront investment of Rs 200 million. Central government funding was the key catalyst that enabled the project champion to sell the idea within the state. Healthy competition with the neighbouring state of Andhra Pradesh, which seemed to have moved much faster with reforms and e-government, was another reason that spurred Karnataka into action.

The World Bank, which has provided a structured adjustment loan to Karnataka, has also been quietly supportive of Karnataka's e-government programme. The bank has been providing technical assistance in the form of periodic review of major e-government initiatives. The project leaders have been open to feedback from the bank's team. Some of the new initiatives like connectivity to rural kiosks have a strong bank endorsement. A bank-funded evaluation conducted by an independent agency was seen as a very useful exercise for establishing the credibility of a fledgling system.

External recognition in the form of awards and positive feedback has been a major motivator for the Bhoomi team.

## LESSONS LEARNED

Success of Bhoomi flies against the traditional wisdom of improving service delivery to the poor which emphasises more investments to create a greater reach of delivery points. Bhoomi has reduced service delivery points from 9,000 to 177 and is now in the process of providing 1,000 points, and consumer satisfaction has increased. Bhoomi reinforces some of the ideas put forth for improving services for the poor (World Bank 2004). Often large numbers of delivery points cannot be monitored centrally. Unless there are ways in which monitoring can be done by the community (presuming that an equal voice can be created for all groups) such large systems become inefficient.

Implementation of land record computerisation has been difficult in India. Bhoomi succeeded with the efforts of the project champion (the departmental head) who worked a 15-hour day for over 12 months, devoting 80 per cent of his time to the project. The fact that the project champion has had a tenure exceeding six years (and is still continuing) has been a very important factor in stabilising the system. Minimising resistance from staff by harnessing political support was an important contributory factor. Extensive training, coupled with a participatory style, also helped to diminish resistance.

Project managers need to balance the potential benefits against the risk of implementation failure in deciding how much reform (re-engineering) to tackle at any one time. In Bhoomi significant benefits are delivered in issuing RTCs, but much of the old mutation process remains unaltered. There is no change in the role of revenue inspector in passing the mutation order. Some other changes in process may impact corruption in the mutation process. Bhoomi has reduced the discretion of public officials by introducing provisions for recording a mutation request online. Requests are processed on a first-come-first-serve basis. Another officer can pass a mutation order if the revenue inspector delays it beyond a limit. Farmers can now access the database and are empowered to follow up. They can also detect fraudulent mutations. Reports on overdue mutations can point to errant behaviour. Still, supervisors must examine the reports and take appropriate action. In remote areas, operators may turn away citizens by saying that the system offering online service is down. Strict field supervision is needed (through empowered citizens committees and NGOs) to curb such behaviour. Ultimately, the only recourse that a citizen has against such practices is to lodge a complaint. The process for lodging a complaint should be facilitated through the Web. The backend has to be geared up to handle complaints received electronically.

As an implementation strategy, manually written RTCs were declared illegal from the day on which the computerised system became operational in a taluk. The notification was issued on a taluk-by-taluk basis as and when the scheme became operational there. This forced the department and the farmers to completely rely on the new system. The strategy worked because the application design was robust and did not falter.

There was some concern in Karnataka about raising the user fee to Rs 15 from Rs 2 in the manual system. Often these fears about user fees are exaggerated, particularly if services have genuinely been improved. The response of the farmers at taluk level has been overwhelming. Soon after the initial success, elected representatives, district officials and farmers made demands that Bhoomi be extended to the sub-taluk level. Presumably, the project was considered an unqualified success. However, this expansion would have increased the costs without necessarily increasing the number of RTCs that would have been issued. The department did well to resist the temptation as it would not have been able to monitor and support a geographically spread-out operation. In any case, systems should be allowed to stabilise and prove their sustainability over a two-year period before attempting any replication. In the 1980s, a DRDA (District Rural Development Agency) computerisation project called CRISP (Computer Retrieval of Information on Scientific Projects) was replicated in 500 districts in a hurried manner. The expansion turned out to be a failure.

The department did well to explore other possibilities, short of direct expansion, that could make RTCs available at sub-taluk level. Plans to allow private rural kiosks to issue copies signed through the territorial village accountants may never have come about if a hurried expansion of the Bhoomi system had been made. If such copies can be accepted by banks and verified by accessing the departmental database, the need for signed copies will be reduced. A solution may emerge through wider consultations with the ultimate consumers of these documents.

Bhoomi succeeded because its design is robust and it targeted a critical need for farmers and delivered significant benefits by re-engineering land record processes.

Projects that are intended to benefit rural populations need to recognise the high level of effort that is needed to make rural population aware of the reforms that have been instituted. There is some feedback that in spite of considerable publicity of Bhoomi, farmers may still not understand the implication of all the reforms that have been carried out. The farmers need to be made aware that there is no need to pay bribes because the functionaries would no more be able to misuse their authority to benefit or wrongly penalise any one.

# REPLICATION OF BHOOMI IN INDIA AND OTHER COUNTRIES

The potential of information and communication technologies in impacting the lives of rural poor has been recognised, but harnessing it has been a challenge. By its ability to serve as a *killer application* that can make a large number of privately owned rural Internet kiosks economically viable, Bhoomi has shown the way to bridge the digital divide in poorer countries.

Although, the direct impact of Bhoomi on rural poverty cannot be easily measured, there are many ways in which Bhoomi helps the poor farmers, as was discussed earlier. Recognising the importance of accurate land records, the Ministry of Rural Development, Government of India, funded many projects, including Bhoomi, to computerise land records in different states in India. After the success of Bhoomi, the Ministry of Communication and Information Technology (MCIT) has also taken up the replication of Bhoomi in other states under a special programme titled 'Roll-out of successful e-government initiatives.' Under this programme Bhoomi is one of the three e-government initiatives identified for a countrywide roll-out. MCIT is providing funds for pilot implementation of Bhoomi in one district of each of the 13 states that have volunteered to implement Bhoomi. Leading management-consulting companies have been chosen to support the roll-out effort. MCIT is providing the funding for these consulting agencies.

The consultants are expected to capture knowledge and experience from successful projects and transfer such knowledge to the agencies involved in pilot implementations. The project recognises that the replication need not necessarily involve the use of the same software as was implemented in the successful application. It is more important to capture the processes that lead to successful implementation such as digitisation of manual data, re-engineering of processes, involvement of all stakeholders and management of change. The consultants will prepare a report outlining the implementation plan, which defines the scope, outcome and the technology, and business model for the proposed pilot implementation.

One of the key problems in replicating the Bhoomi system is the fact that the documentation of procedures that govern the mutation of land is poor across all states. In addition to legal provisions which are documented, there are several procedures developed on the basis of conventions that have evolved over many years. It requires significant efforts to understand and document such procedures for designing a computerised mutation process. The computerised system needs to have the ability to handle different ways in which a mutation can arise. It took almost seven years for the Bhoomi project to understand and document these procedures. In most other states the tenure of project managers is very short to allow them to undertake such an exercise.

In considering Bhoomi for replication it should be noted that Bhoomi does not lead to security of land tenancy for the farmers who till the land of other owners. During the land reforms in 1970s and 1980s in India, tenancy system was scrapped and land was granted to the tiller. However, in terms of ground reality there could be a large number of tenants still tilling land of other farmers without having any legal rights. The reforms needed to establish tenancy rights are more fundamental in nature. Clearly Bhoomi has little impact on securing such rights.

It must also be emphasised that Bhoomi does not provide a title. The RTC issued by Bhoomi has only a presumptive value. In the titling system the accuracy of the database such as that maintained by Bhoomi will be guaranteed by the state. In case an owner loses the ownership of a land because of legal process or otherwise, the state would be required to compensate such owners. A land titling system can only be built upon records that are clean and maintained in a manner that they cannot be tampered with.

Given the poor quality of land records in many states of India, there is no state (and, in fact, only a few countries) which has moved to a title system. Encouraged by the fact that Bhoomi will further clean up the data because of constant usage and openness of the land records, Karnataka has now embarked on this journey to move to a land titling system in the next few years.

# CONCLUSION

The Bhoomi project of online delivery of land records in Karnataka demonstrates the benefits of making government records more open so that citizens are empowered to challenge arbitrary action. It also illustrates how automation can be used to take discretion away from civil servants at operating levels.

The Department of Revenue in Karnataka has computerised 20 million records of land ownership of 6.7 million farmers in the state. In the past, under the manual system, land records were maintained by 9,000 village accountants, each serving a cluster of three to four villages. Farmers had to seek out the village accountant to get a copy of the record of rights, tenancy and cultivation—a document needed for many tasks such as obtaining bank loans. Nearly 2,500 bank branches in Karnataka loan approximately Rs 40 billion to farmers as working capital every year.

Village accountants were not easily accessible, as their duties entailed travelling. The time taken by village accountants to provide RTCs ranged from three to 30 days and bribes ranging from Rs 100 to Rs 2,000 had to be paid. If some details were to be deliberately written in an ambiguous fashion, the bribe could go up to Rs 10,000. Land records in the custody of village accountants were not open for public scrutiny. In the Bhoomi project, a printed copy of the RTC can be obtained online by providing the name of the owner or plot number at computerised land record kiosks in 177 taluk[15] offices, for a fee of Rs 15. A second computer screen faces the clients to enable them to see the transaction being performed. In the next phase of the project, all the taluk databases will be uploaded to a web-enabled central database. RTCs will then be available online at Internet kiosks in rural areas, which will be able to connect to the central database.[16]

Earlier, mutation requests to alter land records (upon sale or inheritance of a land parcel) had to be filed with the village accountant. The village accountant was required to issue notices to the interested parties and also paste the notice at the village office. Often neither of these actions was carried out, nor any record of the notices was maintained. Although an update to the land records could be carried out after a 30-day-period by a revenue inspector, in practice it could take one to two years for the records to be updated. Bhoomi has reduced the discretion of public officials by introducing provisions for recording a mutation request online. Farmers can now access the database and are empowered to follow up. A farmer can check the status of a mutation application on a touch screen provided on a pilot basis in 20 of the computerised kiosks. If the revenue inspector does not complete the mutation within 50 days, a farmer can now approach another officer at the taluk level to authorise a mutation. Now, mutation requests are to be handled strictly on a first-come-first-served basis. These measures limit opportunities for collecting bribes. After computerisation, there is a 85 per cent jump in the number of mutation requests. This change would seem to indicate a level of approval of the new system by the population, and willingness to update changes in land were previously left undocumented.

The system of collecting crop data printed at the back of the RTC is also being computerised on an experimental basis. Greater accuracy in crop data would lead to a more equitable distribution of crop insurance claims. In 2002–03, nearly 1 million farmers (15 per cent of the farming community) insured their crops. Earlier farmers could obtain falsified crop records from village accountants to boost their claims. With the implementation of Bhoomi, crop data on the back of the RTC is the only document that can be used to back a claim.

Bhoomi will facilitate a quicker disposal of land disputes in courts by enabling faster retrieval of documents required by courts such as notices issued for mutation to affected parties. More than 70 per cent disputes in courts are land-based. The number of disputes will also come down because of the open access to data and the transparent and traceable mutation process.

Bhoomi has demonstrated a sustainable way of computerising land records. By the end of April 2004, the total user fee collected through issuance of RTCs was Rs 270 million. This amount not only covers the investments made in computerisation but leaves enough surplus for further development.

By enhancing transparency and providing greater access to information, Bhoomi has empowered poorer farmers and increased accountability of the revenue department. Operators of the computerised system are made accountable for their decisions and actions by using a bio-login system that authenticates every login through a thumbprint. A log is maintained of all transactions in a session. By and large, Bhoomi has been portrayed positively by the media and has won several prizes.[17] Independent evaluation studies have shown that Bhoomi has significantly reduced corruption and improved service delivery.[18] The Government of India is making special efforts to replicate Bhoomi in other states of India.

# NOTES

1. The chief revenue officer for a taluk.
2. Figures in brackets indicate the percentage of records signed by different officers.
3. N-Logue Communications Pvt. Ltd. is a private company promoted by the Telecommunications and Computer Networking Group of Indian Institute of Technology, Chennai.
4. Most of the users spend Rs 25–50 in travelling to a taluk kiosk. Some of the users when questioned about the additional fee indicated that an additional charge of Rs 10 would be totally acceptable to the farmer community if the RTC could be delivered through a rural telecentre. To make sure that farmers are not overcharged, the stationery used by the telecentres to print RTC would be stamped with the maximum price that can be charged for a RTC just like the maximum retail price stamp on product packages sold in India.
5. User fee being collected by Bhoomi is approximately Rs 100 million in a year. If 50 per cent of the RTCs are issued from 1,000 rural kiosks that are proposed to be set up, each kiosk will earn an average annual revenue of Rs 50,000. Accounting for variability across kiosks, the floor earning could be in the range of Rs 30,000. At this level of earning, a kiosk can be viable.
6. The Report Card on the Bhoomi initiative sought to assess benefits derived by users of Bhoomi Centres in relation to improved quality of service and satisfaction. A sample survey was carried out with citizens who have used Bhoomi kiosks, as well as a control sample of those who have used non-computerised land record providers. Quality of service and user satisfaction was compared across these two groups, to derive conclusions on the impact and benefit from the Bhoomi initiative. Data was collected from six districts reflecting geographic regions of Karnataka, and two Bhoomi kiosks were selected through sampling (weighted by intensity of use) among the kiosks operating in each district. A total of 198 respondents were interviewed across the Bhoomi kiosks. For the non-computerised facility user sample, four taluks were selected and 59 respondents interviewed. A team from AC Nielsen-ORG-MARG carried out the field survey and preliminary analysis.
7. When the delegates of a workshop in Bangalore in February 2004 held in preparation for the Shanghai conference visited a rural kiosk issuing RTCs in Mandya, Karnataka

an old farmer demanded that data be corrected in Bhoomi records as the printout in his RTC had misspelt his name.

8. National Informatics Centre is a central government department with offices in state capitals and districts to provide technical assistance in developing ICT applications.
9. Source URL: *http://www.expresscomputeronline.com/20030324/focus3.shtml*
10. Source URL: *http://www.expresscomputeronline.com/20030324/focus3.shtml*
11. Rs 1.1635 billion [up to 31 December 2001].
12. One example in which he demonstrated his commitment was that he signed letters to revenue collectors regarding Bhoomi while he was sick in a hospital.
13. The data-entry software should not be confused with the back-end Bhoomi software, also developed by NIC, which operates on data, create reports, handles mutations and tracks applications.
14. Based on a propriety software developed by HP Labs India. The image is printed using the private key of the kiosk operator. The public key is attached to the decoder, enabling it to decode the contents of the image and authenticate the source as the kiosk operator.
15. Sub-unit of a sub-division of a district.
16. Internet kiosks are being set up in rural areas by the department of agriculture, NGOs and the private sector but the numbers are very small. See *The Hindu* (2002).
17. Commonwealth Award.
18. Report card on service of Bhoomi kiosks: *www1.worldbank.org/publicsector/bnpp/Bhoomi.pdf*

## REFERENCES AND SELECT BIBLIOGRAPHY

**Bhatnagar, S.C.** (2003a). 'Administrative Corruption: How Does E-Government Help?', The World Bank. Source URL: *http://www1.worldbank.org/publicsector/egov/Corruption %20and %20egov't%20TI%20Paper%20Subhash.doc*
———. (2003b). 'BHOOMI: Closing the digital divide through innovative reforms and partnership', 11th International Anti-Corruption Conference, Seoul, Republic of Korea, 25–28 May. Source URL: *www.11iacc.org/download/0618/ WS_11.3_Bhatnagar_Final_Paper.doc*
**Chawla, Rajeev** and **Subhash Bhatnagar.** 'Bhoomi: Online Delivery of Land Titles in Karnataka, India', Case study available on World Bank's e-government website. Source URL: *http://www1.worldbank.org/publicsector/egov/bhoomi_cs.htm*
**Checchini, Simone.** (2002). 'Bhoomi: Preliminary Findings on Costs', Poverty Reduction Group, The World Bank, July.
**Government of India.** (1985). Seventh Five Year Plan (Chapter on 'Land Reforms'). Planning Commission.
**Gupta, Vivek.** (2002). 'E-governance: Lessons from District Computerization', IFIP Newsletter, Volume 12, No. 1, April, International Federation for Information Processing.
**Hanstand, Tim.** (2001). 'How are Rural Land Sale Markets in Karnataka Impacting the Poor's Access to Land?'. Discussion paper. Rural Development Institute, University of Washington, School of Law. October.

**Hanstand, Tim** and **S.B. Lokesh.** (2002). 'Computerization of Land Records in Karnataka: Observations from a Simple Field Study'. Unpublished. Rural Development Institute, Bangalore.

**Islam, K.M. Baharul.** (2003). 'Information Age Government: Success Stories of Online Land Records & Revenue Governance from India', Executive Summary, Third Meeting of the Committee on Development Information (CODI), Economic Commission for Africa, United Nations Economic and Social Council, Ethiopia, 10–17 May. Source URL: *http://www.uneca.org/codi/Documents/PDF/Information% 20Age%20Government.pdf*

**Lobo, Albert** and **Suresh Balakrishnan.** (2002). Report Card on Service of Bhoomi Kiosks: An assessment of benefits by users of the computerised land records system in Karnataka, Public Affairs Centre, Bangalore, November.

**Ministry of Rural Development.** Website. *http://rural.nic.in/book00-01/ch-20.pdf*
———. Website. *http://rural.nic.in/book01-02/ch-24.pdf*

**Rai, Kuldip** and **D.K. Bhalla.** 'Computerization of Land Records in India'. http://www. gisdevelopment.net/application/lis/overview/lisrp0015.htm.

**The Hindu.** (2002). 'IT for agriculture: Karnataka move', 3 April. Source URL: *http:// www.hinduonnet.com/thehindu/2002/04/03/stories/2002040303460600.htm*

**World Bank.** (2004). *World Development Report.*

# 4

# Bhoomi: A Case Study

## A. RAMA MOHAN RAO AND P.V. BHAT

## BACKGROUND

The majority of the population of India lives in rural areas and depends on the agricultural sector for their bread and butter. The cultivation or ownership right of farmers depends upon the land records maintained by the revenue department. If there is any mismanagement of this important document, the farmer will not know what to do as he is illiterate and can't fight against the powers that be. To counter this, the government has stepped in at various levels to provide better management of land records with the help of information technology.

In Karnataka alone, there are 17 million land records documents covering 30,000 villages and 2 crore farmers. A land record document has valuable information, which includes ownership, tenancy, cultivation, irrigation, trees, liabilities, crop and soil details including the details of government lands.

---

For all figures in lakhs and crores, please note that 1 lakh = 100,000 and 1 crore = 10,000,000.

## Importance of the Land Records

- A land record is required to be produced for obtaining the crop loans from any recognised financial institution, as proof of ownership and existing liabilities.
- Traditionally, people are satisfied as regards their ownership of land by having the land record issued by the revenue department.
- The majority of legal disputes are settled on the basis of sequence of land records issued for a survey number.
- The government has a liability to protect the ownership of land based on the information maintained in land records books.
- The survey department maintains the schedule of property and carries out division of land for any survey number, based on the public demand during inheritance, partition, etc., and accordingly informs the revenue department.
- The revenue department collects revenue from the respective owners subject to the extent of land owned by them.
- The registration department registers the sale-deed after verifying the ownership from the copy of the land record produced by the seller.

## MANUAL VERSUS COMPUTERISED SYSTEM

Not too long ago, a farmer had difficulty in procuring his land record from the village accountant (VA) or *patwari*, despite waiting for a long time. The manual system had the following drawbacks:

- The issue of land records depends on the availability, mood and interest of the VA/patwari.
- The individual is asked for extra money, sometimes by the VA.
- The manually written land record may not be legible.
- Land records books are not maintained properly.
- It takes a long time to reproduce the land records for the succeeding year after incorporating the current year crop details and liabilities, and changes in ownership or cultivators, etc., that happen through mutations.

- It is very difficult to prepare cross-tabulated registers or reports.
- No quick analysis for decision making or planning is possible.
- The manual system is a low cost and slow delivery system, operated from the bottom-most layer of government administration.
- Multi-level consolidation of information is just impossible.
- No clear-cut procedures exist to pinpoint tampering of documents.
- The entire process results in monopolistic management, with VA at the helm of affairs.

In the new system, however, the farmer can collect his land records within a couple of minutes at the land records centre, without any hassle or delay. Also the farmer can submit the request to carry out the mutation on his land records at the land records centre and collect computer-generated acknowledgement number for reference. This makes officers accountable for carrying out the mutation as per request within the specified period.

In addition to this, the farmer can see his land records documents and status of the mutation-in-process without the intervention of the officials on touch screen kiosk, set up at the entrance of *taluk*/block office. This brings total transparency to the maintenance of land records documents. Of course, the current system of computerisation of land records forced a villager to go (send some one) to taluk office in order to get the copy of land records.

The modern system helps the administrators in evolving tamper-proof mechanism for easy maintenance and updating of land records. The valuable data on the land records documents supports in developmental programmes of government. It also helps in monitoring the government lands from encroachments.

## BHOOMI—LAND RECORDS MANAGEMENT SOFTWARE

Bhoomi, the software for land records management has been fully designed and developed in-house by National Informatics Centre, Bangalore, a central government organisation, using state-of-the-art technology. The following features are incorporated into the Bhoomi software:

- Bhoomi is an online system to carry out the mutation on the live data.

- It has built-in workflow automation, which moves transactions from one officer to another on the system (see Figure 4.1).
- The process of mutation on the Bhoomi will get fully synchronised with the fieldwork done by the revenue officials (see Figure 4.2).
- It also facilitates the scanning of the field mutation order passed by revenue authorities and notice served on the public and storage into database, so that it can be referred to easily in future for various purposes.
- It has also been integrated with fingerprint (bio-metrics) technology to ensure foolproof authentication system instead of traditional password system. This enforces the concept of non-repudiation.
- The software is in local language (Kannada) for easy use by officials.
- Various analysis reports can be generated in text format and also viewed in graphical style.
- It has two modules for public interface:

  - One module is used by revenue official at the land records centre to issue the land records documents on demand from the public and accept the request application for mutation from the public.
  - The other module will run on touch screen kiosk, set up at *taluk/ block* office. This module can be easily operated by even the person/farmer having little knowledge of computer as this is developed using the Keep It Simple (KIS) concept.

**Figure 4.1**

*Bhoomi: Workflow Automation for Smoother Functioning*

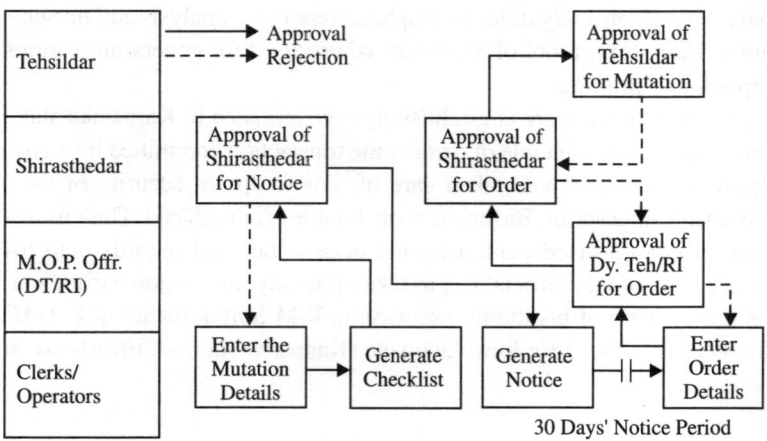

30 Days' Notice Period

**Figure 4.2**

*Bhoomi: Keeping Track of the Mutation Process*

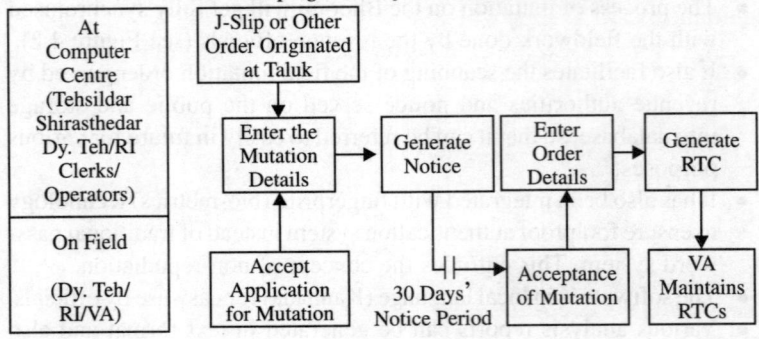

## TECHNOLOGY

Online process of land records system has been built using state-of-art technology. It is designed and implemented using client/server architecture. It uses one of the powerful Relational Data Base Management System (RDBMS), Microsoft SQL Server 7.0, as a back-end tool to maintain the data. The front-end GUI based Bhoomi software is developed using Microsoft Visual Basic 6.0 for effective transaction processing. MS-Graph tools have been extensively used for graphical reporting, analysis and presentation. Data Report tool of Microsoft is also used for generating various reports and printing.

As Bhoomi software is establishing e-governance in Karnataka state, the fundamental principle of owning the transaction committed by a government official is well taken care of. For foolproof security of data, Compaq's fingerprint (Bio-metrics) technology is interfaced. This ensures that an unauthorised person cannot access the land records data for modifying, and the official has to own up to any transaction carried out, on the strength of his thumb impression. ISM Soft software of C-DAC has been interfaced for local language (Kannada) support. Efforts are in the pipeline to have the Kannada data transliterated into other Indian languages by using 'Unicode' at an advanced level, depending upon such requirements as may come up subsequently.

## IMPLEMENTATION STRATEGY

The implementation process of computerisation of land records (see Figure 4.3) starts with digitising the legacy data. This is a laborious process as there are around 100,000 documents in each taluk/block, whose data is to be fed correctly and properly into the computer. The Government of Karnataka has assigned this work to private data-entry agencies. The village accountants will go to the premises of data-entry agency and ensure that data is fed correctly from the good old land record books. The checklist of documents will be printed by the data-entry agency and submitted to the VA. The village accountant verifies the printed checklist with that of original record and corrects the checklist accordingly. The correction of wrongly entered data will be carried out by the data-entry agency. Once the data is corrected, the agency will take the final print of land records documents. Again the VA verifies the printed data for correctness. The process is repeated till all the data-entry errors are eliminated. The data-entry agency hands over the digitised data in CD form to the revenue authority. The revenue officers/officials cross-verify the final printed land records documents with the manual documents on random basis.

Once revenue officials certify the accuracy of the digitised data, the CD data is ported into SQL database for online operations. During this stage all logical errors such as duplicate records, etc., and those RTC data not confirming to validation criteria are either eliminated or clearly marked for possible corrections. Those records marked for correction will not be allowed for transaction processing till they are cleared and properly certified. The system maintains the log of those corrections and authority that approves their correctness along with dates.

Now, the online mutation process on Bhoomi starts after porting the data provided by the data-entry agency into the Bhoomi system. Meanwhile

**Figure 4.3**

*Implementation Strategy for Computerisation of Land Records*

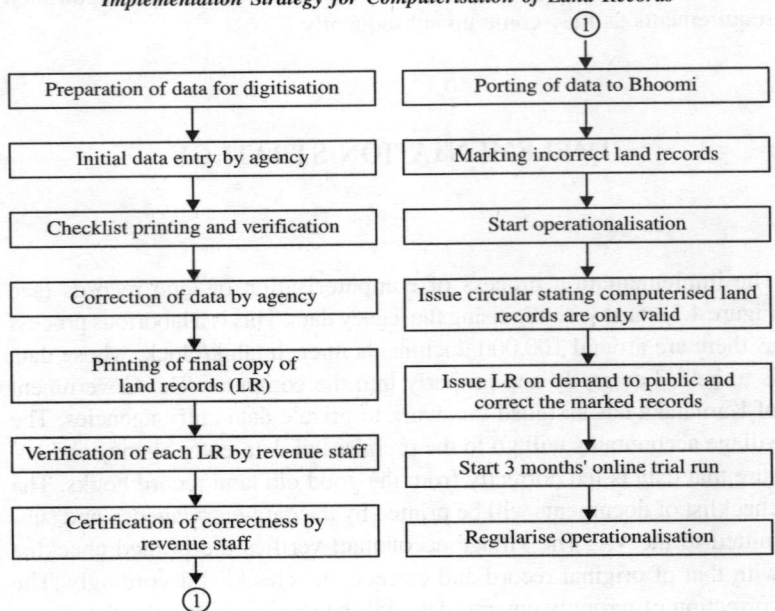

the revenue department issues the taluk/blockwise circular saying that only the computerised land records documents are valid for all legal purposes. This puts pressure on the revenue staff to carry out the mutation on Bhoomi system; the Bhoomi system will always have live and up-to-date data.

The Bhoomi online mutation system has three components (see Figure 4.4):

- The first one is the back end where the revenue officials will carry out the updating activities on the Bhoomi. To support these activities, server, client, printer and scanner with UPS are integrated.
- The second component is the land records centre set up at the entrance of taluk/block office with a client, a printer and UPS, and operated by a village accountant. This provides the public interface from where one can collect the signed land records document on demand or submit a request to carry out the mutation on his/her land.
- The third component is the touch screen kiosk, established at the entrance of taluk/block office. The farmer can use this to see his document and status of the mutation-in-process without intervention of revenue officials.

As Bhoomi works on client/server architecture, all the clients and kiosk interact with the server through an ethernet-based local area network (LAN) implementing TCP/IP.

**Figure 4.4**

*Components of Bhoomi*

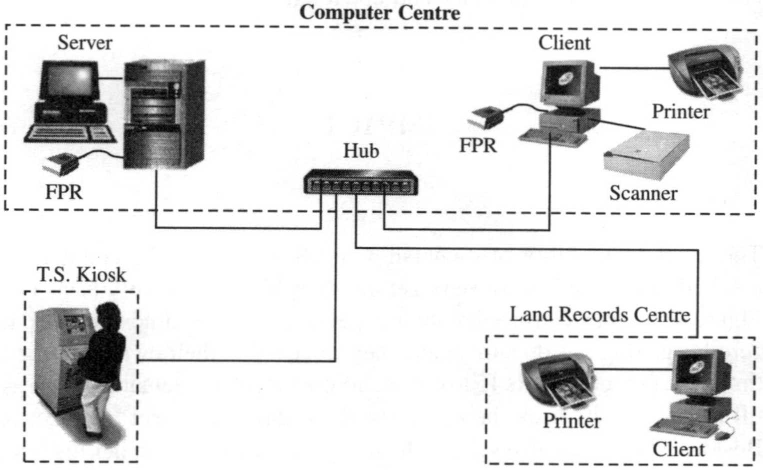

(FPR—Finger Print Reader)

## KEY PLAYERS

There are three players in bringing this project to this stage:

- Ministry of Rural Development, Government of India, has sponsored and funded the scheme from the initial stage.
- The revenue department officials of Government of Karnataka, from the village accountant to the secretary, have played an important role in successful implementation of this project.
- Karnataka state unit and district centres of NIC have provided the full technical support for software, training and assistance in its implementation.

## COST OF THE PROJECT

This is one of the most important projects to serve a major section of the population. Roughly, the cost of project for one taluk/block works out to Rs10–12 lakh. This includes initial data entry of land records, supply of systems, site preparation, training, etc. The major portion of the project cost goes for initial data entry and updating.

## IMPACT

The quick availability of ownership certificate across the counter has resulted in hundreds of owners getting their RTCs on a daily basis (see Figure 4.5). They can see that their dependence on VA almost reduced to zero for getting this document and they can get it at their own convenient time. The farmer pays Rs 15 to collect his documents on demand. Whereas, till a few months back, he had to wait for days to collect his records. Besides, she/he can also submit the request for mutation on her/his land.

**Figure 4.5**

*Ownership Certificates are Now Easily Available Over the Counter*

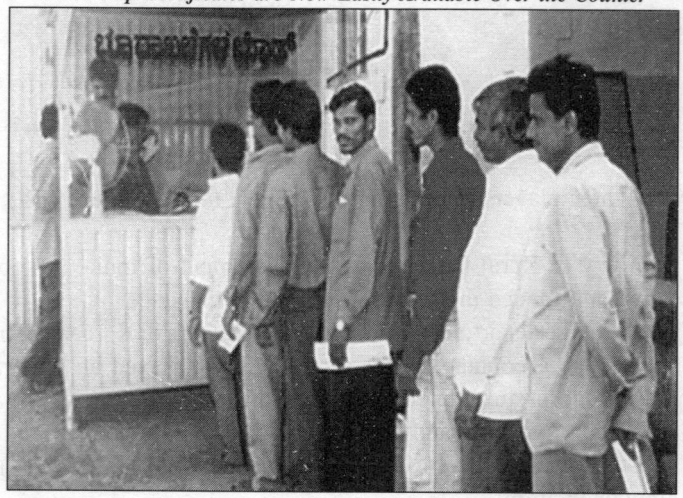

The collection of more than Rs 2.5 lakh at the land records centres in some of the online taluks itself says how the public has accepted the new system. The smile and satisfaction of the farmer after collecting the computerised document at the land records centre is also telling.

Use of Touch Screen Kiosk by the public at the taluk office indicates the enthusiasm and the interest of farmers (see Figure 4.6). Farmers are themselves learning how to operate the kiosk by observing the operations carried out by the previous person. This is also helping the rural people to understand, know and use the computer without much difficulty.

**Figure 4.6**

*Using a Touch Screen Kiosk*

## HURDLES

The whole process of computerisation of land records depends on how accurately the legacy data has been entered by the data-entry agency. In most of the districts, the data-entry agency was not well equipped with the required infrastructure and technical staff to carry out the work correctly and properly, which has delayed the process of making the taluk/ block online.

Another important step is how correctly the checklist (generated by the data-entry agency) is verified with the original records by the revenue authority. Even if there is a small mistake in data, the village land records may not be made online. A number of workshops have been conducted to explain to village accountants how to provide the land records for digitisation and how to verify digitised data for correctness. Awareness and training programmes to the revenue officials is an important step in a smooth switchover to the new system and its operation. This will help in overcoming the resistance by the revenue staff towards computerisation and building up confidence in the new system. More than 6,000 officers ranging from divisional commissioners to village accountants have undergone the awareness-training programme on various aspects of Bhoomi project conducted jointly by the revenue department and NIC at various levels. Besides this, more than 350 revenue staff have been trained on Bhoomi application software by NIC.

Non-availability of continuous and quality power supply will create problem in providing regular service to the public. Improper and irregular maintenance of the system for longer period will spoil the project.

## FUTURE

The land records documents are required basically to purchase/sell the land, to take loan and for legal purposes. Hence, connectivity will be shortly provided to financial and legal institutions to access the land records details easily to provide better service to the public.

Further, Government of Karnataka is thinking of extending the service up to sub-block/hobli levels so that the farmer does not need to come to the block to collect the documents. A pilot scheme is in progress for this purpose. The data centres at the district level will be established to provide this data on Internet.

# 5

## Evaluation of Computerisation of Land Records in Karnataka: A Study from Gulbarga District*

### MANOJ AHUJA AND A.P. SINGH

### INTRODUCTION

Application of information technology to government functions can lead to better governance. Nearly 63 per cent of Indian population is dependent on agriculture. Land records therefore affect the largest number of people in our country. These records are required for a variety of purposes like security of tenure, seeking crop loan, bail in criminal cases, planning purposes, etc. With the objective of streamlining the maintenance and updating of land records, Ministry of Rural Development, Government of India, sanctioned a scheme for Computerisation of Land Records (CoLR) in 1991 in many states, and the scheme was implemented with the assistance of National Informatics Centre (NIC). The progress made in different

* This chapter is an extract of the published report.

For all figures in lakhs and crores, please note that 1 lakh = 100,000 and 1 crore = 10,000,000.

states has been uneven. But in Karnataka, the progress made in the computerisation of land records project is remarkable. Karnataka has 67 lakh owners of rural land spread across 177 *taluks* in nearly 30,000 villages. Together they account for 2 crore records of RTC (records of rights, tenancy and cultivation). A printed copy of the RTC can be obtained online from a computerised land record kiosk (Bhoomi centres) in 177 taluk offices after paying a fee of Rs 15. The state government legally abolished all handwritten records after the implementation of this project. Karnataka's CoLR programme has attracted widespread recognition in the country as well as internationally. Recently, this programme was one of six award winners among 150 global entries in a competition on innovation in governance, instituted by the Commonwealth Association of Public Administration and Management.

## CoLR IN KARNATAKA

Computerisation of land records in Karnataka started in 1991 when the first pilot was initiated in Gulbarga through a centrally sponsored scheme of CoLR of Government of India. By 1996, projects for computerisation of land records were sanctioned for all districts in the state of Karnataka. However, earlier efforts failed to achieve required objectives of creating a clean, up-to-date database. Later after assessing the earlier efforts, the state government consented that all taluks would be computerised by March 2002. By now, all 177 taluks have been computerised.

Now, due to massive efforts of the revenue department of the state, Karnataka's 67 lakh farmers can access 20 million land records at all 177 taluks of the state through Bhoomi e-governance project. This software has been designed fully in-house by NIC, Bangalore. The first records of Rights, Tenancy and Cultivation (RTC) information kiosks centre started in Maddur taluk of Mandya district on 6 February 2001. An amendment made to the Karnataka Land Revenue Act 1964 by the state government recognises only the computerised land records and RTCs duly signed by the authorised signatory as valid for all legal purposes and manually written RTCs have no legal validity. The state government has gazetted the notification in this regard and the amended Karnataka Land Revenue (Amendment) Rules 2002 have come into force from 13 June 2002. Prior to this, the computer-held information had been given legal sanctity. For this, government issued taluk-wise notifications when the new system became fully operational in a particular taluk. The notification declared that only computer-generated RTCs duly signed by the authorised signatory would be valid for all purposes.

The Government of Karnataka lists the following benefits of CoLR system for the farmers:

1. farmers can get all necessary records whenever they need it without having to wait for weeks after applying to kiosk operator;
2. these records are free from human arbitration;
3. the updating becomes easy as farmers' records can be updated by applying at the RTC information kiosk and their request is directly registered into the land records database;
4. the computerised records are free of harassment from government officials, touts, middlemen, village-level leaders, etc.;
5. farmers have direct access to all information about their property; and
6. farmers are able to query and get all necessary information about their land.

According to the Government of Karnataka, the revenue officials get the following benefits:

1. they can access information about any land or revenue property at any given point of time;
2. they can retrieve updated information at any point of time;
3. revenue officials access and use the RTC system only by providing their thumb impression, as against most other forms of security that use passwords and can therefore be manipulated. This also safeguards against any kind of data manipulation, pilferage and loss; and
4. revenue officials are able to monitor the land record work of their subordinates and therefore have better control over their work.

## CoLR IN GULBARGA

Computerisation of land records in Gulbarga started in 1992 in the first phase when the first pilot was initiated in Gulbarga. Gulbarga University was the agency appointed for entering the data, which was completed in

August 1993. But corrections could not be made to the records, as printouts were not taken. After a gap of nearly four years the programme was again taken up in 1996. After obtaining the printouts the necessary corrections were carried out, and this work was completed by March 1996. Further implementation was hindered as the permission then sought by the districts from the government for the purpose of computers was delayed. Consequently in the third phase of computerisation, the government supplied all the necessary hardware to all the 10 taluks in the district. Gulbarga district has 1,394 villages and 248,931 survey numbers.

Sedam became the first taluk in the district to have the computerised land records facility on 4 July 2001. Now, all 10 taluks have been computerised. In all there are 7.88 lakh RTCs in the district with Yadgir having the highest with 1.04 lakh and Chincholi the least with 59,650 RTCs.

## Field Study in Gulbarga District

All the 10 taluks of Gulbarga district were selected for the study with the following objectives:

1. to examine the extent and impact of computerisation of land records on revenue administration and cultivators;
2. to examine the ease and speed with which the cultivators are able to obtain the land records;
3. to examine the human resource development, capacity building and awareness-generation taken up for implementation for the programme, and the adequacy of the same;
4. to examine the procedure for making mutation and the time taken for the same;
5. to examine the extent to which the data generated through the computerised land records system is helpful in planning and decision making; and
6. to find out the extent to which:

   i. CoLR has reduced and changed the workload of the village accountant, *tehsildars* and other revenue functionaries
   ii. the way in which the role of village accountant has been affected in mutation and maintenance of land records

   iii. it has minimised the possibilities of interpolation of land records and rent-seeking behaviour

   iv. a comprehensive database on various facets of land is available for helping in land reforms

   v. the system has cultivated a sense of awareness among cultivators and prompted them to exercise their rights

   vi. support has been extended or resistance put up by various official agencies and other interest groups to the functioning of the system

The Centre for Rural Studies with the help of Karnataka Rajya Vijana Parishat (KRVP), Bangalore conducted a field study in all 10 taluks of Gulbarga during the period of 25 February to 15 March 2002. During our field study we visited Sedam taluk, which was computerised first in the district as well as Surpur taluk which was the last taluk to be computerised. Sedam and Surpur were made operational in July 2001 and March 2002, respectively. Thus, the implementation of CoLR can be termed as quite recent and the study while making an attempt to assess its success keeps this in mind. This study is a modest attempt to critically assess the highly acclaimed efforts for CoLR in Karnataka. This paper is an extract from the report built on extensive field work in rural areas of Gulbarga district of Karnataka. We conducted field studies in more than 100 villages and the kiosk centres located at the taluks. The total number of respondents is 1,478.

## ANALYSIS OF DATA

### General Awareness about the Computerisation of RTC

This indicator is very important for us as the study was taken up soon after the implementation of the programme. Sedam was the first taluk to be computerised in Gulbarga in July 2001 and Surpur the last, made operational in March 2002. Farmers need a copy of their RTCs for: (*a*) obtaining a bank loan; (*b*) conducting a survey of their land; (*c*) obtaining a certified income statement necessary to receive numerous types of government benefits; (*d*) making land transactions; (*e*) producing in court or a police station during a land-related dispute; and (*f*) for various personal references. As such, farmers typically seek an official copy of their RTCs at least once per year and sometimes even more often. A majority of the farmers obtain RTCs only for the purpose of crop loan. Therefore, they approach for RTCs at the time of applying for a crop loan. The time for crop loan starts every year after June. Overall, 85 per cent respondents were aware of the computerisation of RTC at taluk headquarters. Thus it can be safely deduced that within a year of the implementation of this programme, awareness about the computerisation of land records has become almost universal.

### Procedure for Obtaining Computerised RTCs

The awareness about the procedure for obtaining computerised RTCs is directly related to the general awareness about computerisation of land records. A majority of the respondents (78.8 per cent) knew that the taluk had one computer kiosk from which they could take computerised RTCs and *khata* details after paying Rs 15 per holding. Some of the respondents (5.9 per cent) knew about the computerisation but not exactly the procedure for obtaining RTCs. Half (50.6 per cent) of the total respondents obtained RTCs directly from kiosk for self or for other persons. Landless persons obtained RTCs for other persons after charging some extra money, in addition to the prescribed fee.

We find that there is a small though not very significant positive correlation between the landowning class and computerised RTC obtained. More or less around 40 per cent to 55 per cent of the farmers from each category were obtaining computerised RTCs. It can be safely concluded that farmers, irrespective of the size of their landholdings, were aware of the procedure for obtaining RTCs and nearly half of them had also obtained a copy of the computerised RTC from the taluk office.

## Information Flow

It is seen that within the existing institutional framework, enhancement of information flow has a multi-dimensional impact. This affects other factors like rent-seeking behaviour, improvement in record management, and storage and reduction of the dispute burden.

'It is the best thing to happen for people like us', says Sangappa Mali Patil, a farmer from Sargadagi village of Gulbarga taluk, located about 16 km away from Gulbarga, on receiving a computerised record of rights and tenancy and cultivation certificate at a kiosk in Gulbarga. He received the RTC within a couple of minutes without any distress or by bribing the government officials, especially village accountant.

At the time of our survey, only 50.6 per cent of the respondents had obtained a copy of the RTC. Out of the total respondents, 55.3 per cent stated that RTC was available without delay, 35.3 per cent did not know if computerisation made the availability of RTC any easier. Some (9.3 per cent) of the respondents indicated that there was a delay in obtaining RTCs after computerisation. We found that there was a clearly positive correlation between the persons who had obtained RTCs and were having a positive opinion about the availability of RTCs after the computerisation. The correlation co-efficient between these two is (+0.676). This correlation is also significant at 99 per cent level of significance (2-tailed).

Now we will discuss the cross-tabulation between these two for the whole district. From Table 5.1 we find that *86.8 per cent of the persons who had obtained RTCs opined that this system is less time-consuming as compared to old system because they did not have to search for the village accountant.* Those who had not obtained RTC till the field study (22.7 per cent) also had a positive opinion about the availability of RTCs after computerisation. They also reported that previously they found it difficult to obtain RTC on the same day. Even persons residing more than 5 km from the taluk office stated that after reaching the office, there was no delay but the total time consumed due to long distance of taluk from their villages was longer. Details can be seen in Table 5.1.

We asked the respondents about the amount of time required to obtain their land records after computerisation. There were two factors regarding the time spent: (*a*) travelling time; and (*b*) waiting time.

We exclude the factor of travelling time since everyone knows that kiosk centres are established in the state at taluk headquarters. Therefore we will only discuss the reasons for waiting time. The option of five minutes was adopted by only 18.4 per cent of the respondents. It clearly implies that these people have a very good impression in terms of time spent for obtaining RTC. Similarly, 24.8 per cent spent one hour for the RTC; the reason may be due to a queue in front of the kiosk. About 26.5 per cent of the respondents spent half to two days. The reasons for this are: lack of power supply and absence of kiosk operator. Since only one person had received computer kiosk training, his absence for lunch or any other reason led to delays for the farmers. Of these respondents some returned to their village in search of village accountant to ask for their survey number for obtaining RTC. Some of the farmers found mistakes in their RTC; therefore they visited the taluk another day to obtain a correct RTC. About 30.3 per cent of the respondents were unable to say anything because they had not visited the kiosk. In Table 5.2, we will see the pattern of opinion of the persons who have already obtained RTCs.

Table 5.2 reveals that amongst the persons who already obtained RTCs, 67.5 per cent stated that obtaining RTCs only took five minutes to one hour.

**Table 5.1**

*Cross-tabulation between Persons who Obtained Computerised RTCs and Availability of New Computerised RTCs without Delay (in per cent)*

| Persons who obtained computerised RTC ↓ | Opinion about the availability of RTC without delay ↓ | | | |
|---|---|---|---|---|
| | Yes | No | Don't know | Total |
| Yes | 86.8 | 8.4 | 4.8 | 50.9 |
| No | 22.7 | 10.3 | 66.9 | 49.1 |
| **Total** | **55.3** | **9.3** | **35.3** | **100.0** |
| Correlation co-efficient | | | 0.676** | |

** Correlation is significant at the 0.01 level (2-tailed).

**Table 5.2**

*Cross-tabulation between the Time Required for Obtaining RTCs and Persons who Obtained RTCs (in per cent)*

| Persons who obtained computerised RTC ↓ | Time ↓ | | | | | Don't know | Total |
|---|---|---|---|---|---|---|---|
| | 5 minutes | 1 hour | ½ day | 1 day | 1–2 days | | |
| Yes | 30.5 | 37.0 | 6.0 | 12.5 | 11.2 | 2.9 | 50.9 |
| No | 5.9 | 11.8 | 3.7 | 11.8 | 7.6 | 59.1 | 49.1 |
| **Total** | **18.4** | **24.8** | **4.9** | **12.2** | **9.4** | **30.3** | **100.0** |
| Correlation co-efficient | | | 0.603** | | | | |

** Correlation is significant at the 0.01 level (2-tailed).

The time taken for obtaining RTCs is still quite long. This may be due to the fact that the process is in the early stage of implementation. Thus it is evident that a majority of the farmers are able to obtain RTCs within one hour. Once the errors in RTCs are reduced with time, farmers will not have to return for a correct copy. Further, training of another person and provision of a generator will also reduce the time required for obtaining RTCs.

The time taken by village accountant to provide RTC prior to computerisation ranged from one day to 30 days. According to Basavarajappa of Mudagola village of Shahapur taluk:

> Village accountant came only once a week, due to this reason it used to take a week to get a land record copy. Therefore it was very difficult for the villagers to obtain RTC whenever it was necessary. The village accountant used to demand 50,100 or even 500 rupees—sometimes for one copy. The village accountant informed about the latest order of Government only to the elected members and large farmers only. He discriminated between the large and small farmers.

The study shows that 59.7 per cent of the farmers were getting RTC on the same day. For the remaining, the time taken extended in some cases up to 30 days also. Further, as stated by Basavarajappa, in reality the service of the village accountant in many cases also depended upon the amount of money provided by the farmer.

## Opinion about Accuracy of Computerised Land Records

In the entire district 44.2 per cent of the respondents were quite sure about the accuracy of computerised land records. They said that the new system was more accurate. About 11.3 per cent were not confident of the accuracy of computerised RTCs. These respondents found many errors in the computerised RTCs and therefore they contacted the village accountant for the required corrections. The remaining respondents were not able to say anything about the accuracy of the system, the system being at an early stage of implementation. Gouda of village Madana claimed: 'There was a mistake in my document and I'm unable to get the certificate'. Subam Reddy of village Irakpalli of Chincholi taluk also complained about the misprinting in the computerised RTC. In his RTC, Ambanna was misprinted as Anjamma. An overwhelming number of respondents, however, expressed faith in the authenticity of information through the computerised process. The errors which are present in the RTC's are expected to decrease with time as the system stabilises and the initial errors in the database are rectified.

## Opinion about Harassment in the Computerised System

Less than half (43.8 per cent) of the respondents said that the new computerised system was free from any type of harassment. Farmers said that they paid only Rs 15 to the kiosk operator and were able to get their RTC without any harassment from any person or any official. They reported that it took less time to obtain RTC under the new system because they did not have to go in search of the village accountant. Some (15.1 per cent) respondents stated there was still harassment from officials and middlemen. They reported that in the old system the village accountant, who issued the RTC was easily accessible, if the RTC was needed urgently. Now they had to travel to the taluk to get their RTCs. Many (41.1 per cent) had either never visited the kiosk or were unable to say anything about the harassment because the system was in an early stage of implementation. Mahalingappa of Chincholi taluk expressed the opinion that the new computerised system was good and there was no possibility of any type of harassment by any official, including the village accountant. Table 5.3 details the opinion of persons who obtained computerised RTC, about the harassment faced in obtaining RTC in the computerised system.

**Table 5.3**

*Cross-tabulation between Persons who Obtained Computerised RTCs and their Opinion that the New System is Free from Harassment (in per cent)*

| Persons who obtained computerised RTC ↓ | The computerised system is free from harassment | | | |
|---|---|---|---|---|
| | *Yes* | *No* | *Can't say* | *Total* |
| Yes | 67.6 | 18.9 | 13.6 | 50.9 |
| No | 19.3 | 11.2 | 69.6 | 49.1 |
| **Total** | **43.8** | **15.1** | **41.1** | **100.0** |

Table 5.3 indicates that the persons obtaining computerised RTCs have a positive opinion of computerisation. On the other hand, persons who have never visited a kiosk centre were not in a position to say anything about the harassment in computerised system. Some respondents who had obtained computerised RTC (18.9 per cent) stated there was harassment in the computerised system. The reasons are: the significant distance of the computer kiosk, the delays caused by power failure and the increased travel cost. Table 5.3 also confirms that after computerisation, farmers going to the taluk office to obtain RTCs were facing much less or no harassment as compared to earlier.

According to *shirasthedars*, computerised land record information is more accurate than manual records. They also said that irregularity (non-attendance) of village accountant to their area of operation made it difficult sometimes for farmers to obtain RTCs, and for the village accountant it was easier to prepare wrong documents. Computerisation has resulted in eliminating manipulation of records. The village accountants can now concentrate on other work. On the other hand, they also said that farmers often have to travel long distances to obtain RTCs. Corrections and changes in the records due to land transactions also require a lot of time. They also said that frequent power failures shut down the system. Due to this, inconvenience was caused to both users and operators. Delay was also caused due to necessity of the tehsildar's thumbprint for entries and as he was often unavailable, many entries were delayed. After computerisation, even small corrective revisions to RTCs required significant time and delay. For crop information, it was difficult to issue a RTC with the current year's information because the crop information had to be communicated by the village accountant to the computer operators which takes time. These are some of the issues which need to be addressed in the future.

According to the village accountants, RTCs could be issued quickly to farmers and in their own locality by the old manual system. With the introduction of the computerised system, many farmers must travel long distances to obtain RTC. This causes wastage of time and money for the farmers. Corrections of land records could be done more quickly and easily in the old system. After computerisation, no work pertaining to RTCs remains with the village accountants now. *This reasoning can be understood in the context of the arbitrary and discretionary powers of the village accountants being reduced by the computerised system.*

All the tehsildars opined that after computerisation, accuracy rate of the RTCs was higher and updating had become easy. For the accuracy of data, data verification was carried out three times at the time of data entry. On an average, 40 per cent RTCs were found with errors during first verification and about 20 per cent were found with errors during second verification. Computerisation has also helped them greatly in monitoring and controlling the work of their employees. Thus, both the farmers and revenue officials are confident about the accuracy of the new system and are also of the view that harassment has been considerably reduced in the new system.

The manual system of land records maintenance has been described as highly opaque. The village accountants have been perceived as monopolising the records, which were not open to public scrutiny. Several inaccuracies had crept into old manual system due to improper manipulation by the village accountants. In the newly computerised system, there is no possibility of any type of manipulation by a village accountant or kiosk operator or any other person. Therefore, when we asked the beneficiaries whether they thought the computerised RTCs could be manipulated, only 13.4 per cent gave negative response, 37.1 per cent of the beneficiaries were quite sure that no manipulation was possible by a village accountant or kiosk operator, and 49.5 per cent of the beneficiaries were unable to respond since they did not know the details about the programme. They said that they did not know the power of the officials in the new computerised system.

## Rent-seeking Behaviour

Rent-seeking behaviour is especially pronounced at the grassroots level in the revenue administration. The findings clearly establish that the village accountant had been in a position to seek rent for transactions. This was perhaps true for some other revenue officials as well. Now, after computerisation, costs include the fees for the records (Rs 15 per record) and the travel costs. Before going into the details of the new system, we will discuss the rent incurred by the farmers during the old manual system. The costs for obtaining an RTC in the old system ranged from Rs 2 to more than Rs 100. About the new system one farmer, Mahalingappa of Chincholi taluk expressed 'It is wonderful. Now we need not be at the mercy of the village accountant to get a copy of RTC. The system has

102 • MANOJ AHUJA AND A.P. SINGH

done away with the customary bribe, nearly up to Rs 500, or, worse, the endless wait for the village accountant to appear. We can get it instantly by just paying Rs 15'. According to tehsildars, computerisation has also decreased corruption. Overall, 20.5 per cent of the respondents were paying within the prescribed charges for obtaining RTC prior to computer-isation. Out of these, 11.6 per cent were not paying even the prescribed fees. The remaining farmers were paying more than the prescribed charges.

The amount of bribe paid to the village accountant depended on the importance and urgency of records. If a person wanted to obtain the RTC immediately then he had to pay more money to the village accountant. About 11.6 per cent of the farmers had paid nothing for obtaining an RTC. Why had the village accountant taken no bribe? We found in our field study that the village accountant never charged any money from the influential persons of the village. In some of the cases we also found that village accountant provided free RTC to the poor or the marginal farmers of the village. In Table 5.4, we will see the behaviour of rent with respect to land size of the farmers.

**Table 5.4**

*Behaviour of Rent with Respect to Land Size Prior to Computerisation*

| Land size class | Rent (in Rs) prior to computerisation | | | |
|---|---|---|---|---|
| | None or prescribed fee | 10–25 | 25–50 | > 50 |
| Marginal | 20.7 | 50.5 | 15.3 | 22.4 |
| Small | 20.2 | 51.4 | 13.2 | 15.8 |
| Semi-medium | 21.4 | 48.4 | 15.6 | 14.5 |
| Medium | 17.0 | 51.9 | 18.4 | 12.7 |
| Large | 26.2 | 51.0 | 12.1 | 11.3 |

**Note:** The figures indicate the percentage of total respondents.

According to Table 5.4, 26.2 per cent of the large farmers paid either nothing or only the prescribed fee to the village accountant. While on the higher side of rent, 22.4 per cent of the marginal farmers paid more than Rs 50. Therefore, we can conclude that the old system was good for large farmers as well as for influential persons. But now, in the new sys-tem, there is no possibility of issuing of RTC without any charge. Thus, this is a case of technology bringing equity. During our field study, we found that many of the large farmers were against the new computerised system. The reason may be the facilitation provided by village accountants to them. Therefore, it is evident that in the old system, service was extended to the farmers on the basis of their influence and money power. But in the new computerised system there is no discrimination in issuing a RTC. We also found that all the farmers are obtaining RTC paying only Rs 15 throughout the district. However, the total cost of the RTC is more for the farmer as he also pays for the travel cost.

We asked respondents about the amount paid by them in case of RTC obtained through other persons or village accountants. The average cost paid by them is Rs 24.57 and the maximum amount paid by the farmers is Rs 80. There were many cases in which farmers paid only Rs 15 to the persons obtaining RTC directly from the computer kiosk. About 51.80 per cent of the farmers paid actual charges to the person obtaining computerised RTC. The remaining 48.20 per cent paid more than Rs 15.

There is quite a difference in the expenditure between cases where the RTC was obtained through other persons or village accountants, and where the farmer visited the computer kiosk personally. The difference is just double in terms of money in cases where the RTC was obtained through other persons or the village accountant. The reasons are: the other persons or village accountants were engaged in work which required regular visit to the taluk. Therefore, they charged only nominal money from the farmers. Inspite of that many of the persons were charging more than Rs 15. In some cases, we also found that one person obtained the RTCs for four to five holders of the village in one visit and money spent on travelling and other items was divided proportionately. Therefore, the cost of the RTC together with travelling and other item costs becomes less, as compared to the cost incurred in the personal visit of the actual RTC holder. Thus, it is an added advantage of the system that any representative of the landowner can obtain a RTC on his behalf. Due to this facility, obtaining a RTC costs less and results in saving time for the farmers. Basically, the expenditure on obtaining a RTC depends on distance of the villages from taluk headquarter office. For Gulbarga district, the average cost of the RTC for a person visiting personally is Rs 47.58 and average time spent is four hours and 30 minutes. In other words, we can say that visiting a kiosk also results in cost on travel as well as in time for the farmer. This problem can be overcome by taking the kiosks to the hobli or web, enabling the RTCs and allowing the village accountant to issue the RTCs from his headquarters. This would solve the problem to a large extent.

In Karnataka, the revenue department assesses fee per land plot instead of per landholding. This is causing two problems: first the Rs 15 fee was typically multiplied many times depending on the number of plots a farmer had. In our field study we have found that there were many respondents who had more than five plots. Two respondents had 17 plots, another two had 12 plots and so on. The farmers having 17 plots were paying Rs 255 for the copies of their RTCs. Second, the farmers seeking RTCs for multiple plots occupy the computer kiosk for a considerable time. The computer kiosk operator and the dot matrix printer take at least five minutes in generating a RTC. For a farmer to obtain 17 RTCs, it would take one hour and 35 minutes, thus delaying the farmers in the queue behind him.

In Gulbarga, around 46.27 per cent villages are located within a distance of 20 km radius from the respective taluk headquarters. For covering this distance the farmer has to spend a maximum of Rs 16 and about two hours in terms of time.

In these villages the RTC will cost between Rs 15–31 for the farmers having only one plot. If we compare this cost with the cost of old manual system, we found that in the old system about 71 per cent of the respondents claimed that they had paid up to Rs 25 for obtaining a RTC. But in the new system only the farmers residing within the distance of 20 km can obtain the RTC for Rs 15–31, without spending much time. According to the farmers Kudali, Nagendra, Kallappa and Mallamma of Chincholi taluk it was better to make arrangements through the village accountant as their village was situated 26 km away from the taluk office. Farmers would have to spend at least Rs 100 for the computerised RTC. According to several farmers from villages, which are far away from taluk office, unnecessary expenditure in getting a RTC is unavoidable. This problem can be easily solved if more kiosks are set up or the project is web-enabled.

## Land Reforms

The purpose is to determine whether CoLR has contributed to improved implementation of land reforms. It appears that in Karnataka, CoLR till date has done little to promote further implementation of land reforms legislations. Revenue department officials reported not a single case of surplus land detected as a result of CoLR. This may be due to the fact that implementation of CoLR is very recent and information is available only talukwise as yet. Once the database is integrated at the district level or state level, there might be emergence of new cases. But CoLR has definitely enhanced the knowledge of the use of government land. About 21 per cent of the respondents reported that CoLR helps in generating awareness of encroachment over government land while 79 per cent denied that CoLR has helped in generating awareness of encroachment over government land. This signifies that the level of information about government land has gone up though awareness is still restricted. The findings are clear that the respondents welcome CoLR as a positive step but this had not resulted in any change in the revenue administration. Several respondents specifically stated that there were cases of encroachment over government land but no action was being taken. Several have reported that they did not see how CoLR would overcome this problem if the will to take action was lacking. It can be inferred that CoLR has not had any impact on implementation of land reforms legislation as yet. Moreover, there has been a marginal increase in the awareness of the use of government land, though as yet the general population has been unable to use this information to put pressure on the government machinery to act and remove encroachments on government land.

## Reduction in Disputes

Any form of dispute imposes a burden upon the efficiency of the village economy. Many of the disputes originate from a faulty record system. For this indicator, we asked the respondents about land-related disputes. About 26 per cent of the respondents are sure that computerisation has reduced the land-related conflicts. Some (7.4 per cent) respondents opined that computerisation is not helping in the reduction of disputes. The remaining respondents (66.6 per cent) were unable to say anything about computerisation since it was in the early stages of implementation.

However, in terms of conflicts related to government land, only 18.3 per cent of the respondents said that computerisation definitely reduced the conflicts related to government land, 5.6 per cent gave a negative reply, and remaining 76.1 per cent were not in a position to comment on the same.

Land tenancy could be one of the points of conflict. During our field visit, 81 per cent of the respondents confirmed that the practice of tenancy still exists in Gulbarga. In our study, we interviewed the persons still involved in the practice of land tenancy. One hundred and five households

(7.1 per cent) are taking land on lease from landowners. The area involved under 'leasing in' is 5.84 per cent (431.072 ha) of the total area owned. Forty-four households (2.98 per cent) reported that they give their land to tenants. The area involved under leasing out is 3 per cent (222.349 ha) of the total area owned. The leasing out is underreported since respondents quell information about leasing out. During our field study we found that only 18 tenants were recorded prior to computerisation and same status is continuing after the computerisation. It is obvious that computerisation of land records would not result in detection of concealed tenancy in the state as the data is the same as given in manual RTCs. As far as reduction of the tenancy-related conflicts is concerned, only 10.9 per cent of the respondents were of the opinion that computerisation reduced conflicts of land tenancy; 3.5 per cent of the respondents thought that there was no effect of computerisation on tenancy-related disputes; while 85.60 per cent of respondents were unable to say anything one way or the other. Again as the project has been implemented fairly recently, any significant impact on reduction of land-related disputes is not apparent.

## Institutional Finance

Bank loans are given on the basis of RTC; therefore, landowners need copies of RTCs for applying for loans. It was also learnt that the state plans to connect the land records database to databases accessible to various courts and banks in order to facilitate their work relating to land records. It was noted through our findings that there had been some positive impact on the flow of institutional finance. We asked the respondents a very simple question about the easy availability of finance after computerisation. Since the project was in an early stage of implementation, there were many farmers who had never been to a kiosk. About 62.9 per cent of the respondents found it easier to obtain a loan after computerisation. Only a very low percentage (2.1 per cent) found there was no change, and 35 per cent did not make any comment as they had never applied for a bank loan. On the basis of this survey, one can safely conclude that computerisation of land records has facilitated availability of loans from banks for the farmers. This is basically because of the easy availability of RTC after computerisation.

## Facilitation in Sale/ Purchase of Land

Sale and purchase of land has been a problem in the village society. The seller and the purchaser have to incur high expenditure in the form of search and uncertainty costs. While 38.5 per cent of the respondents opined that the new computerised system facilitated sale or purchase of land, only 6.8 per cent were not in agreement with this view. The remaining were unable to say anything. It is obvious that as accurate and updated records are available, this has facilitated sale and purchase of land by reducing search and uncertainty costs.

We also asked farmers about the number of days and the amount of time spent in obtaining information regarding the land after and before computerisation. Overall, 68 per cent of the respondents were able to get land-related information for sale and purchase purpose within a day, before computerisation. After computerisation of land records, 97.29 per cent of respondents have either got or have a hope of getting the information within one day. Before computerisation there were many respondents (5 per cent) who got information in more than 10 days, the remaining got information in 1–10 days.

The landowners have to spend less time in obtaining information about land after computerisation. Besides our observation was that the purchaser was more easily convinced with a computerised printout of RTC. We also asked if there was any increase in information clarity regarding the land being purchased, after computerisation. While 32.8 per cent agreed that there was an increase in clarity regarding the land being purchased, 3.7 per cent did not agree with the above statement. The remaining were not in a position to give response. It is clear, therefore, CoLR that has been of some assistance to conveyancing.

**Table 5.5**

*Cross-tabulation between Persons who Obtained Computerised RTCs and Increase in Clarity Regarding the Land Being Purchased After Computerisation (in per cent)*

| Persons who obtained computerised RTC ↓ | Increase in clarity | | | |
| --- | --- | --- | --- | --- |
| | *Yes* | *No* | *Don't know* | *Total* |
| Yes | 46.1 | 3.9 | 50.0 | 50.9 |
| No | 19.0 | 3.4 | 77.5 | 49.1 |
| **Total** | **32.8** | **3.7** | **63.5** | **100.0** |

It is clear from Table 5.5 that 46.1 per cent of the respondents who had obtained computerised RTC thought that computerisation had increased the clarity regarding information of sale and purchase. We can say that respondents have a more positive opinion about the new system after visiting the computer kiosk. (The favourable percentage increases from 32.8 per cent to 46.1 per cent.)

## Planning Process

It is definite that CoLR will result in the availability of more timely and usable data for planning purpose. Converting land records data into digital form, will almost certainly make such data easier to review, collate and analyse for various administrative and planning purposes.

The computerised system generates various types of reports of land-ownership, types of soil, crops, etc., which will be useful for planning purposes. The Directorate of Statistics and Agricultural Census and other bodies rely upon this data for the compilation of state data, for state statistics is ultimately used for state-level planning. Sometimes land data is needed for Poverty Alleviation Programmes (PAPs) for verification. Now after computerisation, verification of land at taluk office will become easy. Planning is also required to be done at the village level under the new dispensation of Panchayati Raj. At the *panchayat* level, land data will be helpful in the identification of beneficiaries as well in the formulation of programmes. Therefore, we can say that CoLR will make data and information readily available for planning at different levels from panchayat to the state government.

## Transparency in Decision Making

Administration is governed by an old dictum that 'not only should justice be done but it should also appear to have been done'. This appearance of 'justice being done' is summed up by the terminology 'transparency'. There had been serious transparency-related problems in revenue administration, a subject that has been the central theme of concern so often in the past. CoLR system in the state definitely has contributed a lot towards transparency in the revenue administration. It has taken away discretionary and arbitrary use of powers from the revenue functionaries and made land records accessible to one and all.

## Mutation

One of the unique features of 'Bhoomi' software is the 'online mutation' module which is incorporated in the software. There has been a synchronisation of computerised activities with the manual activities. Even though the land records system is computerised, the revenue officers have to carry out their field work as usual. There has not been any change in their roles and responsibilities. We specifically asked the respondents about the time taken for mutation before and after computerisation.

About 88.5 per cent farmers indicated that time required for finalisation of mutation prior to computerisation was within three months. Very few respondents (11.5 per cent) opined that time needed for mutation prior to computerisation was more than three months.

We studied the online mutation in Sedam taluk. Sedam was the first taluk to be computerised in Gulbarga. Other taluks were in the process of completing the exercise of online mutation. The process for updating the computerised RTCs generally follows the old process with a few added steps. In case of a sale registered with the registration office, the registration officials now send the J-slip along with copies of the deed and other relevant transaction documents directly to the tehsildar from where they are forwarded to the computer operator. The computer operator prepares a checklist for the transaction using the information form J-slip and verifying it against the current computer records. The checklist is then verified and approved by the shirasthedar.

The taluk level officials then send the J-slip along with a blank no-objection form, a blank mutation form, the checklist, and other accompanying forms to the revenue inspector. The revenue inspector, in turn, informs the parties to the transaction and passes the information to the concerned village accountant.

The village accountant then posts a notice of the transaction for 30 days in his village office, inviting objections. If objections are received, he makes an entry in the dispute register and passes the information along to the revenue inspector. If there are no objections, the village accountant, completes the blank mutation form and gives it along with the rest of the file to the revenue inspector, who inspects the forms, signs his approval, enters his statement and gives the entire file back to the village accountant.

The village accountant then takes the file to the taluk office and gives it to the computer operator for making necessary changes in the RTC. The computer operator scans relevant documents and makes the necessary entries in the computerised records. The entries must first be approved by the concerned revenue inspector who does so by entering his thumb impression. After the revenue inspector approves the entry, the shirasthedar and tehsildar, in turn, must approve the entry by providing their thumb impressions. After the tehsildar's approval, the changes are automatically entered in the computerised RTC record.

The entire process of updating the RTCs following a land transaction now takes less than two months. Sometimes there are delays due to the tehsildar's non-availability due to other engagements, including 30 days' period for the statutory notice. Other reasons for delay include technical problems with the computer and inadequately trained computer operators.

It does appear that CoLR has succeeded in making the mutation process less cumbersome. Computerisation of land records has enabled the tehsildar to monitor the pendency of mutation cases. By reviewing the same regularly he can ensure that mutation cases are disposed of expeditiously.

Now we will see rent-seeking patterns in mutations prior to computerisation. It indicates that rent paid by the farmers to get their mutation was very high. No one was able to get his corrected RTC without paying money. The majority of people paid more than Rs 200 for their mutation. Some paid up to Rs 5,000 for the finalisation of their mutation. The average cost for the finalisation of RTC is Rs 651. People are of the view that the CoLR programme has definitely led to the reduction in rent-seeking behaviour for getting mutation done. Therefore we can conclude that CoLR makes land transactions easier, less expensive, timely, simpler and more effective.

## POINTS OF VIEW OF LOCAL REVENUE FUNCTIONARIES

### Advantages

1. *Enhancement in transparency:* The manual system of land records maintenance has been described as highly opaque. The village accountants have been perceived as monopolising the records, which were not open to public scrutiny. But, after computerisation, everyone can see his or her RTC on computer screen without any harassment. Land purchasers and sellers can more easily verify land and land ownership information. Land rights information is more accurate now.

2. *Complete avoidance of malpractice and manipulations:* Observers note that several inaccuracies crept into the old system through improper manipulation by the village accountant. Computerisation does not leave any room for manipulation. Prior to computerisation farmers bribed the village accountant for obtaining RTC. After computerisation, they have to pay only Rs 15 as fee to obtain RTC.

3. *Increase in collection of revenue:* The government is getting a good amount of revenue as RTC fees, as compared to previously.

4. *Reduction in the workload of village accountant:* After computerisation, there is less work pertaining to RTCs for village accountants. Now they can concentrate on other work.

### Disadvantages

1. *Delays due to power outages and breakdown in the system:* The taluk centre is plagued by regular, almost daily, power outages. Since the computer kiosk does not have a battery or generator back up power supply, the process of obtaining RTC often involved long

delays. For example, in Chincholi taluk, the system broke down in the month of October 2001 for a period of 10 days. When-ever any problems related to software as well as hardware occurred in the computer system, no expert was available at the taluk office, and one had to be called in from the district headquarter to tackle the problem.

2. *Difficulty in issuing RTC with current year's crop information:* There was some difficulty in issuing a RTC with the current year's crop information because the crop information must be communi-cated by the village accountant to the computer operators, which takes time. Crop information for only one crop season is entered in the land records.

3. *Glitches in software:* The software contained a few initial glitches related to the transfer and inheritance of land.

4. *Significant distance of computer kiosk from villages:* Farmers often have to travel a long distance to obtain RTCs, resulting in greater costs in terms of time and money.

5. *More time lost in making corrections:* Corrections and changes in the records due to land transactions require a lot of time. Small corrective revisions to RTCs are also time-consuming, causing greater dependence on the village accountant to change land records. He has to visit taluk at least twice a week.

6. *Delay in getting tehsildar's thumbprint:* Because the tehsildar's thumbprint is necessary for entries and since he is unavailable most of the time, many entries are delayed.

## POINTS OF VIEW OF FARMERS

### In Favour of Computerised System of Land Records

- The new computerised system of land records is more explicit and transparent. The village accountant and other officials have no chance to manipulate the land records.
- Any representative of the landowner can obtain land records under the new, computerised system of land records.

- Obtaining RTCs under the new, computerised system of land records is more time-effective because farmers do not have to go in search of the village accountant.

### Against Computerised System of Land Records

- Cost of RTCs is more under the new computerised system of land records. In the past, the village accountant issued RTCs for a very nominal fee. The travel cost was very little or nothing. The fee of Rs 15 per plot in addition to travel cost makes the computerised system more costly.
- The time spent for obtaining RTCs is more under the computerised system because most of the farmers have to travel long distances to the computer kiosk at taluk office.
- In the past, the village accountant, who issued the RTC, was easily accessible even in the case of urgency.
- Farmers needed information like survey number from the village accountant to obtain a RTC from the computer kiosk. Therefore, they have to visit village accountant first and then go to a computer kiosk at taluk office in case they do not know their survey numbers.

## CONCLUSION

After the field study of all the taluks of Gulbarga district, we can say that CoLR is dealing with some of the deficiencies of the old manual records system. Now, land records are more transparent and open to public scrutiny.

It is also noted that CoLR will do very little to promote further implementation of land reforms. We found not a single case related to land tenancy or land ceiling surplus detected as a result of CoLR.

CoLR has made land records less prone to manipulations. The village accountants have very little scope to manipulate or harass people. This is an important advantage of the computerised land records.

In general, it has been found that CoLR has made it easier for farmers to obtain RTCs. However, in many cases due to significant distance of computer kiosk from their home villages, farmers have to spend time and incur extra expenditure for travelling to the kiosk. Since the Government of Karnataka is in the process of extending this up to hobli level, the farmers will be extremely benefited by this. The great majority of the revenue personnel felt that the farmers will be able to appreciate the benefits of CoLR fully only in the next two years.

We also found that CoLR had made land records current as compared to the manual system. This was because mutations were being disposed of faster. Once a mutation application is entered in the system it is tracked until it is disposed of. This system also enhances monitoring by the tehsildar, thereby improving the accountability of the revenue administration.

The online mutation was in process in Sedam, Chincholi, Jewargi and Afzalpur taluks. Many of the farmers were happy with online mutation where this process was under implementation. They reported that the existing level of harassment by village accountants in the manual system was quite high. They said that village accountants charged up to Rs 500 and it even took up to two years for the mutation under the manual system.

Definitely, CoLR will result in easy and timely availability of usable data for planning process. Conversion of land records data into digital form has made it easy to review, collate and analyse for various administrative and planning purposes.

The Government of Karnataka is in the process of addressing the problems of power backup for the computer kiosk, additional computer kiosks and additional computer operators. Whenever the government sorts out these problems, the farmers will be immensely benefited from these. It will be essential to monitor farmers' satisfaction with the CoLR and ask for their suggestions and feedback for improvement.

In the end, we can say that CoLR is to a large extent a remedy for the multiple problems of the Indian land record system. CoLR has improved land records systems in Karnataka. The CoLR programme in Karnataka is a successful application of information and communication technology to government work. It has succeeded in making a 'closed' system 'open'. The CoLR programme has succeeded in bringing about administrative accountability, checked corruption and harassment and has provided equitable access to all concerned.

One aspect which has made CoLR successful in Karnataka, besides the dedication shown by the revenue department officials under the leadership of Additional Secretary Rajeev Chawla, Revenue Department, Government of Karnataka, has been the incorporation of online mutation module with the software. This has ensured that the database is as current as possible and reflects the reality. The workflow automation process also has been designed excellently and synchronises the manual process with the computerised system. Other states would do well to follow Karnataka's example and successfully computerise their land records.

Besides, some of the factors which have made CoLR programme successful in Karnataka are:

1. the incorporation of an online mutation module in the software has ensured that the database is dynamic and current. As soon as mutation is approved, the database gets updated and thus reflects the actual ground position;

2. the workflow automation system design has been excellent and the computerised system synchronises very well with the manual system. The basic mode of functioning of revenue personnel remains the same;

3. implementation of any new system/ process gives rise to a number of issues/ problems which need to be sorted out. The project team at the state government level has been proactive in clarifying and sorting out issues and overcoming teething problems;

4. the project conceptualisation and design in terms of security features, training, overcoming resistance to change, hardware configuration, etc., has been done in a meticulous manner after a thorough study of the existing system; and

5. though the success of Bhoomi is due to team effort, the role of Rajeev Chawla, head of the project, has been one of the major factors which has resulted in the successful conceptualisation, design and implementation of the project.

## RECOMMENDATIONS

- Farmers often have to travel long distances to obtain RTCs resulting in delays and greater cost. Therefore additional computer kiosks must be established to reduce the distance and travel time for farmers. It will be better to find out the location, which will be within a radius of 20 km from the villages instead of setting up the kiosk at hobli.

- The taluk centre is plagued by regular, almost daily, power outages. Since the computer kiosk does not have a generator backup for uninterrupted power supply, the process of obtaining RTCs often involved long delays. UPS generally cannot work for more than two hours. It is therefore necessary that 5 KVA generators should be provided in every taluk.

- Depending on the workload, the number of computer kiosk operators can be increased so that RTC-seekers do not have to wait while the operator is taking a break or is on leave.

- The RTC copies should be issued on per landholder basis rather than on per land plot basis.

- Establish a ticket number queuing system to establish efficiency and equity in the queuing process at the computer kiosk.

- Extra printer should be provided to overcome the problem of any fault in the existing printer.

- Farmers need up to date RTC in terms of crop details. At present the updating takes some time and there are also some errors in updated crop details. The system needs to be further streamlined.

- Whenever any problems related to software as well as hardware occurred in the computer system, no expert was available at taluk office, an expert had to come from district headquarters to tackle the problem. Due to this, inconvenience was caused to the users. Therefore, a trained person should be available at taluk level to sort out these problems or the government should tie up with computer agencies at taluk level to provide solutions.

- At present the computerisation of land records in Karnataka is restricted to non-spatial data. At the most, attempts are being made to give a copy of the plot map in a scanned image. For comprehensive computerisation,it is necessary that in the next phase digitisation of maps is taken up either by scanning and digitising the existing maps or by resurvey/fresh survey through modern survey equipment like Total Stations, etc., for generation of new maps.

- There should be a mechanism to upgrade the hardware in view of technological advancements and also to take care of new and unavoidable requirements, for example, higher capacity hard disks, new OS, RAID controllers, etc.

- To empower farmers, touch screen kiosks should be installed in all taluks as has been done in Bangalore, South Taluk.

- MPs/MLAs can finance the extension of kiosk at sub-taluk or other level under the MP/MLA LAD (Member of Parliament/Member of

Legislative Assembly Local Area Development) scheme so that access to the farmers is enhanced.

- After the implementation of the programme in taluks it would be necessary that computers be maintained all the time. The downtime should certainly not be more than 24 hours. Annual maintenance contract has to be entered into with competent parties which should be stationed at taluk level so as to rectify computers and peripherals in less than 24 hours. Ten per cent of the machine's cost should be provided for the maintenance of the hardware every year. This maintenance cost should be payable every second year onwards for at least five years.

- There is a need to integrate departments dealing with lands, such as survey and land records, registration department at village, taluk, district and state levels which could facilitate simultaneous updating of land records caused by mutation, sale of property, conveyance, partitions, exchange, gifts, settlements, release deeds, etc. This may also help in the faster updating of land records, which may be useful to landholders.

- There is a need to train land survey and revenue officials including village-level functionaries for upgrading their skills in computerisation of land records.

- The computerisation process should integrate registration of land titles. Land laws/mutation process should be simplified for easy and fast implementation of computerisation.

- The land information data should be web-enabled. This will provide easy access via Internet.

- The state government should explore the possibility of providing Simputers* (the common man's computer), to the village accountants for data entry of crop information.

## REFERENCES AND SELECT BIBLIOGRAPHY

**Appu, P.S.** (1995). *Report of the National Committee on Revitalisation of Land Revenue Administration*, Ministry of Rural Development, GoI.
———. (1996). Land Reforms in India. New Delhi: Vikas Publishing House.
**Aziz, Abdul** and **Sudhir Krishna** (eds). (1997). *Land Reforms in India; Karnataka: Promises Kept and Missed*. New Delhi: Sage Publications.

* The Simputer is a full-featured, powerful hand-held computer. It is an acronym for simple, inexpensive, mobile, people's computer. The Simputer is a low cost portable alternative to PCs, by which the benefits of IT can reach the common man.

**Bhoomi.** (Version 2.0): Land Records Computerisation System, NIC, Karnataka and Revenue Department, Government of Karnataka.

**Centre for Rural Studies.** (2001). 'Contributory Papers of National Workshop on Computerisation of Land Records', November. LBSNAA, Mussoorie.

**Chawla, Rajeev** and **Subhash Bhatnagar.** 'Bhoomi: Online Delivery of Land Titles in Karnataka, India,' online at *www.worldbank.org*

**Singh, S.K.** (2001). *Dictionary of Land Revenue Terms in India*. Dehradun: Greenfield Publishers.

**Sinha, B.K.** (1998). 'Evaluation of Computerisation of Land Records in Morena District', Land Reforms Unit, LBSNAA, Mussoorie.

———. (2000). 'Dynamic Land Records Management System: A Pressing Need', in B.K. Sinha and Pushpendra (eds), *Land Reforms in India: An Unfinished Agenda*. New Delhi: Sage Publications.

**Government of India.** Ministry of Rural Development, Annual Reports from 1995–2001.

———. Ministry of Rural Development, Conference of Revenue Ministers on Land Reforms, 1985 and 1992.

———. (1999). Ministry of Rural Development, Vision Document.

———. Planning Commission, the First, Second, Third, Fourth, Fifth, Sixth, Seventh, Eighth and Ninth five year plans (Chapter on Land Reforms).

# 6

# Computerisation of Land Records in Haryana

## MAHA SINGH

## INTRODUCTION

Efforts seem to have gathered momentum to walk in the wake of e-governed states. However, so far not much has been achieved in terms of a vision of paperless transactions. The potential to achieve far outweighs accomplishment. A step forward, however, is that procedures seem to have been made less complex. There are opportunities for growth galore. One stark reality that cannot be overlooked, however, is the absence of infrastructure for the free flow of information.

To harness growth it is essential to build infrastructure. Overall, the economy benefits. The pattern of government management is getting remapped. Communication system's compatibility with public interface is critical to the whole governance delivery chain.

Age-old procedures of communicating and transactions are becoming obsolete. It is extremely important to keep up with contemporary technologies in communication, as practised in national and international arena. India has recently adopted an IT policy compatible with international standards. This is supposed to be of help to the administration as well as to the public in general. Timely delivery and quick response to the dynamic needs of the public has assumed a greater significance in the emerging scenario. And it is in this context, that computerisation of land records has become highly relevant and significant. In fact, paperwork involved has become so cumbersome and cost-ineffective that we are forced to think in terms of IT-enabled environment for making governance meaningful and effective.

## CURRENT STATUS OF COMPUTERISATION OF LAND RECORDS

Broadly, the computerisation of land records took off in the year 1989 under the aegis of NIC. The funding pattern has been in the shape of budgetary support from Government of India to the state governments. Since 1989, the RoR data has been, more or less, put on the hard disk. Beyond this little has been achieved. Even the data needs to be validated by verifying and comparing with the original records. I do not agree with the argument that computerisation of land records is just putting the RoRs on the hard disk. In fact, this is the preliminary stage; at this stage the data is frozen on a particular date after due verification and a printout with due signature of the concerned revenue authority is kept for reference. The maintenance and updating of records is continuous and is the real issue that needs to be addressed.

Registration of a deed is the beginning point that triggers the process of updating of the land records. Well, this is the crucial stage and offers an opportunity for online updating of land records. As would be seen later in this chapter, registration of documents provides the key to the needed funds for the whole project of computerising land records. The idea is simple: registration of a document needs pre-operations that costs money to the buyer and as per analysis the transactional costs are significantly higher than the user charges needed for the project to take off. The model is: at the heart of the strategy for the development of the project of computerisation of land records is 'technology'; technology is available in the market and registration of documents would be the cash cow. There would be enough cash to go ahead with the project as against the present piecemeal approach. As would be seen later, the sustainability issue stands addressed. I shall first discuss the transactional costs the buyer has to incur in practice and then reason out as to how the user charges are going to be significantly less than what they are presently. In a way it is going to be a win-win approach.

## FORECASTING REGISTRATION TRANSACTIONS

Decision making requires foresight in the form of forecasting. The quality of looking into the future depends on the methodology of crystal gazing. Broadly, there are three techniques: qualitative techniques, time-series analysis and projection, and the causal model. The first uses expert opinion and information about the special events, and it may or may not use historic data. The second is based on historic data and the third makes use of special information relevant to the elements in the system, and the past data as well. The forecasting of the documents to be registered in the future is very relevant and crucial to the whole model of financial sustainability of the project of computerisation of land records and registration of documents.

### Purpose of Forecast

The project of computerisation of land records and registration of documents by way of project financing is a new concept in the field of land records. However, it promises good results. As of now, funds are meagre and are received by the states in trickles. The piecemeal approach just does not work: computerisation of land records took off in the year 1989 and till date results speak about its not being as functional as was expected. In fact, unless we achieve online updating of land records, there is limited use of computerisation. For online updating, we need significant funds that do not seem to be forthcoming. Another, bigger issue is of sustainability—financial as well as technical. In the proposed concept the lifeline for both of these problems is the cash cow that will shape up by charging reasonable charges for the services to the customer at the time of registration of documents. It is the trigger mechanism that spurts out from the registered document. The change in the ownership of immovable property arises from the document, which comes out of the process of registered deeds like sale deed, gift deed and so on. As a consequence of this, the mutation process takes off and after the attestation of the mutation the land records are updated. The process is depicted in the following flowchart (Figure 6.1).

**Figure 6.1**

*Flowchart of Manual Registration and Mutation Process*

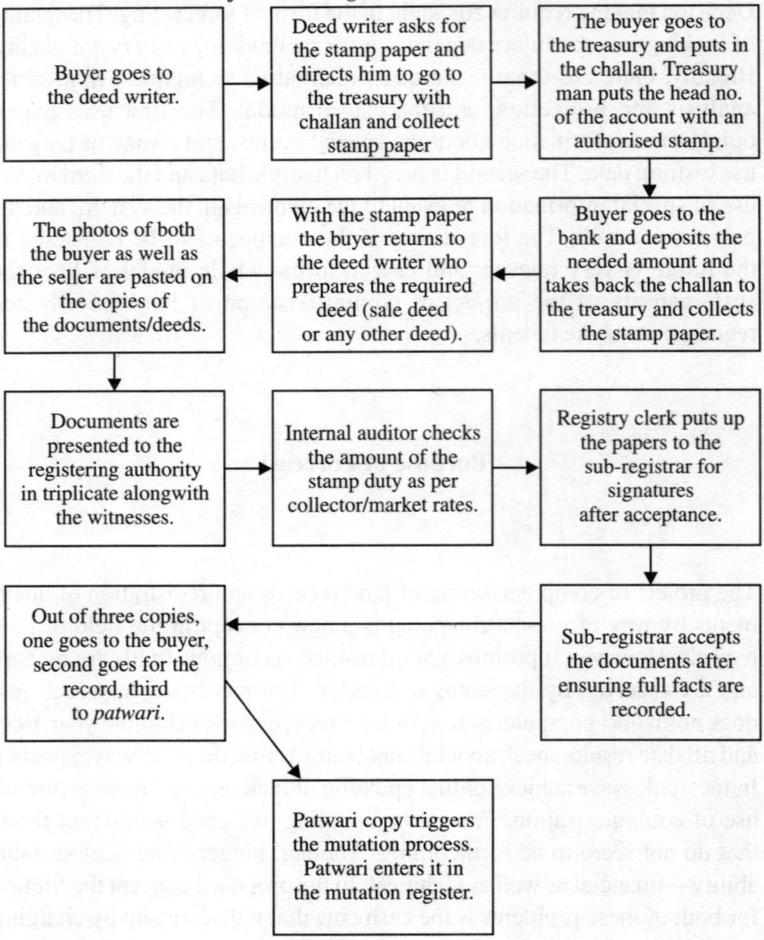

| Buyer goes to the deed writer. | → | Deed writer asks for the stamp paper and directs him to go to the treasury with challan and collect stamp paper | → | The buyer goes to the treasury and puts in the challan. Treasury man puts the head no. of the account with an authorised stamp. |

| The photos of both the buyer as well as the seller are pasted on the copies of the documents/deeds. | ← | With the stamp paper the buyer returns to the deed writer who prepares the required deed (sale deed or any other deed). | ← | Buyer goes to the bank and deposits the needed amount and takes back the challan to the treasury and collects the stamp paper. |

| Documents are presented to the registering authority in triplicate alongwith the witnesses. | → | Internal auditor checks the amount of the stamp duty as per collector/market rates. | → | Registry clerk puts up the papers to the sub-registrar for signatures after acceptance. |

| Out of three copies, one goes to the buyer, second goes for the record, third to *patwari*. | ← | | | Sub-registrar accepts the documents after ensuring full facts are recorded. |

Patwari copy triggers the mutation process. Patwari enters it in the mutation register.

## Transactional Cost Analysis

From Figure 6.1 we see that there are a number of transactions that precede the presentation of the documents for the final registration. These activities involve financial expenditure for the buyer and we can call it the pre-operation expenditure that is incurred by the buyer trying to get the documents for registration at the office of sub-registrar. In other words, we can say the expenditure is involved for various transactions till the stage of not-ready-to-register document. Till this point no fees or stamp duty is involved. It is purely a pre-expenditure. This is crucial to understand how much the buyer spends. I will explain it in the following model:

Spending model:
transactional expenditure = cost of deed writing + cost of photos + cost of transport + opportunity cost of time foregone

I conducted an informational/exploratory study in the state of Haryana on the foundations of random sampling. The transactional costs varied from Rs 300 to Rs 1,000 per deed. This presents an opportunity for the computerisation of land records. Herein lies the trick. The computer can perform all the activities and the project cost can be capitalised at much less rate of transactional costs to the buyer. This is good for both the buyer as well for the project of computerisation of land records. The road map is like this: the registered document that triggers the process of land records updating would lay the foundations for cash generation, which would generate enough funds for the project for its capitalisation and sustainability.

## Economic Evaluation

All projects are feasible, if there are unlimited resources and infinite time. Unfortunately the real world is different. Economic feasibility is an evaluation of development cost (project cost) weighed against the ultimate income or benefit desired from the project. It is generally associated with bottomline consideration—whether it will be acceptable to the investors. The other considerations of interest would be how the project is going to impact on the other sectors of economy. It needs to be evaluated with a long-term perspective. A myopic consideration leads to disastrous consequences. Organisational planning should be able to see beyond the horizons.

In the present case the number of deed transactions had been collected from the historic data. From the historic data, based on the least square method, a future forecast has been worked out. And on the forecast figures the income has been calculated by charging the customer, for the deed registration activity, Rs 200 per deed. This amount is quite reasonable as compared to the cost to the customer on the pre-activities for the purpose of registration of a document. Financial analysis worked out to be an IRR (internal rate of return) of 27 per cent. This makes it economically viable to go ahead with the project. The cost includes all the capital expenditure on hardware as well as software. The project is thus based on the simple fact that registration of the document triggers the updating process of land records and it generates cash. The cash charges would form a pool of fund that would finance the project. The customer would welcome it, as it would cost him less. It would save him time and unnecessary hassles.

## Project Financing

Now in the given scenario of cash generation by the activity of registration of documents a question that needs to be addressed is: how to finance the project of computerisation of land records? Finance engineering is the answer for how to raise required funds from the lenders: the financial institutions, commercial banks or any other source. The sponsor's interest lies in low exposure and the lender's in advancing credit with normal risks associated with the credit industry. The creditors are less interested in ROI (return on investment) than the usual credit risks. There is always a risk premium with project-specific risks. This increases the cost of capital for the project. In such a framework project financing seems to be a feasible strategy and government guarantee seems to give some hope.

Project financing, a major innovation of recent times, offers considerable promise to meet the needs of the project. Project financing is the financing of major independent capital investment that the sponsoring organisation has segregated from its assets and general-purpose obligations. The economic prospects of the project, combined with commitments from third parties, provide the support for extensive borrowings carrying limited financing recourse to the parent organisation.

Several characteristics distinguish project financing from traditional government financing:

- The undertaking (project cell) is established as a separate entity and relies heavily on debt financing ranging from 65 to 75 per cent of its capital needs.
- The borrowing is linked to the assets and cash flow potential of the project.
- A commitment by third parties (major players in the venture and the government agencies) and the sponsor makes up important elements of the credit support.
- The sponsor's guarantee to the lenders usually does not cover all the risks involved.
- The debt of the project is differentiated from the parent organisation for the purposes of balance sheet.

Each project has a unique risk and capital needs. Different sources of funding will suit various needs of the project. It now depends on the economics of the venture how the project cell is structured. The role of revenue department is of strategic importance. The revenue department has the potential of a cash cow for the flow of liquid funds in the shape of user charges for the processing of the documents. It needs to be emphasised again here that the user charges would be for the activities/transactions that are prior to the registration of the document. Anyway, the user is currently paying more than what is proposed to be charged. The user also benefits.

Therefore, it is a worthwhile approach: the user pays less and the entire updating system of land records becomes simpler. The new flowchart is shown in Figure 6.2.

Technically the source of funds can be any financial institution or a commercial bank. Escrow mechanism would only motivate the lender to lend. However, there are any number of financial products available that can be compatible with the unique needs of the project. The continuous and daily cash flow offers opportunity both for the project as well as the

investor. Thus funds need not be a problem for the project of computerisation of land records. Experience has shown that the funds required
are more than the small amount that the Government of India sends across
to the states. Also a piecemeal approach has led us nowhere: computerisation started in the year 1989 and till date results are not encouraging.
Unless online updating of land records is done, it is no computerisation.
In fact, it only increases the work: first you do it manually as has been
the practice and then feed the data in the computer. What the computer
does nobody has been able to understand in the revenue department. It
would be meaningful only when online updating is in place.

**Figure 6.2**

*Flowchart of Computerised Registration and Mutation Process*

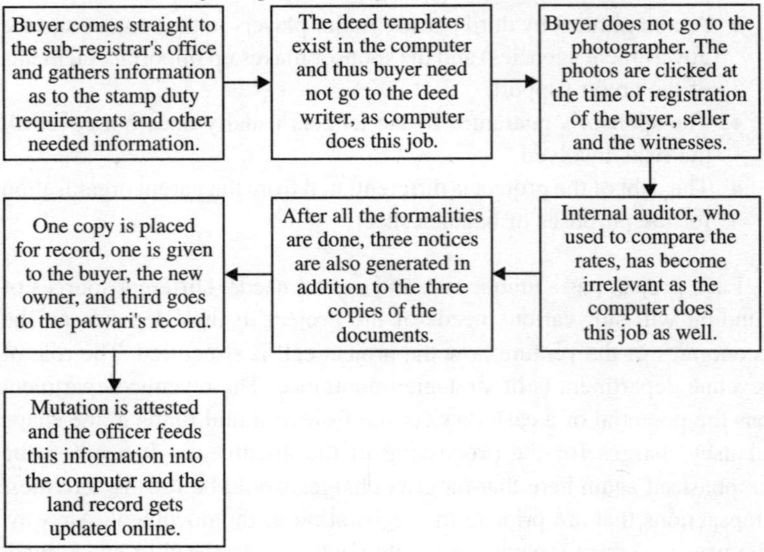

| Buyer comes straight to the sub-registrar's office and gathers information as to the stamp duty requirements and other needed information. | The deed templates exist in the computer and thus buyer need not go to the deed writer, as computer does this job. | Buyer does not go to the photographer. The photos are clicked at the time of registration of the buyer, seller and the witnesses. |
|---|---|---|
| One copy is placed for record, one is given to the buyer, the new owner, and third goes to the patwari's record. | After all the formalities are done, three notices are also generated in addition to the three copies of the documents. | Internal auditor, who used to compare the rates, has become irrelevant as the computer does this job as well. |
| Mutation is attested and the officer feeds this information into the computer and the land record gets updated online. | | |

# DOES IT WORK?

The test of steel lies in fire. The million-dollar question, 'does it work?'
can only be answered by an example of practice. I shall take the example
of Haryana where it has been put to practice and is working very well,

although many technical aspects still need to be addressed. However, these are just procedural matters that have got to be handled continuously as per the needs of the occasion. Computer societies (there can be any number of variants for having this kind of arrangement at the district headquarters) exist at each district headquarter level. In fact, the Red Cross Societies have been found handy for the time being as they already are functional with deputy commissioner as its chairman and controller of functions. The computer society thus, so far, technically is not a separate society from the Red Cross Society. However, its functions are performed by the Red Cross Society by keeping separate accounts both for income as well as expenditure. This is because the income from the registration of documents can only be utilised for the legitimate purposes of land records maintenance. It has been done because we raised the funds also from these societies as they had surplus funds. Now 30 per cent of the income goes to the Red Cross Society and the remaining 70 per cent is appropriated for the exclusive use for the operations and maintenance of the computers. It gives the much-needed sustainability, both financial as well as technical. The deputy commissioner is the chief controller. This gives him the flexibility of using funds as and when required depending on the local conditions, an example of a totally decentralised system. It gives the much coveted advantage to the government to fix responsibility of the officers at the district level. The district commissioner cannot say that the funds were not available in time. In fact, funds are being generated adequately and the needs of replacement of the hardware and software can easily be taken care of. As of now, in the state of Haryana, all the *tehsils* have started functioning on the computerised model as regards the registration of documents. The much-desired issue of online updating of the land records is under implementation.

Another issue that needs to be addressed is whether NIC is the only agency that should be responsible for this kind of a project. In fact, so far the major role in this direction has only been played by NIC. But the limitations are obvious: the manpower available with NIC does not meet the needs at the tehsil/*taluk* level. Outsourcing is a must both for development of the software as well as operations and maintenance. NIC would always be there as a big brother to guide and lead.

# 7

# Centrally Sponsored Scheme of Computerisation of Land Records in West Bengal

## S. SURESH KUMAR

## THE BEGINNING

The Ministry of Rural Development, Government of India had approved the pilot project on Computerisation of Land Records (CoLR) as a first step in the district of Burdwan in the financial year 1990–91. Burdwan is one of the largest districts in West Bengal and has the kind of diversity in agro-climatic zones as well as in the land-utilisation pattern not seen elsewhere. The government staff did the initial data-entry work, which presented a massive problem as it involved overcoming a number of barriers related to technology, training and perception itself. By the time the next three projects were sanctioned in 1993–94 in Jalpaiguri, Hughli and Nadia districts, vendor support for data entry could be developed and the progress became more rapid. In 1994–95, sanction was given under CoLR for the district of Howrah. In 1995–96, another eight districts were sanctioned, namely Darjeeling, Malda, Birbhum, Bankura,

For all figures in lakhs and crores, please note that 1 lakh = 100,000 and 1 crore = 10,000,000.

Medinipur, Tamluk, North 24-Parganas, and South 24-Parganas. By 1996–97, the scheme was sanctioned for all the remaining districts of West Bengal.

## STATUS AND UTILISATION OF FUNDS PLACED UNDER CoLR PROJECT

The number of *mouzas* (revenue villages) attested or which are baseline records are 39,600 and the number of finally published mouzas are 38,892 of which data of 39,151 mouzas was entered (98.86 per cent), printouts for 38,168 mouzas were generated (96.38 per cent), checking of printouts of 35,088 mouzas (88.60 per cent) was completed and validation of 31,909 mouzas (80.57 per cent) was done. Funds to the tune of Rs 15.96 crore received till date were expended as per the old guidelines, and a further fund of Rs 5.56 crore was received under the revised guidelines. Initially the work was estimated as shown in Table 7.1

**Table 7.1**

*Districtwise Status of Computerisation of Land Records Project*

| Sl. no. | District | No. of blocks | Total no. of mouzas | No. of mouzas attested | No.of individual records (interests) (in Rs lakh) | No. of plots (in Rs lakh) |
|---|---|---|---|---|---|---|
| 1. | Bankura | 22 | 3,847 | 3,842 | 51.8 | 43.2 |
| 2. | Burdwan | 31 | 2,827 | 2,779 | 64.4 | 21.9 |
| 3. | Birbhum | 19 | 2,489 | 2,488 | 44.8 | 29.9 |
| 4. | Darjeeling | 12 | 615 | 610 | 1.3 | 4.96 |
| 5. | Howrah | 14 | 836 | 827 | 16.3 | 8.3 |
| 6. | Hughli | 18 | 1,998 | 1,998 | 39.9 | 15.1 |
| 7. | Jalpaiguri | 13 | 774 | 698 | 15.3 | 5.1 |
| 8. | Kochbehar | 12 | 1,170 | 1,168 | 27.8 | 8.8 |
| 9. | Malda | 15 | 1,815 | 1,794 | 17.4 | 14.1 |
| 10. | Medinipur | 24 | 8,129 | 8,108 | 50.9 | 39.8 |
| 11. | Tamluk | 30 | 3,890 | 3,888 | 55.9 | 39.9 |
| 12. | Murshidabad | 26 | 2,289 | 2,279 | 45.0 | 23.1 |
| 13. | Nadia | 17 | 1,406 | 1,405 | 31.9 | 14.4 |
| 14. | Purulia | 20 | 2,700 | 943 | 51.4 | 13.5 |
| 15. | N. 24 Parganas | 22 | 1,828 | 1,746 | 31.5 | 31.1 |
| 16. | S. 24 Parganas | 29 | 2,292 | 2,046 | 40.8 | 39.8 |
| 17. | D. Dinajpur | 8 | 1,646 | 1,639 | 21.5 | 10.3 |
| 18. | U. Dinajpur | 9 | 1,516 | 1,342 | 13.0 | 8.1 |
| | **Total** | **341** | **42,067** | **39,600** | **367.7** | **624.56** |

## REASONS FOR SUCCESS

- *Tight administrative set-up:* The Directorate of Land Records and Surveys at the state level and the district land reforms set-up were tightly bound layers which had previously implemented very successful programmes such as Operation Barga and re-distribution of vested land programme. A direct and single chain of command existed which was outside the normal functions/emergency role of the district collectorate. Therefore they could concentrate on the job at hand in a sustained manner.

- *Innovative role of some of the officers:* The leadership displayed at certain crucial junctures by some of the directorate officers and the district-level officers played an important role in stabilising the programme and in giving the right direction to it. To some extent continuous monitoring and pressure from the directorate and some of the district-level officers went a long way in ensuring that planned progress went ahead steadily.

- *Condition of record of rights:* The present record of rights were framed in the current settlement operation, which started in the year 1974. Thus, the RoRs were in a relatively good condition and had not suffered any significant damage. This made the job of handling the records by the data-entry operator much easier, and also made the need for government staff at the time of data entry a matter of just a token presence.

- *Data entry through private vendors:* Initially for nearly one and a half years the data entry was taken up departmentally but the progress was extremely unsatisfactory, so much so that private vendors had to be appointed. This process reduced the involvement of staff to some extent in the programme, but there was no other option, considering both the attitudinal problems prevailing then and acute staff shortage. In fact it took some time to gear up even the data-entry operators considering their lack of familiarity in the Bengali keyboard but once this initial hurdle was overcome the next problem was to supply adequate corrected records and fresh records for data entry.

- *Thorough checking by the staff:* The checking done was very thorough and meticulous. Initially, even if the printouts had more than 2 per cent errors prima facie, the data-entry operator was made to do fresh entry or to correct the records himself. After the receipt of a printout of a mouza, a clerical staff scrutinises all the individual records, which is followed by 10 per cent sample checking by a revenue officer. Printouts of the corrected record of rights also go through the same cycle after which the record of rights are validated to the extent of 100 per cent.

- *Software development:* The software went through as many as nine versions of development before a GUI version was developed by the NIC. Throughout, continuous interaction with the NIC and communication of the field necessities for software development to take care of all the intricacies in the record of rights had to be made without which there would have been a serious dislocation in the endeavour.
- *Technical spin-offs:* The process itself generated some formats, which could be used for checking the errors involved in framing the record of rights. The process of framing of RoRs as well as checking the accuracy is painstaking and tedious. The validated data could be utilised to generate the plot index and the *khasra*, which reduced the tedium as well as the time taken to finalise RoRs. Some standardisation of the classification of lands in different districts had to be evolved perforce. As the computerisation of the RoRs required some standardisation, some form of uniformity had to be used for easy search facility and many superfluous classes of land were renamed. This exercise also was of great utility for the computerisation project of the registration department.
- *Attitudinal change in the staff:* The prospect of supplying certified copies to the public quickly brought a lot of pressure on them initially but they became reconciled to it when the computerisation process became a part of their routine itself. Work related to the computerisation, such as checking, also became a part of their routine.

## TECHNICAL SPIN-OFFS FROM THE DATA

- *Detection of defects in the survey and settlement work:* Computerisation has proved to be a boon for quick detection of mistakes made at the field level. Manual preparation of an index of the land records based on certain key fields is very time consuming and is fraught with errors. Hence, if the data entry is correct, then it generates an exact plot index which gives us the actual picture of the records. This has given us a list of plots which need to be checked due to changes in ownership, cases where joint property has been declared but individual ownership has not been decided, cases where there is incomplete ownership of plots due to non-reflection of the appropriate tenant's share. Interestingly the printout generated is not at all a time-consuming process and it can be used to pinpoint the defects unlike the previous manual system.

- *Standardisation of land classification in the state:* A list of classes of land is approved for use prior to every survey and settlement operation. In practice, however, it has been found that there is no uniformity or one-to-one correspondence between the description of a class of land over all the districts in the state. Therefore, all redundant and obsolete land classifications were merged with a suitable land class. This has resulted in tremendous benefits as some parity between land classes could now be maintained for assessment of land value, data mining, etc.

- *Generation of registers:* The ease with which certain crucial survey and settlement registers could be generated is another great spin-off. The plot index which is the plotwise list of the number allocated to each RoR, the khasra which is the plotwise list of the individual landowner and the sub-tenancies created and the Register III which is the demand register for the land revenue and taxes payable by each landowner. All three registers presently have great utility.

- *Generation of individual record of rights:* A change had been engineered in the present settlement operation where the RoRs are prepared individually for a *raiyat* instead of joint ownership. However, in the transferred areas of Purulia and Uttar Dinajpur districts where the current settlement operation is still continuing, a software package was developed by the NIC called Joint 01.exe which is being utilised to great effect. The software package converts the data in joint ownership RoRs into individual RoRs very easily and quickly which is the first step in revising the RoRs. This has a great advantage in that it not only saves time significantly but it also liberates a significant manpower from an otherwise laborious job for other work which is extremely crucial.

## ANALYSIS OF THE GAPS/DEFICIENCIES
## IN THE CoLR SCHEME

### Related to Computer Hardware

- *High obsolescence rate of hardware:* The CoLR project had started off with 286 series machines in the early 1990s and has currently reached the Pentium IV series machines. Hardware development has also faithfully followed the Moore's Law whereby a processor's capacity would double every 18 months leading to the necessity of frequent upgrading. Moreover, due to the short product cycles of only three to four years, maintenance is well nigh impossible after that period due to the non-availability of various components. Wherever components become incompatible, the whole machine has to be junked and a new machine has to be purchased which requires additional investment, which the revised guidelines do not take into consideration. Thus, a paradigm change in the configuration is necessary to obviate frequent upgrading. The best alternative is to work towards the three-tier architecture based on a server and their clients. The architecture would consist of a thin client with little hard disk space in Graphic User Interface (GUI), an application server in Java Database Connectivity Bridge (JDCB) and a database server. The advantages are many and there is easy change management in hardware and software; easy and dynamic load balancing of the network, improved data protection and security, and flexibility in changes in storage strategy, etc.
- *Use of GIST (Graphic and Intelligence based Script Technology) cards:* This hardware solution for the conversion of data is prone to defects and needs frequent replacement. Not only are GIST cards unreliable but they also slow down the printer's speed by half. Hence, a GUI solution is the need of the hour and GIST cards should be phased out. Any investment required for this comprehensive solution would only be possible if the guidelines were to make a provision for the expenditure.

- *Machine maintenance:* It is unfortunate but true that the penetration of information technology goes rarely beyond the state capital and some major towns, due to which the availability of technical manpower for maintenance in the districts is negligible. Nor is there any inclination on the part of hardware manufacturers to undertake service contracts in the rural areas. This has resulted in enormous costs in maintenance after the guarantee period is over and the downtime due to non-operation is also very high. This should be considered in the guidelines.

- *Erratic power supply:* Power supply disturbances due to fluctuations such as surges/drops and long periods of load-shedding lead the computer system to be idle and non-productive, and create a negative impression on the service-taker. A stand-by arrangement is very much necessary which ought to be included in the guidelines.

- *Higher hardware requirements:* Presently only textual database is being delivered to the user. Shortly, after the digitisation of maps and the integration of the textual and graphic data into a land information system it would require a more powerful multi-user architecture at the *tehsil*/block level, rather than the existing stand-alone computer.

- *Unsatisfactory data archiving:* Presently there is no reliable method of backing up data when changes to the database are being made on a daily basis. The use of floppy disks is unreliable and could lead to data loss. What is required is a good solution such as DAT or a CD writer, which can be a trouble-free solution.

## Related to Software

*Non-conversion of existing software platform:* The code for the software package had been written in FoxBASE, a third generation programming language on a DOS platform, since the inception of the CoLR. The Vision Document has also recognised that the FoxBASE platform was suitable (from those available) 8–10 years back but is no longer suitable presently due to the following reasons:

- The use and access of the files is not particularly user-friendly due to which there is still a lot of resistance to typing out any code by the user. Novice, older users particularly, have found it very intimidating and do not relate well with the user unlike a windows-based (GUI) software which primarily uses a point and click technique.

- Training input is much heavier and the retention of the inputs is also not very satisfactory, to the say the least. Hence, frequently the trainees have relapsed into their original state of ignorance or indifference to errors when using the package, if they are not in constant touch.
- There is no data security in the existing software package based on FoxBASE. As the data is highly valuable, it should be made tamper-proof and free from unauthorised access. Security packages as an add-on can be developed but a good Relational Database Management System (RDBMS) like Oracle and MS SQL Server can ensure the security as well as manage the date exceedingly well.
- The amount of data at the block/tehsil level is nearly 1 GB alone and the proper maintenance of the data integrity from corruption in the present open database created in a FoxBASE platform is becoming extremely necessary. Migration to a standard RDBMS platform would be an effective solution. Not only that, if the conversion to a multi-user RDBMS is made now then the spatial database would also get better organised.

*Computerisation of land records per se is not just sufficient:* The entry of textual data and its generation as a printout is a very limited exercise being undertaken at the moment. There are a host of other activities related to the maintenance of RoRs which can be derived from the existing database created. In addition, other administrative routines can also be computerised to make the utilisation of computers more pervasive and widespread.

## Networking

The revised guidelines make a brief mention of the concept of networking but have not gone into the details of it with the result that there are no clear-cut ways to go about it, such as the connectivity links to be followed by the blocks/tehsils to the districts and as to how the districts would in turn be connected to the state. It has also been well recognised that there would be a marked improvement in monitoring system in place. The work output should in turn be reflected in the website of the revenue department or the state-level organisation maintaining land records.

## Project Management Under the CoLR

- *Training of the officers and the subordinate staff:* This aspect has been repeatedly emphasised but has not got the importance it has deserved. The primary objective is to equip the personnel, but equally important is the necessity to bring about an attitudinal change in them to give up an age-old system of following certain procedures and pick up a technological solution. The training of supervising officers has been neglected with the result that most of them are unable to relate properly with the scheme either, in accessing the data or in properly monitoring the scheme itself. Hence, training in the use of the software should be from the topmost rung to the lowest functionary involved in the scheme. Some other incentives and checks should be improved to bring in proper forms and an attitudinal change in the officer cadre. Training of the lower level functionaries has not always been fruitful if they are hostile or feel intimidated, or if they have to recall and type lengthy commands to use the existing software package. Probably the conversion of the software into a GUI-based package would result in better receptivity among the trainees.
- *Monitoring and evaluation:* Though it has been emphasised in the CoLR scheme, the fact is that the monitoring and evaluation of CoLR activity has become just one component among the gamut of activities involved in the survey and settlement process, with the result that its emphasis has been diluted to some extent. There is a need for a special mechanism to ensure that the milestones are achieved within the fixed time frame.
- *Lack of trained manpower:* The scope of the scheme has increased to such an extent that for the maintenance of infrastructure or for the maintenance of the database itself some specialists are necessary

at the district and the state level. Existing recruitment practices in the state are not particularly conducive for the intake of such professionals nor is it advisable to employ such professionals permanently. Hence some kind of consultants need to be engaged to fill the gap.

- *Exclusion of certain administrative levels:* Some levels of the administrative set-up involved in the survey and settlement process have been left out in the CoLR scheme. The sub-divisional officers, assistant commissioners of survey and assistant directors of land records who are important supervisory officers in the revenue/survey set-up need to be also involved in the process. At the apex level in the state headquarter, there is no provision for a central data warehouse exclusively for the land records data, with the result that proper screening of data for data quality and data mining is not possible at present. Hence a separate set-up at the state level is very much a felt need.

- *Involvement of NIC:* The National Informatics Centre had pioneered the process of developing the software for the CoLR scheme in Indian languages all over India and in specifying the basic hardware specifications too. However, it has been a common complaint that the NIC has not been adequately responsive to making necessary changes in the software within a reasonable time due to which there is a loss of interest in the user. The NIC could be overburdened due to the demands of other users or due to its own infrastructural problems, and hence it is time that the CoLR scheme is weaned away from reliance on NIC. In fact a significant portion of funds had been transferred to the NIC for the installation of computer hardware at the district set-up, which is yet to be accounted for.

- *Integration of the CoLR scheme with other computerisation activities:* The computerisation of land records should develop cross-departmental linkages with the registration department regarding the property details or the property changes where the computerisation process has been going on under the Eleventh Finance Commission funding, the Irrigation Department or the Minor Irrigation Department which need to raise a demand for the raiyati-wise water usage rates, the agriculture department which needs the statistics for crop survey and agricultural census, the forest department, the municipalities and *panchayat* bodies, etc. Thus the mobilisation of the activities of various land-related agencies in a coordinated manner to collect all the necessary information under their respective jurisdiction is becoming a necessity. This would prevent the development of 'islands of computerisation' and would provide the cross-platform infrastructure for users of land information to get access to data regardless of the location of these distributed databases, and not establish separate data collection mechanisms and avoid replication of efforts and expenses. This would go a long way in promoting a state land information system.

• *Introduction of e-governance:* The basic *taluk*/tehsil/block level revenue department agency has the maximum number of transactions with the general public, other than the police station or the sub-registry office. Basic information should be made available through the information kiosks for citizen interface. However, an objective system to answer the basic query of any citizen who would like to know what action has been taken on the application made by him is yet to be developed and only an IT based e-governance solution can bring about a radical change. This would also ensure that information is quickly available, so as to be able to take decisions without depending on the lower-level functionaries.

## VARIOUS COMPONENTS TO BE INCLUDED IN THE GUIDELINES FOR CoLR

### Hardware

• *Increase in unit cost of tehsil/block/taluk level computerisation:* In every state, the unit cost is highly inadequate to fund the following items: (*a*) UPS; (*b*) furniture; (*c*) wiring and networking; (*d*) air conditioners; (*e*) site preparation; (*f*) software; and (*g*) scanners and fingerprint readers. It is suggested that all states should be allowed to purchase the equipment and the Government of India can fix the unit cost approximately, based on the ballpark market rates. The schedule of suggested configuration and unit costs for various levels is given in Appendix 7.1 and Appendix 7.2.

- *Fund for maintenance of hardware:* Once the land records project is made operational in taluk/tehsil/block it would be necessary for computers to be maintained all the time. The downtime should certainly not be more than 24 hours. Annual maintenance contract has to be entered into with competent parties who should be stationed at district and divisional level so as to rectify the computers and the peripherals in less than 24 hours. Of the machine's cost, 10 per cent should be provided for maintenance of the hardware every year. This maintenance cost shall be payable every second year onwards for at least five years.
- *Generators:* In rural areas the quality of power supply is very bad and erratic. Commonly, electricity not available for as long as 10 hours in a day. UPS can certainly not work for more than two hours. It is therefore necessary that 2 KVA generators should be provided in every taluk/tehsil/block at the cost of roughly Rs 40,000 per generator.
- *District office computerisation:* While the scheme has a provision of Rs 10.2 lakh for providing computers to district offices, Government of India has not been releasing the above amount. The Government of India should release this amount after deducting the cost (if any) of the computers supplied to deputy commissioner's offices for computerisation of land records by NIC.

## Project Management

- *Monitoring cell:* As the scheme is now growing in size, there is a need to monitor it closely from the state level. Funds for the running of the monitoring cell should be immediately provided by Government of India in every state. An earmarked senior officer should be made available by the state for regular visits and close monitoring.
- *Training of personnel:* It is very important that village accountants and lower-level revenue functionaries and other officers should be trained comprehensively on the software to be used in the state. There is a need for training them comprehensively in all the states and therefore provision should be made in the scheme for this purpose.

The funds to be allotted should be categorised separately to identify their expenditure.

- *Provision of computers to sub-divisional officer (SDO)/assistant commissioner (AC)/assistant director of land records (ADLR):* At the moment, the scheme does not provide for computers to the SDO/AC/ADLR. Due to this, the supervision process is not improving. Therefore, it is necessary that the scheme should have provision to supply computers to these middle tiers. The unit cost would approximately be as per the cost of funding a district office.

- *Rate fixed for data entry:* The rate fixed for data entry is Rs 10 lakh for a district, which is probably a rough estimate. This being a guideline for the whole country, it would be best if a more rational guideline based on the data to be entered in bytes/KB is worked out as the size of a district in terms of the number of records of rights in it or the size of the data in the records of rights varies significantly from state to state and district to district. It is suggested that the payment should be Rs 3 per KB of the data entered, if done in the local language.

- *Front-end land records shop:* In the computerisation of land records scheme, Government of India has not provided for such a shop, where farmers can buy their land records. Such a shop would provide more transparency in land records ad-ministration and empower farmers. The cost of such a shop would be Rs 1.5–2 lakh, including the shop preparation which would consist of the following:

  - one PC
  - one extra 15" colour monitor with monitor multiplexer
  - Wipro 1050 + DX dot matrix printer
  - table-top 650 VA UPS
  - suitable furniture
  - site preparation

- *Touch screen kiosk:* To empower farmers, touch screen kiosks should be installed in all taluks/tehsil/blocks in a phased manner during Tenth Five-Year Plan. The cost of the touch screen kiosk may work out to be Rs 1.5–2 lakh.

- *Consultants in every district:* The district informatics officer is overburdened in every district and therefore, to ease the pressure it is very necessary that a private consultant is engaged for a period of one year at a time. The cost of consultants so appointed would be Rs 2–3 lakh per year per district.

- *Consultancy services for security design of software:* The Government of India should enable the state government to hire consultancy services from Microsoft, Wipro, Satyam Computers, CDAC, etc., so as to take care of security and customised software applications. As the land records database is sensitive and large, farmers and other agencies depend upon this database and it is very important that the software designed should have rugged features so as to ensure integrity of the data. After putting the hardware infrastructure in place at great expense and labour, the whole effort could be put into jeopardy if a professional approach is not adopted for the application of software development. Individual proposals should be taken up by the land reforms division when forwarded by the state government.

- *Amendment of relevant acts:* Relevant state acts have to be amended to make handwritten land records illegal or irrelevant and give necessary evidence value to digital records. This is extremely important as in any system in which handwritten and computerised records are allowed to co-exist, it is bound to make computerisation of land records scheme redundant.

- *Constitution of a core group at Government of India level:* A small team should be constituted at the level of Government of India consisting of GOI officers and state government officers who would go around to different states and advise state governments regarding various corrective measures required for computerisation of land records. This will result in experience-sharing and better results.

- *Annual inspection report:* The annual inspection reports of deputy commissioner/collector/revenue department should have a separate page on the efforts made by the district administration on land records' computerisation.

- *Reporting in Annual Confidential Report:* The Department of Personnel and Training, Government of India and the Home (Personnel)/ (General Administrative Department) may be requested to include a paragraph in the Annual Confidential Report of deputy commissioner/Collector/sub-collector on the efforts made by them for computerisation of land records.

- *Recruitment rules:* The recruitment rules of all the states should be amended to ensure that computer knowledge is made a pre-requisite for new recruitments at the clerical and officer level. The rules should also be amended to ensure minimal computer skills for promotion.
- *Study tour:* The Government of India should arrange for study tours to states where computerisation of land records has progressed well so that the staff and officers can learn from those states and also implement land records in an effective manner. The study tours of the state-implementing officers to other countries where computerisation of land records is being implemented should be arranged periodically so as to learn important lessons and the Government of India should fund this scheme.

## Networking

- *Connectivity:* The database needs to be connected at the sub-divisional, district and state levels to make a more meaningful use of the database. The guidelines will have to be amended to provide funds for this purpose. A schematic approach is given in Appendix 7.3. It has been suggested that the block/tehsil/taluk and the sub-division could be connected through dial-up modems to the district headquarter which would in turn have a 30-channel ISDN (Integrated Services Digital Network) PRI (Primary Rate Interface) connection for interacting with the blocks as well as providing it with the band-width for connecting with the state. The state website could post all the necessary information which would not be maintained centrally but through online updating. The state-level server could have two ISDN PRI connections, one for interacting with the districts and the other for connecting with the Internet and the Land Reforms Division. This would provide for a statewide network for data transmission which in turn would be linked right up to the Land Reforms Division in Delhi.

# APPENDIX 7.1

| Items of approved expenditure | For the tehsil/ block/taluk Rs in lakh | For the district level Rs in lakh | For the state level Rs in lakh |
|---|---|---|---|
| Hardware server & clients | Server – 2.0 5 Clients – 2.0 | Server – 3.5 Clients – 4.0 | Server – 8.0 Clients – 4.0 Server connectivity –7.0 |
| Software (operating system & RDBMS) | OS – 0.3 Oracle – 1.3 MS Office – 0.3 | OS – 0.6 Oracle – 1.3 MS Office – 0.3 | OS – 0.6 Oracle – 1.3 MS Office – 0.3 |
| Power management (UPS, servo stabilisers, etc.) | 0.60 | 1.00 | 1.25 |
| Networking (Local area network, etc.) | 0.50 | 0.80 | 1.0 |
| Connectivity (charges to be paid to BSNL for local/ISDN connection, network cards, etc.) | 0.05 | 2.8 | 5.6 |
| Maintenance cost of the hardware & software for 5 years (@ 10% of M/C cost). | 2.0 | 3.80 | 6.0 |
| Peripherals (printers, fingerprint scanners, scanners, touch screen kiosks, etc.) | 3.0 | 5.3 | 4.65 |
| Site preparation (including air conditioning, etc.) | 1.00 | 1.00 | 1.00 |
| Furniture | 0.50 | 0.50 | 1.00 |
| Documentation costs | 0.15 | 0.25 | 0.50 |
| Miscellaneous expenditure including stationery, office costing, training of staff, etc. | 0.25 | 0.25 | 0.50 |
| Data entry cost @ Rs 3 per KB | 13.35 | 24.9 | 42.85 |

# APPENDIX 7.2

## SUGGESTED CONFIGURATON FOR COMPUTER HARDWARE, PERIPHERALS

### Block/Tehsil/Taluk/Sub-Division/Others

*Hardware*

1. Back-to-Back Servers – 1 no. (i.e., 2 servers in one for backup)
   Intel Pentium III based machine
   Dual Processor Server motherboard
   128 MB ECC SDRAM
   1.44 MB FDA
   52 × CD ROM
   8 × EIDE CD Writer or 4/8 GB SCSI DAT
   1 × 18 GB Ultra 160 SCSI HDD (1000 RPM)
   14" Colour Monitor flat screen non-inter laced 0.20 micro metre
   do pitch SVGA Keyboards/Mouse
   Modem 56 KBPS
   P4 AT × Cabinet
   1Parallel, 2 serial and 2 USB ports

2. Client Machines – 5 nos.

   Intel Pentium-III 933 MHZ
   Intel 815 chipset motherboard
   128 MB SDRAM
   20 GB Hard Disk Drive
   1.44 MB FDD, 5 × CDROM
   2 Serial, 1 Parallel, 2 USB Ports
   14" Colour Monitor
   Bilingual Keyboard
   Mouse
   10/100 MBPS E-net Card Intel/3 com

3. Local Area Network Items

   Switches 8 port unmanaged 10/100 HBPS desktop switch
   Patch chord – 2 per client / server
   Info" outlet each client / server
   Label as required
   Patchpanel – 8/12 ports

4. Power Management

   UPS = 7 × 500–600 VA @ Rs 8,000 each
   At least 1 hour backup

5. Peripherals

   7K Scanner A4 Scanner – USB @ Rs 7,000
   70 Duplex A4 Laser Printer (optional) HPLJ 2200DN @ Rs 70,000
   16–17K 24 Pin High Speed 136 Col. DMP @ Rs 20,000
   30K Bio-metrics fingerprint reader @ Rs 30,000
   5KVA Generator @ Rs 20,000

6. Software

   Oracle 9 5 user
   MS Office 2002 5 User @ Rs 30,000
   Win 2K Professional (OEM) 5 Nos. @ Rs 6,000 each

## District Level

### *Hardware*

1. Server –1 no.

   Dual Intel P-III processor
   3 × 18 GB, 1000 RPM, Ultra 160 Hard Disk with hot swap
   capability, in RA 105
   64 bit PCI RAID controller with 128 MB ECC SDRAM
   2 nos. of Power Supply (Hot Swappable)

1Keyboard and 1PS2 mouse port
12/24 GB internal DAT Drive on SCSI
52 × IDE CD ROM drive
128 bit sound card and speakers
2 × 10/100 Ethernet controller with load balancing and link
aggregated support
17" colour monitor
1.44Mb Floppy drive
Windows Keyboard
VGA Controller with 4 MB video memory
Tower Cabinet with locking facility on front and back and on
motherboard

2. Client –10 nos.

   (Same configuration as in the block-level machines.)

3. Power Management

   10 × 525VA UPS for clients @ Rs 8,000 each
   2 × 525VA UPS for server @ Rs 8,000 each

4. Peripherals

   24 Pin High Speed 136 Col. Line Printer @ Rs 110,000
   Duplex Network Laser Printer (Optional) @ Rs 70,000
   24 Pin High Speed 136 Col DMP @ Rs 25,000
   A4 Scanner USB Port @ Rs 7,000
   Iomega Print Reader – @ Rs 30,000 –Rs 60,000
   Touch Screen Kiosk – 1 no. @ Rs 150,000
   5KVA Generator @ Rs 30,000

5. Networking Hardware

   LAN-PRI interface adapter card on PCI – Rs 200,000
   16 Port 10/100 Mbps switch – Rs 20,000
   13 I/0
   26 Patch Cards
   18 port patch panel Rs 40,000
   9 U Rack
   Cable as required

6. PRI Charges to be paid to BSNL

| | |
|---|---|
| Application Fee | Rs 2,000 |
| Registration Fee | Rs 45,000 |
| Installation Charges | Rs 4,000 |
| Wiring Charges | Rs 4,000 |
| Initial Deposit | Rs 15,000 |
| ISDN Internet Access | Rs 8,000 |
| **Total** | **Rs 78,000** |

7. Software

Oracle 9 10 user @ Rs 130,000
MS Office X P 10 user @ Rs 30,000
Wins 2K Professional (OEM) 10 nos. @ Rs 6,000 each

## State Level

### *Hardware*

1. Cluster Server – 4 nos. (Server would be in a cluster and a fault in any of them would not bring down the whole system)

2. Each Server

   1U high Rack mounted server
   Intel Pentium III dual processor 256 MB ECC SDRAM
   Slim line CD Rom /FDD Combo Drive 2 × 18 GB ultra 160 SCSI
   HDD (1000 RPM) (Hot swap)
   Dual Ethernet adapters integrated on board
   Dual Channel Ultra 160 SCSI Controller
   RAID Controller
   200 W Power supply
   Integrated video controller with 4 MB RAM Provisions for atleast
   on free full length PCI slot for PRI ISDN
   Sound Card.
   Approx Cost = Rs 200,000

3. Inter-connectivity of Servers

   10U Rack 800 mm deep with adequate cooling
   Layer – 4 switch (12 ports)
   Approx. cost = Rs 700,000

4. Clients – 10 nos. @ Rs 40,000 each

   Same configuration as in block level machines

5. Local Networking

   16 Port 10/150Mbps Switch = Rs 20,000
   13 I/O
   26 Patch Cords          } Rs 100,000
   18 Port patch panel
   9 U Rack
   Cable as required

6. Peripherals

   24 Pin High Speed 136 Col Line Printer @ Rs 180,000
   Duplex Network Laser Printer (Optional) @ Rs 70,000
   24 Pin High Speed 136 Col DMP @ Rs 25,000
   A3 Scanner USB Port @ Rs 150,000
   Fingerprint Reader – 2 nos. @ Rs 30,000 each = Rs 60,000

7. Power Conditioning

   10 × 525 VA UPS for clients @ Rs 8,000 each
   4 × 252 VA UPS for server

8. Networking

   ISDN PRI Cards – 2 nos. @ Rs 2 lakh each
   ISDN PRI Charges – 2 nos. @ Rs 80,000 each

9. Software

   Oracle 9 10 user @ Rs 130,000
   MS Office X P 10 user @ Rs 30,000
   Windows Small Business Server @ Rs 60,000

# APPENDIX 7.3

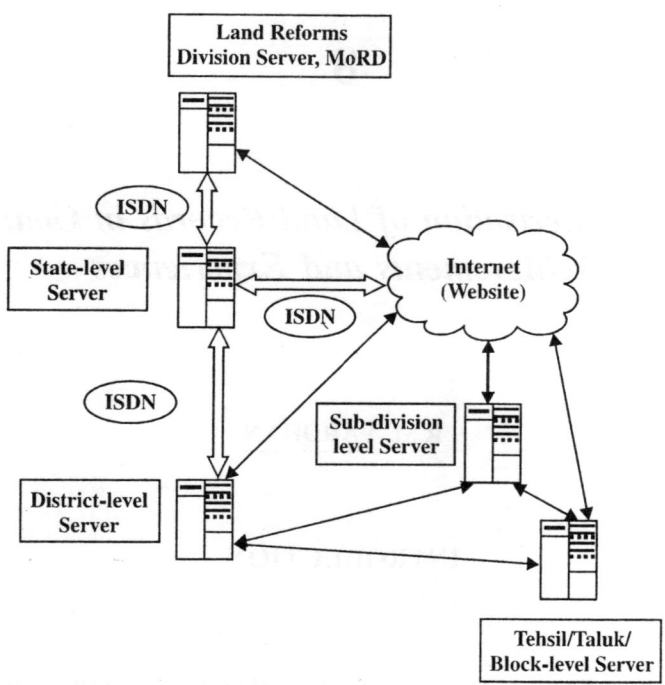

➤ Dial-up TCP/IP THRO' Modem

⟺ ISDN Connection

# 8

## Computerisation of Land Records in Goa: Achievements and Experiences

### R.M. VARDHAN

### INTRODUCTION

Goa is a small state with an area of 3,702 sq km. As per the latest census, the population is roughly 15 lakhs. There are only two districts: North Goa district and South Goa district, the former having a jurisdiction of six revenue *taluk*s and the latter having a jurisdiction of five revenue taluks with 429 revenue villages. The length of the state is about 120 km and the breadth-wise distance is approximately 60 km. The people of the state are highly literate. There is a great sense of awareness regarding public rights, especially related to land matters. People are prone to litigation. Besides, land values are steep as it is a popular tourist destination and as the state is on the path of development, land transactions taking place are large. Under the circumstances, there is a high public demand for land records. The prevalence of tenancy laws and other laws protecting the underprivileged enhances the value of land records.

For all figures in lakhs and crores, please note that 1 lakh = 100,000 and 1 crore = 10,000,000.

## LAND RECORDS

Goa is a cadastral state. After liberation in December 1961, a fresh land survey of the state was undertaken in late 1960s and early 1970s. This led to the preparation of record of rights (RoRs) known as Form I and XIV and cadastral maps known as plane table sheets (PT sheets). The RoRs contain details of a village, survey number, sub-division number, tenure, occupant, tenant, other rights, area, classification and record of cultivation. The details like survey number, sub-division number, area and classification and other features on the ground are graphically reflected in the plane table sheets. All the land records numbering about 8 lakh holdings have been promulgated except for a few stay cases. The RoRs are being periodically updated. There is one inadequacy in the case of cadastral maps in the sense that these are not fully updated. To address this issue, it has been decided by the Government of Goa to undertake revisional survey using latest surveying tools, and for this purpose financial assistance of the Government of India has been sought.

## THE SCHEME

The scheme of computerisation of land records (CoLR) fully sponsored by the Government of India was introduced in Goa in the early 1990s. Its objectives were: (*a*) to ensure safe and space-saving storage of records; (*b*) to better the security of records by reducing the possibilities of tampering and manipulation; (*c*) to make land data accessible easily and quickly to landholders for their personal use and to administrators for micro- and macro-planning; (*d*) to facilitate easy and quick updating of records; (*e*) to promote accuracy of records and minimise errors; and (*f*) to reduce heavy workload on the revenue staff.

Initially, only the project of computerisation of RoRs of all taluks was taken up. Later, in the year 1999–2000, Government of India sanctioned a pilot project of computerisation of cadastral maps in one taluk.

## Implementation

The implementing department in the state of Goa is Directorate of Settlement and Land Records. This department proceeded to implement the project of computerisation of RoRs with the help of National Informatics Centre (NIC) step by step at the taluk level *mamlatdar* offices in the following manner: (*a*) setting up of furnished air-conditioned computerroom in mamlatdar offices; (*b*) undertaking the work of data-feeding of RoR and its validation; (*c*) installation of appropriate hardware and software; and (*d*) imparting training to staff by the NIC.

Regarding the project of computerisation of cadastral maps, the department undertook the work in technical collaboration with a private professional agency involved in the work of GIS. The work involved scanning and digitisation of each PT sheet followed by software-aided mosaic process to generate village maps and taluk map. It also involved development of software modules to take care of the requirements of the department like generation of accurate and reliable printouts of survey numbers and sub-division numbers, or any parcel of land.

## Achievements

In December1997, when computerised RoR of Tiswadi taluk was inaugurated, it became the first taluk in the state where public could receive computerised certified copies of Form I and XIV within minutes of applying. This was the first evidence of information technology in the state having benefited the common man. However, the completion of work in this taluk was delayed because data-feeding work was undertaken departmentally. Considering problems like inadequate and untrained staff and lack of coordination between the mamlatdar offices and directorate offices, the exercise of data-feeding was time-consuming. The government then took the crucial decision of handing over the work of data-feeding to private agencies as provided in the scheme. This effectively speeded up the process of data entry. Consequently, the directorate was able to complete and commission the remaining 10 taluks within four years.

At the time of commissioning all the data was converted from Visual Foxpro to MS SQL Visual Basic. The last taluk was commissioned in December 2001 and Goa was declared to be the first state in the country to have completed the computerisation of RoRs of all 11 taluks of the state by the Minister of Rural Development, Venkaiah Naidu.

At the same time the pilot project on computerisation of cadastral maps of Tiswadi taluk was commissioned by the union minister. In order to facilitate public benefit from this computerisation a software module was developed by a private agency to extract and print any survey number/ sub-division number or land parcel that may be required by an individual landholder. The public now has the facility to quickly receive certified copies of computerised plans of any village in the taluk of Tiswadi.

Tiswadi taluk has become the first taluk in the state to have a complete Land Records Information System (LRIS). The work of integration of textual and graphic data, that is, non-spatial and spatial, is in progress and will be completed soon.

A notable step taken by the Government of Goa in the direction of delivering the benefits of information technology to the common man is the opening of Electronic Information Centres in the cities of Panaji and Margao. The centres are being run by a private agency with the support of the government. At these centres the land records and other services are available across the counter on demand by the public. It is proposed to extend this service to other places in the state in the long run.

## Updation

While the taluks were being completed and commissioned one by one, the significance of updating the records was not lost. If this was not done the whole exercise of computerisation would be self-defeating. Initially updating was centralised in the sense that all mutations effected at the taluk level were being periodically sent to the head office of the directorate for updating. However, as the state was nearing completion of all taluks, the directorate realised the need to decentralise the updating to the taluk level. In this regard, a software programme was designed and installed at all taluks with the active cooperation and assistance of the NIC. As per the designed programme, only authorised persons are allowed to use the system.

In Goa, mutation details normally include partitioning of the parcels of land, addition/deletion of names of occupants, tenants, other rights holders, cultivators, etc. Facility has been provided to carry out all the changes only after proper authorisation. For this purpose, two users have been created. One user can only enter the mutation details (at the level of lower division clerks [LDC]/upper division clerks [UDC] or any other subordinate revenue officer). The second user is usually the mamlatdar (taluk revenue officer) or a joint mamlatdar or an authorised officer who has to verify and approve each and every transaction. Only after proper authorisation will the transaction be received in the database tables. This updating programme is very user-friendly. The switchover form Visual Fox Pro to Microsoft SQL Visual Basic was done because the latter system had additional security features and facilities for public use. To further strengthen security, Finger Print Readers have been introduced on experimental basis in one of the taluks.

Regarding updating of the cadastral maps, the software Vision Map Maker is user-friendly and has got the facility to edit the maps, that is, add or delete any feature in the map, and allow for updating by authorised persons.

## COMPUTERISATION—BEFORE AND AFTER

To understand the impact of computerisation of land records it would be necessary to analyse the situation before and after the computerisation. First, under the manual system landholders were not provided untroubled access to land records and, therefore, delays and inconvenience to the public in attaining authenticated land records was common. Computerisation has now enabled the public to obtain land records quickly, especially from the electronics information centres promoted by the Government of Goa, where land records are available instantly across the counter. Second, the manual preparation, maintenance and updating of land records was a tedious and time-consuming job. It was expensive and prone to errors, willful or inadvertent. Moreover the records, stored in shelves and dusty rooms and constantly handled, were liable to damage or mutilation. After computerisation, the preparation, maintenance and updating has become quick, easy, accurate and cost-effective. The problem of safety and storage of records has also been solved as all the data can safely be stored in the computers and also a backup created by means of CDs. Besides this, the data is also secure and less prone to unauthorised changes. The adequate security precautions are incorporated into the programme to protect the data. Third, the computerisation has proved to be useful for administrators, planners and policy makers, as any kind of data regarding land records for better land management is available at the click of a button. This has made administration more efficient, effective and responsive. Previously the manual process of collecting data for decision making was rather slow and causing unnecessary delay. In short, the salutary effects of computerisation of land records are being felt by public and it has facilitated financial, legal, administrative and operative aspects of land records system.

## FUTURE PLANNING

In the near future it is planned to set up intranet connecting all the 11 taluks so that any person from any taluk office will be in a position to get records of any part of state. Besides this, it is also planned to computerise the entire mutation process so that long delays are eliminated and on-line updating is available. For this purpose the Government of Goa has sent a proposal for financial assistance to the Government of India. It is also proposed to undertake the digitisation of cadastral maps of remaining 10 taluks on a war footing and for this purpose the Government of Goa has moved a proposal for financial assistance to the Government of India.

## REASONS FOR SUCCESS

The reasons for the success of computerisation of land records are many. However, the main factors are as follows: (*a*) the state of Goa is a cadastral state; (*b*) the record of rights and the cadastral maps were in good condition; (*c*) timely financial assistance from the Ministry of Rural Development, Government of India; (*d*) the data entry through private vendors ensured a speedy completion of the work; (e) the smallness of the state has facilitated close cooperation and coordination between all departments and people involved in this exercise; (f) positive attitude of officers and officials involved in the task of computerisation; (g) regular monitoring and periodical review of the scheme at the field as well as state secretariat level; (h) determination and commitment of all directorate staff, NIC staff, mamlatdars staff and the personnel of the private agencies; (i) availability of power and other infrastructure; and (j) motivation and leadership factors have also contributed to the success of this project.

## CONCLUSION

In conclusion, it may be said that the state of Goa has reached a milestone. But this is just a beginning. The state has still miles to go and the road is paved with growing public demands, new challenges and fast changing technologies. We have also much to learn and gain from experiences of big states which are in the forefront of information technology.

Nevertheless it is hoped that the events in Goa would not only encourage those states that have very little or no land records at all to undertake or expedite the work of preparation or reconstruction but also be useful to those states that have land records but have not been able to make much headway in computerisation due to various reasons. It is also hoped that the achievements of Goa will add impetus to the mission of computerisation of land records at the national level.

# 9

# *Appraisal of Computerisation of Land Records in West Bengal: A Micro Study**

MANOJ AHUJA AND A.P. SINGH

## INTRODUCTION

Computerisation of land records (CoLR) is a programme that aims at implementing e-governance at the grassroots level within the domain of land management in India. One of the major drawbacks in the land management system in India is the opaque, slow moving and corruption-ridden methodology for the maintenance of land records.

The data concerning land records in India can be broadly classified into two categories—spatial and non-spatial or attribute data. The spatial data consists of maps of each plot and non-spatial data consists of details about ownership, size of plot, rent payable, irrigation status, crop status, etc. Through this programme, it is expected that the government can reach out to the rural population specifically and provide better services in

* This chapter is an extract from the report, 'Evaluation of Computerisation of Land Records: A Micro Study' by Ahuja and Singh (2004). It is advisable to look up the original report at LBSNAA, Mussoorie.

For all figures in lakhs and crores, please note that 1 lakh = 100,000 and 1 crore = 10,000,000.

terms of efficiency, time, transparency and reduction in corruption. Once the land management system is responsive and transparent, and defines property rights correctly, it will ensure good governance in one of the most significant sectors of the Indian economy. It may also have spin-offs in improved land productivity by removing asymmetric information in land rights.

In India landownership is in the name of individuals and not the state. In 1985, it was resolved at the Conference of Revenue Ministers to take up a project to computerise land records on a pilot basis. Thus a centrally sponsored scheme on CoLR was started in 1988–89, with the intention of removing problems inherent in the manual system of maintenance and updating of land records, to meet the requirements of various groups of users. It was decided that efforts should be made to computerise core data contained in land records, so as to assist development planning and to make records accessible to people/planners/administrators. The focus here was on computerisation of non-spatial data.

## CoLR IN WEST BENGAL

Computerisation of land records in West Bengal started in the financial year 1990–91 when the first pilot was initiated in Burdwan through a centrally sponsored scheme of CoLR as a first step in the district of Burdwan. In 1993–94, the scheme was extended to Jalpaiguri, Hugli and Nadia districts. The CoLR project was started in Howrah in the year 1994–95. In 1995–96, the project was sanctioned for the districts of Darjeeling, Malda, Birbhum, Bankura, Medinapur, Tamluk, 24-Parganas (North), and 24-Parganas (South). By 1996–97, the scheme of computerisation of land records was sanctioned for all remaining districts in the state of West Bengal.

As per the information of state government, the scheme has been operationalised in all blocks. The computerised certified copies of RoRs are being provided to farmers in these blocks.

The Directorate of Land Records in West Bengal has computerised 94 per cent of the 367 lakh land records for 35,077 *mauza*s (revenue villages) of 341 blocks. Records of rights are required to facilitate sale and inheritance or to provide proof of ownership to avail of credit. Earlier, upon sale or inheritance of a land parcel, requests to alter land records had to be filled with the revenue inspector (RI) or directly with revenue officer (RO). Previously, farmers had to seek out the RI or RO to get a certified copy of the RoR. There were delays and harassment. Bribes had to be paid. The RO/RI could afford to ignore or delay action on these 'mutation' requests and delay the requests for certificates. Land records in the custody of RO/RI were not open to public scrutiny. Over time, several inaccuracies crept into the old system through improper manipulation by the RO/RI. In practice, it could take one to two years for the records to be updated. It used to take 30 days to 90 days, to provide RoRs depending upon the importance of the record for the farmer and size of the bribe.

Therefore, the Directorate of Land Records, started the computerisation of land records in the district of Burdwan in 1990–91 with 100 per cent financial assistance of Ministry of Rural Development, Government of India. Now, the scheme has been implemented in all districts of the state with the following objectives:

1. to facilitate easy maintenance of land database and updation of changes in land database on account of legal changes like transfer of ownership, partition, land acquisition, etc.;
2. to provide comprehensive security to make land records tamper-proof;
3. to provide certified copies of land records to the landowners (*raiyat*s) quickly and at cheaper rate;
4. to facilitate preparation of annual set of records for recording details such as land revenue, cropping pattern, etc.; and
5. sharing of land records database with other departments to facilitate planning in the area of infrastructure development, agricultural census and implementation of development programmes.

In addition to the above-mentioned objectives, the West Bengal government has taken up a pilot project to integrate CoLR with the Registration Department at Rajarhat, 24-Parganas (North) district. The project is in the last stages of completion.

One touch screen kiosk has been installed at Thakurpukur Metiabruz (TM) block, Kolkata for providing land record information. A farmer will be able to operate this kiosk himself or herself. The farmer has to feed a *khatian* number and after that can view his/her land record. The touch screen kiosk is very easy to operate and a farmer with minimum education can operate it. Once the system is operated, it will guide the farmer through instructions in Bangla on the screen.

## CoLR-related Land Laws

The West Bengal Land Reforms (WBLR) Act is primarily related with the land records of West Bengal. The land records in West Bengal are formed through KB, that is, Khanapuri Bujharat u/s 50 of WBLR Act which is followed by Attestation (u/s 51), Draft Publication (u/s 51A), Objection hearing of Draft Publication petition [u/s 51A(1)], Final Publication [u/s 51A (3)], Objection hearing of Draft Publication petition [u/s 51A(4)]. The records may be corrected/ modified u/s 51B and 51BB before or after the final publication of records of rights.

After this stage the records are normally corrected through the process of mutation u/s 50. The classification of a plot is changed/ modified/ corrected by means of the process of conversion u/s 4(c). The *patta* is granted to a farmer u/s 49 and the *barga* (tenancy) is allowed u/s 21(d) but the record should be corrected under any of the above mentioned section, that is, under Section or Sub-sections 50 and 51. And lastly a new Sub-section 50(2) has been added to the WBLR Act to empower the revenue officer to preserve the handwritten mother copy of RoRs after activating the computerised one.

# MICRO STUDY

The Centre for Rural Studies conducted a brief field study of CoLR in six blocks of Hooghly, Nadia and Burdwan districts of West Bengal in May 2003. These blocks are: Mogra Chinsruha, Polba Dodpur of Hooghly, Chakdah and Nakashipara of Nadia and Khandaghos and Burdwan-I of Burdwan. The total number of respondents is 210. Thirty-five beneficiaries were interviewed from each block. The computerisation of land records was expected to speed up delivery of RoRs and reduce delays, harassment and bribery. This assessment study highlights the benefits that accrued to users of computerised land records and the existing deficiencies and drawbacks in the system.

The objectives of the study are as follows:

1. to examine the extent and impact of computerisation of land records on revenue administration and cultivators;
2. to examine the ease and speed with which the cultivators are able to obtain the land records and the procedure for the same;
3. to examine the human resource development, capacity building and awareness generation taken up for implementation for the programme, and the adequacy of the same;
4. to examine the procedure for making mutation and the time taken for the same;
5. to study broadly:

   i. the hardware and software utilised for the computerisation of land records
   ii. the methods of maintenance of the same
   iii. the measures for the security and preservation of the data stored in the computer

6. to examine the changes necessary in existing legal provisions in the revenue laws;
7. to examine the extent to which the data generated through the computerised land records system is helpful in planning and decision making; and
8. to find out the extent to which:

   i. CoLR has reduced and changed the workload of the revenue functionaries
   ii. CoLR has minimised the possibilities of interpolation of land records and rent-seeking behaviour
   iii. a comprehensive database on various facets of land is available for helping in land reforms
   iv. the system has cultivated a sense of awareness among the cultivators and prompted them to exercise their rights
   v. the support extended or resistance put up by various official agencies and other interest groups for effective operationalisation and functioning of the system

# ANALYSIS OF DATA

## General Awareness about Computerisation of RoRs

Only 79 per cent of the respondents were aware of the computerisation of land records. Most of the respondents learnt about the computerisation of land records from the revenue personnel. Some of the respondents reported awareness through friends and neighbours. There is a need to raise the awareness of computerisation of land records amongst the users.

It is important to note that all the blocks of the selected districts were computerised three to four years ago. Therefore, it is really a surprise that even after such a long time awareness amongst the farmers is not universal. The Government of West Bengal abolished the distribution of handwritten RoR by making an amendment in West Bengal Land Reforms Act,1955 by adding a new Section 50(2) in the year 2000. The centre also published a report entitled 'Evaluation of Computerisation of Land Records in Karnataka : A Study from Gulbarga District', by Manoj Ahuja and A.P. Singh in 2003. According to this report, a survey team visited Gulbarga district soon after the implementation of the project. The time of operation ranged from one to eight months for the *taluks* of Gulbarga district. In such a short time the awareness amongst the farmers of Gulbarga district was 85 per cent, which is greater than the awareness amongst the farmers of West Bengal (79 per cent). It clearly indicates that there is a need to raise the awareness regarding the programme in West Bengal.

The awareness regarding the procedure for obtaining computerised RoRs is directly related to the general awareness of the computerisation of land records. The majority of the respondents (70.3 per cent) knew that the block has one computer kiosk at which they can apply for computerised RoRs and plot information. Some of the respondents (8.7 per cent) knew about computerisation but not exactly the procedure for obtaining computerised RoRs. Half (50.9 per cent) of the total respondents obtained computerised RoRs through revenue personnel or middlemen or directly from the block office for themselves or for other persons.

## Information Flow

It has been conceived that within the existing institutional framework, enhancement of information flow has a multidimensional impact. This affects other factors like rent-seeking behaviour, improvement in record management and storage, and reduction of the dispute burden. At the time of survey, only 44 per cent stated that RoR was available without delay, 49.1 per cent could not definitely say whether the availability of RoR was easier after computerisation, and only 6.9 per cent of the respondents indicated that there was delay in obtaining RoR after computerisation.

Table 9.1 details the time required for obtaining RoR after computerisation.

**Table 9.1**

*Time Required to Obtain Land Records After Computerisation*

| Time | Respondents (%) |
|---|---|
| One day | 12.4 |
| Two days | 18.0 |
| Three days | 13.5 |
| One week | 49.4 |
| 15–30 days | 4.5 |
| One month | 2.2 |

In Table 9.1, it is rather surprising to note that only 12.4 per cent of the respondents get the RoR on the same day and for the remaining it takes more than one day to get an RoR. Nearly half of the respondents get their RoRs after one week. According to the revenue personnel, the main reason for taking so long to issue computerised RoR is lack of power supply. Since the supply of electricity is erratic, the revenue personnel asked farmers to come another day for receiving the computerised RoRs. The UPS (Uninterrupted Power Supply) has a short duration battery backup, which does not adequately address the needs. Therefore, it is necessary to equip the block office with a UPS having a minimum of four hours' battery backup, or with a generator. Another reason for delay is absence of computer operator (revenue officer). Since only one person had received computer training, his staying away from office led to delays for farmers.

On the other hand in Karnataka, we found that 86 per cent of the respondents were able to get their RTCs on the same day.

NIC, which is the technical partner for the 'Bhumi' project, has made 10 upgraded versions of the software since the software was first developed in 1989. These changes are not due to any changes in procedures but due to glitches/ implementation problems of the software. One of the reasons for this can be due to the lack of re-engineering of processes. Computerisation of manual system would require a thorough study of the systems, understanding the environment in which it works and re-engineering the systems so that it works effectively when computerised. This needs elaborate and detailed consultation between the parent department, which is the revenue department and the software provider, which is NIC.

However, according to our study the main reasons why copies of RoRs cannot be given over the counter are due to the fact that the data is not updated online and the fact that there are still errors in the computerised data. As the workflow process is not online, the database has to be updated in a batch process, either fortnightly or monthly. This leads to a situation where the database is out of sync with the actual land records and also to some errors due to manual entry of all mutations. As a consequence when an applicant approaches the block office for a copy of an RoR, the mother copy of the RoR is taken as a base and his land record data in the computer is corrected according to this copy. In case there are discrepancies, the computerised records are updated on the basis of the manual record and then a computerised print is given to the applicant. Thus, this procedure generally indicates:

1. lack of faith in the computerised data because it is not updated and has errors;
2. the computerised system has not been fully implemented, as it is the manual system which is being used as a base, and therefore there is duplication of work instead of reduction of work; and
3. total lack of security as anybody can tamper directly with the database. The database should in fact be sacrosanct and nobody should be allowed to tamper with it. In case of extraordinary circumstances where need arises to change the database directly, a proper protocol should be followed to prevent any illegal or arbitrary change in the database.

**Table 9.2**

**Time Required to Obtain Land Records Prior to Computerisation**

| Time | Respondents (%) |
|------|-----------------|
| One day | 1.2 |
| One week | 14.3 |
| 15–30 days | 37.7 |
| Two months | 31.4 |
| Three months | 14.3 |
| Three to six months | 1.1 |

The time required to obtain an RoR in the manual system ranged from one day to six months. The time ranged from one week to three months for the majority of the respondents. Further, according to one respondent, in the manual system the service in many cases also depended upon the money provided by the farmer.

It is true that till now, the information flow has not been as good as it was expected in the beginning of the programme. But if we compare the time required for issuing an RoR after computerisation with time required prior to computerisation, we find that in the computerised system 93.3 per cent of the respondents got their RoRs within one week whereas in the manual system only 15.5 per cent farmers were able to get them within a week. This comparison clearly indicates that information flow has improved. This may be due to the fact that the issue of computerised RoRs is being monitored separately.

## ACCURACY OF COMPUTERISED LAND RECORDS

Less than half (43.4 per cent) of the respondents are confident about the accuracy of computerised land records. They say that new system is more accurate. About 7.4 per cent are not sure about the accuracy of computerised RoRs. These persons found many errors in the computerised RoRs and therefore they contacted the revenue personnel for the required corrections. The remaining respondents were not able to say anything about the accuracy of the system. In other words, further work needs to be done in this area to ensure the accuracy of land records. Once an online mutation system is followed, the errors creeping in due to updating data to mutations would reduce as the database will be automatically updated. However, before the online mutation system is introduced, great care has to be taken to ensure that the legacy data is free from errors. This will be a tedious and time-consuming exercise. Errors in the legacy database may lead to complaints from the citizens and also give cause to vested interests to speak against the system.

## Errors in Documents

The manual procedures had significant implications on the integrity of documents, and the possibility of errors coming out of the indifference of the staff. User feedback indicates that computerised land records system provided error-free documents to 76 per cent users. Among those reporting errors, wrongly spelt names was the most frequent error (47.8 per cent). However, major errors in land details were the issue for 7.4 per cent users. This low error rate in land details could be due to the fact that the computerised database is first compared with the manual ROR copy and corrected if necessary. Therefore, this low rate of error is no indicator of the correctness and authenticity of the database.

### Table 9.3

*Type of Errors in Documents Generated*

| Type of errors found (based on those found errors) | Percentage |
| --- | --- |
| Wrong entry of name/Address/Other particulars | 8.9 |
| Misspellings of name/Address/Other particulars | 47.8 |
| Minor error in the entry of land details(e.g., size, type, etc.) | 31.7 |
| Major error in the entry of land details(e.g., size, type, etc.) | 7.4 |
| Others | 4.2 |

According to revenue personnel, for the accuracy of data, data verification was carried out three times at the time of data entry. On an average, 35 per cent RoRs were found with errors during first verification and 15 per cent were found with errors during second verification.

## Rectification of Errors

Given that errors are not unusual at this stage of development of the Bhumi system, how efficient is the response system when rectification of errors is sought? Timely response is a critical part of service delivery. Only 57.8 per cent got timely response to their complaints.

**Table 9.4**

*Institutional Response to Complaints*

| Response to complaints | Percentage |
| --- | --- |
| Complaint not heard /Official did not give time | 8.9 |
| Complaint heard, no action taken | 8.9 |
| Action was taken; delayed | 22.2 |
| Action was taken; timely | 57.8 |
| Others | 2.2 |

# HARASSMENT IN THE COMPUTERISED SYSTEM

Less than half (44.6 per cent) of the respondents said that new computerised system is free from any type of harassment. Respondents said that they paid only the prescribed fee to the revenue inspector and were able to get their RoRs without harassment. Some of the respondents said that whenever the revenue inspector demanded more money, they themselves went to the block office to collect the computerised RoR. Some of the respondents got their RoRs on the same day, but a majority had to go two times for the computerised RoR. The majority of farmers get a computerised RoR in one week even though they reported that with the computerised system it took less time to obtain an RoR. Earlier, in the manual system, it took more than a month to get RoRs. Some (7.4 per cent) of the respondents stated that there was still harassment from officials and middlemen. The farmer first had to purchase revenue stamps for the prescribed fee and then go to the block office for the submission of application. He had to visit the block office twice or pay extra money to RI for the collection of computerised RoR. Slightly less than half the respondents (48 per cent) were unable to say anything about harassment levels since they had not obtained an RoR after computerisation. Tarapada Roy of Khandaghos block of Burdwan district said that after computerisation there was still same kind of harassment by the revenue officials since the process of issuing RoR was still the same as in the manual system.

## Manipulation

The manual system of land records maintenance has been described as highly opaque. Several inaccuracies had crept into old manual system due to improper manipulation by the revenue officials. In the computerised system, there should be no possibility of any type of manipulation by any revenue official, but presently in West Bengal it does not seem true. The main reason is the lack of workflow automation in the state. In the computerised system only one revenue officer is responsible for all the work. For preventing manipulation, the software should have a built-in workflow automation whereby the work can be moved from one revenue official to another on the computer system. In Karnataka, there is no possibility of any type of manipulation by a village accountant or kiosk operator or any other person; due to workflow automation transactions moving from one revenue person to another on the computer system. According to the beneficiaries, 58.9 per cent of the respondents relied on the present system. It clearly shows good faith of the public in Land and Land Reforms department of the state. Less than half (33.1 per cent) of the respondents were unable to respond since they did not know the details about the programme. Only 8 per cent of the respondents gave a negative response.

## Rent-seeking Behaviour

Rent-seeking behaviour is especially pronounced at the grassroots level in the revenue administration. The findings clearly establish that the revenue officials have been in a position to seek rent for transactions. In West Bengal, the computerised certified copy of RoR and plot information is given against revenue through a court fee stamp. The computerised certified copy of RoR costs Rs 5 as application fee per khatian and Rs 5 per page as authentication fee. Similarly in case of plot information it costs Rs 2 as application fee per plot and Rs 2 as authentication fee. In West Bengal, even after computerisation, the earlier system of issuing RoRs is continuing. The system of middlemen is very much prevalent, wherein money is charged from a farmer as per the urgency of required document. The charges paid by a farmer for receiving an RoR ranged from Rs 10 to Rs 100. Table 9.5 gives the details about the rent paid by the farmers after computerisation.

**Table 9.5**

*Rent Pattern for Obtaining RoR After Computerisation*

| Rent (in Rs) | Respondents (%) |
|---|---|
| 10 | 61.8 |
| 15 | 19.1 |
| 20 | 12.4 |
| 25 | 3.3 |
| 50 | 2.2 |
| 100 | 1.1 |

The costs for obtaining RoR in the old system ranged from Rs 1.5 to more than Rs 100. In Table 9.6 we will see the rent pattern for obtaining RoR prior to computerisation.

**Table 9.6**

*Rent Pattern for Obtaining RoR Prior to Computerisation*

| Rent (in Rs) | Respondents (%) |
|---|---|
| 1.5–10 | 64.1 |
| 10–25 | 10.1 |
| 25–50 | 15.7 |
| 50–100 | 3.4 |
| More than 100 | 6.7 |

Table 9.6 indicates that 64.1 per cent of the respondents were paying between Rs 1.5 to Rs 10. This fee looks reasonable since in West Bengal the cost of RoR depends on the number of pages of RoR. One quarter (25.8 per cent) of the respondents were paying between Rs 25 to Rs 50

and 10.1 per cent of the respondents paid more than Rs 50 for an RoR. The amount paid to the revenue official depended on the importance and urgency of records. If any person wanted to obtain RoR immediately then he had to pay more money.

## Land Reforms

Over the past few decades, while land reform has made little headway in most of India, West Bengal has achieved notable progress. The progress has occurred in three areas: redistributing agricultural landownership, regulating sharecropping relationships and distributing homestead land. Major initiatives in land reforms had already been taken by the state prior to the computerisation of land records. Therefore, it is very difficult to say that CoLR has helped much in furthering the programme.

## Reduction in Disputes

Land from time immemorial has been a source of pride for its owners, and a means to generate revenue for governments. Land has always been considered as a status symbol deriving its strengths from area, location, fertility and other such factors attached to it. Land also has emotional attachments and hence has been a cause of jubilation and miseries, for reward and exploitation. Land has been a cause of many bloody wars between nations and generations of families. A greater part of the agrarian population being inadequately educated or not literate at all, it has been easy for wrong practices to go unchallenged. Boundary or ownership amendments take eons to be legalised, because much of the land records are either untraceable or manipulated due to procedural red tape. All of these shortcomings in the existent system can be effectively alleviated with modernisation of the land records system.

Many of the disputes originate from a faulty record system. About 43 per cent of the respondents are sure that computerisation has reduced the land-related conflicts while 5.1 per cent respondents opined that computerisation is not helping in any reduction of disputes. Remaining respondents were unable to say anything about computerisation.

Land tenancy could be one of the points of conflict. But in West Bengal, the state government has also taken determined steps to bolster the position of sharecroppers (*bargadars*) by regulating the landlord–sharecropper relationship through a programme called Operation Barga. The main components of this regulation consist of tenure security protection for bargadars and control over the share amount afforded to bargadars. The government also placed a near absolute prohibition on fixed rent tenancies. The implementation of such safeguards has been made possible largely through the determined recording of existing bargadars throughout the state. In addition to redistributing some agricultural land in ownership and protecting bargadars, West Bengal has also transferred ownership of homestead land to landless agricultural labourers, bargadars and artisans. The legislation provided that such homestead plots could be up to eight one-hundredths of an acre, about 325 sq m. The Government of West Bengal attaches great importance to the recording of tenancy rights and sorting out conflicts relating to the same. Conflicts relating to tenancy have already been sorted out by the government. Any significant impact on the reduction of land-related disputes is not apparent in West Bengal due to the implementation of CoLR project.

## Institutional Finance

Bank loans are given on the basis of RoR. Therefore, landowners need copies of RoR to apply for loans. We asked respondents a very simple question about the easy availability of finance after computerisation. About 66.9 per cent of the respondents hoped that it would be easy to obtain a loan after computerisation, 6.3 per cent believed that there would be no change, and 26.9 per cent did not make any comment. Computerisation would help in reality if the state government connects the land records database to databases accessible to various courts and banks. This will facilitate the work relating to land records.

## Complexity of Procedures

Government offices have elaborate procedures involving many levels of officials to maintain land records in a secure manner. The multitude of levels of officers that a person had to see for his work was seen as a major problem in the system.

**Table 9.7**

*Number of Officials Met*

| Number of officials met | Before computerisation (in %) | After computerisation (in %) |
|---|---|---|
| None | – | 17.5 |
| 1 | 18.6 | 6.5 |
| 2–4 | 61.0 | 76.0 |
| More than 5 | 20.3 | – |

According to Table 9.7, after computerisation, the situation has not changed much since the state government is not providing a single window service to the farmers for the issue of RoRs. Due to this reason, farmers do not visit block office for issuing of RoR. Feedback from the users indicates that to obtain computerised copy of land records most users (76 per cent) took the help of two to four persons. First, they have to go to purchase revenue stamp as a fee of computerised RoR, after that they have to contact the revenue officer for the computerised RoR. In this process there may be more than two persons. In the case of the manual system 18.6 per cent had to meet one official . The extent of the complexity is reflected in the fact that 61 per cent of the users of the manual system had to meet two to four officials regarding their work. Therefore we can say that the legacy of the manual system has not faded away.

## PLANNING PROCESS

Whenever the deficiencies of the computerised land records system are addressed, the system will provide a reliable information source for both generation of development plans and monitoring to planners and administrators. The system generates various types of reports on landownership, bargadar, *pattadar*, type of soil, etc., which would be useful for the planning of poverty alleviation programmes, supplying of inputs, etc. Banks and other lending institutions could be given electronic access to the database for processing requests for crop loans, and may conduct some advanced planning on the quantum of lending required. The computerised system could also lead to better administration of the Land Reforms Act.

Therefore, we can say that CoLR will make data and information readily available for planning at different levels, from the village to the state government. Further, with such large amounts of data available, techniques such as data mining can throw up interesting and new information for policy makers.

# MUTATION

Even though Bengal was one of the early states to computerise data, the software did not provide the facility for online mutation. Only recently has NIC incorporated online mutation facility with the software. However, this has not yet been put to use by the revenue officials. Online mutation facility is a sine qua non for successful implementation of the computerisation of land records programme. West Bengal would do well to follow the model for online mutation and workflow automation successfully achieved in Karnataka. This would involve changing roles and responsibilities of the revenue officials in view of the additional capabilities and limitation of the computerised system, as well as changes in the process and a workflow automation to ensure that the existing revenue staff can easily adopt the new system. It should also have a provision for scanning and storing of written documents and notices to improve the accountability of the officials involved and also to ensure that legal documents/ proof/ evidence is available in case the applicants later decide to go for appeal. In case online mutation is adopted the system should also provide for non-repudiation by the revenue officials and fixing of accountability. This also could be done by providing bio-metrics identification facility by which different revenue officials can log on into the system. Individual logs would therefore be maintained for each officer.

Updation of land records also depends on filing for mutation after the registration of land. Presently, there are many delays and omissions in applying for mutations; as a result updation of land records becomes tedious. Also, farmers often do not report transactions within the family either because they are discouraged by the attitude of the revenue staff or due to internal family problems. Many farmers do not take an interest in changing their names in the record of rights after registration of land. Therefore, it is necessary to have a system to ensure that registrations are brought to the notice of the revenue personnel automatically.

Registration of a deed is the beginning point that triggers the process of updating of the land records. The change in the ownership of immovable property arises from the document, which comes out of the process of registered deeds like, sale deed, gift deed and so on. As a consequence of this, the mutation process takes off and after the attestation of the mutation the land records are updated. Therefore, there is a need to integrate the registration department with the computerised land records system, which could facilitate simultaneous updating of land records.

## REDUCED WORKLOAD OF REVENUE OFFICIALS

The data which the *patwari*/village accountant/revenue inspector handle and the nature of their revenue work is mostly repetitive and clerical by nature. This introduces monotony and many errors intentional or inadvertent creep in. One of the objectives of CoLR was that the computer would be able to take care of the repetitive and clerical nature of the job and would hence economise on the time of the patwari/village accountant/ revenue inspector. The time saved can be better utilised by the lower revenue official for a number of productive purposes including more field visits, better recording of entries and greater application of mind for quality output. Without workflow automation and online mutation, the workload of the revenue officials cannot be reduced, as he would have to do the same work he was doing in the manual system.

## PROBLEMS AS STATED BY REVENUE PERSONNEL

We also interacted during our field visit with local-level functionaries involved in the distribution of land records and obtained their views about advantages and disadvantages of the programme. The officials who were interviewed were:

- Revenue Officer, who occupies an intermediate position between the BLLRO (Block Land and Land Reforms Officer) and revenue inspector; and
- Revenue Inspector, the lowest level revenue functionary who functions at the *gram panchayat* level and is assisted by one amin and Bhumi sahayak.

The revenue inspectors and revenue officers threw light on certain problems of the computerised land records system. The following are the important views of the officials:

- *Electricity:* In some rural areas of West Bengal electricity is supplied intermittently. The revenue personnel said that since the supply of electricity was erratic, farmers were asked to come again on another day for receiving computerised RoR. Due to this, the process of issuing RoRs often involved delays. The directorate supplied a UPS with short duration battery backup to every block office, which is inadequate for the purpose. Therefore, it is necessary to equip the block office with a UPS with a four-hour battery backup or a generator.
- *Shortage of trained staff:* Since only one person (revenue officer) from each block had received computer training, his staying away from the office led to delays for farmers.
- *Delays due to breakdown in the system:* Whenever any software or hardware related problems occurred in the computer system, no expert was available at the block office, and one had to be called in from the district headquarters to tackle the problem. Sometimes it took three days to one week for an expert to turn up. Due to this, users faced a lot of inconvenience.

- *Infrastructure problem:* There is very poor infrastructure in some of the blocks. Many of the buildings are in bad shape and require repair. In one block, the RAM of the computer became defective due to the dampness in the computer room.

## CONCLUSION

- After the field study, we found that the state had not fully achieved the required objectives of creating a clean, up-to-date database. CoLR in West Bengal has replaced the hand written RoRs with computer printed RoRs. CoLR project was expected to speed up delivery of RoRs without delays, harassment or bribery. But after the field study in the state, we found that delivery of RoR was still not a hand-to-hand service. The farmer first submits his application with a fee in the form of revenue stamps to the block office. After the submission of application, the farmer gets his computerised RoR within one day to 30 days. The system of issuing computerised RoR remains the same as in the manual one; therefore it is very difficult to say that delivery of RoR is free from harassment and bribery.
- Bhumi software in West Bengal provides for printing of land records, and updating the database in offline module makes it out of sync with current status of land records and therefore of not much use. Recently, the state introduced online mutation, which has also not been adopted by the staff.
- Security is provided by the traditional password system, which is prone to hacking. It was seen that the computer in which the Bhumi software was used, was also being utilised for other purposes. There is a real danger of compromising security and also a possibility that the system will be infected by virus.
- The first version of Bhumi software was developed by NIC,WBSU in 1989, which has been continuously upgraded till date. The software went through as many as nine versions of development before a GUI version was developed by the NIC. There have been 10 upgraded versions of Bhumi in West Bengal, but still the software contained glitches.

- Bhumi software is in operation at block computer set-up at BLLRO office. In West Bengal, a majority of the block offices have the DOS system. A very few block offices have GUI software, Bhumi 2000. The DOS version has been written in FoxBASE software, a third generation programming language. There is no data security in the FoxBASE software package. As the data is highly valuable it should be made tamper-proof and free from unauthorised access.

- The problem of erratic power is prevalent in West Bengal, which causes problems in issuing RoR to farmers. The UPS with only 10 minutes power backup is not sufficient to deal with the problem of power failure. Therefore, it is necessary to replace the UPS with some other backup systems or generators. There is very poor infrastructure in some of the blocks. Many of the buildings are in bad shape and require repair.

- The lack of computer literacy among the land and land reforms office staff has been a major challenge. Only 350 revenue officers have been trained. Since only one revenue officer from each block has received computer training, any absence would only lead to delays for the farmers. Therefore, every revenue official should be trained for the computerised system in phases.

- Whenever the deficiencies of the computerised land records system are addressed, CoLR will provide the reliable information on both the generation of development plans and also monitoring the progress, to planners and administrators.

Finally, we can say that there have, as yet, been limited benefits from CoLR in West Bengal; the actual benefits, which can accrue to the masses as a consequence of CoLR, have not yet been attained.

# RECOMMENDATIONS

The implementation of computerisation of land records programme has to be viewed in a project mode. It is necessary to set up a project at the state-government level, preferably manned by a middle-level IAS Officer who is comfortable with information technology. A team should assist him and it should have the full support of the state government to ensure success within a definite timeframe. This would be necessary to ensure the cooperation of the various people involved and also to address new issues related to technology, change management, business processes re-engineering and people management. A project mode approach would also speed up the implementation of the project and make it more successful. Further, it is necessary to ensure online mutation and workflow automation in the Bhumi Software universally, though this facility has been provided in the recent software, which adapts the manual process. However, a second look at this facility is required, keeping in mind the following aspects:

- Mapping the existing manual process and making it amenable to computerisation. A mere mapping of the manual process would not be successful, as problems would arise during implementation.
- Redesigning the process wherever feasible.
- Changing the roles and responsibilities of the people involved.
- The security of data is of immense importance to prevent any unauthorised access or modifications of land records. Access to the database should not be available to any unauthorised person. An audit trail should be made for each transaction. Daily data backups should be taken and data disaster recovery strategy should be ensured through disc mirroring and scheduled backups. Presently, security is provided through the traditional password system, which is prone to hacking. Therefore, it is necessary to supplement this with bio-metrics identification technology.
- It is necessary to provide a front online record shop from where farmers can buy their records. These land records shops would provide transparency in land record administration and empower farmers. If the state government is willing to impose user charges then the front end shop can be set up in a public/private partnership mode. The District Informatics Office of the National Informatics Centre is overburdened in several districts and therefore, to concentrate on land record computerisation, it is necessary that a private consultant is engaged for the initial project duration. The cost of the consultant can be borne by the state government.
- The problem of erratic power supply is quite common in rural West Bengal and it is necessary to provide uninterrupted power supply (UPS) with at least a four-hour power backup or generators

to run the system. There is very poor infrastructure in some of the blocks and some of the buildings are in very poor condition and require repair.

• To sustain the computerised system, adequate training on hardware maintenance and Bhumi should be imparted to relevant personnel. If possible, the Directorate should tie up with a computer agency, at the district and block levels to sort out the software or hardware related problems. There is a need to train other revenue officials for upgradation of their skills in computerisation of land records.

• At present, there are different operating systems being used for the CoLR in West Bengal. There is need to upgrade and standardise the software and hardware being used across the state for this programme.

• An introduction of the new system would throw out new issues which need to be addressed by detailed administrative circulars, so that the district administration can manage the implementation of the programme.

• There is a need to integrate registration department with the land records data to facilitate simultaneous initiation of mutation cases and updating of land records.

## REFERENCES AND SELECT BIBLIOGRAPHY

**Ahuja, Manoj** and **A.P. Singh.** (2003). 'Evaluation of Computerisation of Land Records in Karnataka: A Study from Gulbarga District', Centre for Rural Studies, LBSNAA, Mussoorie.

———. (2004). 'Evaluation of Computerisation of Land Records: A Micro Study'. LBSNAA, Mussoorie.

**Appu, P.S.** (1995). *Report of the National Committee on Revitalisation of Land Revenue Administration*, Ministry of Rural Development, GOI. New Delhi.

———. (1996). *Land Reforms in India*. New Delhi: Vikas Publishing House.

**Bhaumik, Sankar Kumar.** (1993). *Tenancy Relations and Agrarian Development: A Study of West Bengal*. New Delhi: Sage Publications.

**Centre for Rural Studies.** (2001). Contributory Papers of National Workshop on Computerisation of Land Records. LBSNAA, Mussoorie, November.

**Chattopadhyay, Saibal.** 'Computerisation of Land Records in West Bengal with Special Reference to CoLR in Hooghly District', Unpublished Article.

**Government of India.** Ministry of Rural Development, Annual Reports from 1995–2002.

———. Ministry of Rural Development, Conference of Revenue Ministers on Land Reforms, 1985 and 1992.

———. Ministry of Rural Development, Vision Document.

**Government of India.** Planning Commission, the First, Second, Third, Fourth, Fifth, Sixth, Seventh, Eighth and Ninth Five-year Plans (Chapters on Land Reforms).

**Singh, S.K.** (2001). *Dictionary of Land Revenue Terms in India*. Dehradun: Greenfield Publishers.

**Sinha, B.K.** (1998). 'Evaluation of Computerisation of Land Records in Morena District', Land Reforms Unit, LBSNAA, Mussoorie.

———. (2000). 'Dynamic Land Records Management System: A Pressing Need'; in B.K.Sinha and Pushpendra, (eds), *Land Reforms in India: An Unfinished Agenda*. New Delhi: Sage Publications.

*West Bengal Land Reforms Act, 1955.* (1990). Kolkata: Eastern Publications.

# 10

# Land Records—Issues and Innovations: A Case Study of Bhojpur, Bihar

RAJESH KUMAR

## INTRODUCTION

Ownership of land is perhaps as ancient a concept as Indian tribal settlements and has held paramount significance throughout history. British administration put in place a comprehensive and elaborate procedure of preparation and updation of land records. Starting with a brief historical background of the existing system of land records maintenance, this chapter goes on to briefly explain the various documents constituting the existing system of land records. The chapter further dwells upon the issues that seem to ail the present system, followed by the rationale behind computerisation of land records as the most preferred tool for restructuring the existing system. In the concluding part the chapter enumerates the present status of the implementation of NIC developed Bhu-Abhilekh software in the district of Bhojpur in Bihar, followed by its critical evaluation and suggestions as to what more needs to be incorporated in any sustainable restructuring process.

## HISTORICAL BACKGROUND

It has been a universally accepted principle that the rulers of the state are entitled to a portion of the produce of the land, from those who utilise it, as a price for the protection of life and property and also to meet the common expenses of the community. It is this concept of collection of revenue that necessitated the maintenance of land records, although in a rudimentary form, in ancient times.

The *Arthashastra* is the first Indian work that mentions village officers (known as 'gopa') whose duties included preparation of various registers for the village fields, land transfers, due taxes, etc. Attempts to reform the system were first made by Shershah whereby land was categorised, measured and a schedule of crop rates fixed. This was further upgraded during the regime of Akbar, who with the assistance of Raja Todarmal fixed cash rates on a more scientific and rational basis. Elaborate methods were devised for determining the average produce of each class of land and for commuting grain rates into money rates. In fact, Akbar's settlement widely resembles the later settlement effected under British rule. Subsequently during the British era, regulations were introduced for detailed surveys and regulations. The primary interest of the British rulers was the collection of land revenue and consequently the system of land records was organised to serve that purpose. All these factors helped in development of the present-day land records system. Let us now briefly discuss some of the important documents that form the backbone of the existing land records system.

## LAND RECORD DOCUMENTS

Land is a very precious resource and the land records system must safeguard the rights of the legal owner of land. In the land records system prevalent in Bihar, a number of records are prescribed to be maintained at the circle (*anchal*) and district levels. There are more then 20 registers that are being maintained by the revenue department. To put the issue in perspective, it is important to mention how some of these key documents are prepared and updated.

The first stage in this context is the cadastral survey of the concerned village. The objective of the cadastral survey is the preparation of village maps showing the village and field boundaries and preparation of field registers giving the land particulars like ownership, revenue assessment, land classification, etc. The principal records being prepared at the conclusion of survey stage are as follows:

1. *Village map:* A pictorial form showing the village, village boundary and position of identification pillars, plot boundaries, *khasra* number of each plot (every plot is given a unique identification number called khasra number).
2. *Record of rights (khatian):* It is a principal land document in which entries are classified by unique *khata* number(s). Each entry enumerates the names and share of all the *raiyat*s (titleholders) who are owners of all the plots (included in that particular khata number), khasra number of all such plots, area under each khasra number, type of land, name and share of the person(s) who are actually in possession of such plots.

   (After the cadastral survey, revisional survey may be undertaken in which the above-mentioned records are comprehensively updated.)

After conclusion of the survey, true copies of the documents, i.e., the field map and the khatian are sent to the district record room and the respective circle. The circle officer (CO) is legally empowered to prepare subsequent documents and update them periodically. The following important documents are maintained/updated in the circle office:

1. *Register II:* The circle officer has been given the powers to order mutation in case of ownership transfer and any such ownership transfer is incorporated into Register II (also known as 'tenants' ledger'). Every page in this register corresponds to a particular khata number. The land revenue to be paid by each raiyat is periodically updated in Register II.
2. *Khasra panji:* Plot-wise details of the right-holder, type of land, person(s) actually in possession, etc., are maintained in the khasra panji.

There are some other land-related documents pertaining to change in ownership of land. The basis of ownership–transfer can be either will/ testimony of the owner or proof of right to the land by inheritance (*vanshawali* or decree of a competent court) or any of the documents mentioned below that are executed in the registry office:

1. *Sale deed:* Document indicating sale and purchase of a particular land (identified by khasra number, area and boundaries);
2. *Bakhsish-nama:* Document indicating free grant of a particular land to any person;
3. *Badlain:* Document indicating mutual exchange of two pieces of land.

## ISSUES

The present system of record-keeping has not been able to cater to the needs and aspirations of the landholders. Over the years there has been tremendous increase in the volume of land-related documents and land-related disputes have also increased manifold. Let us first enlist the main shortcomings of the present system.

- *Preservation problem:* Land records are maintained on paper/cloth and therefore are in very bad shape. Duplication on similar media is cumbersome and results in similar problems of maintenance after a few years.
- *Updation problems:* Updation of change in plot-boundaries or title by the manual process is highly time-consuming and any error gets propagated in subsequent records. Khatian and the village map can be comprehensively updated only in the next survey. It is important to mention here that the last revisional survey in this district was finalised in 1970–71. The process of mutation is very cumbersome. In practice, the circle officer enjoys de facto discretion of either processing the application for mutation or not. As land records are maintained in a decentralised manner, there is no reporting mechanism available at the collectorate level regarding the pendency of such applications with the circle office. Lack of any effective monitoring mechanism in the manual system has made farmers amenable to all form of pressures and harassment from the officials of the revenue department.

- *Retrieval problems:* Retrieval of relevant information from the existing land records for redressal of any dispute or for any other purpose is a time-consuming affair (due to existence of large volume of records). Furthermore, every retrieval/use has an associated risk of further physical damage of the old records.
- *Prone to manipulations:* Manual record administration is always prone to manipulations. There have been a number of instances of unauthorised entries in the land documents, like cases of government land being shown in the name of individuals. An opaque manual system facilitates such manipulation by unscrupulous employees.
- *Delay in delivery of land records:* There is a general trend of long delays in delivery of copies of land record documents like khatian, mutation order, etc., to the concerned raiyat. This delay could be intentional or, on many occasions, could be unintentional. Even if a revenue official is willing to give such records in time, either it is not possible for the records to be retrieved quickly or the concerned official is not available as he may be manning a number of revenue villages. Therefore, there is no certainty about timely availability of such records when a landholder requires them.
- *Non-confirmation to the planning process:* Land records contain useful data like soil type, irrigation details, trees, crops grown, crop yield, etc. All such data is valuable for various planning purposes. As data is manually maintained, it is not possible to collate and analyse such data and use it in any meaningful way.
- *Cumbersome bank loan mechanism:* Banks often ask for various land records before lending loans to farmers. Farmers in turn have to hunt for revenue officials, with no guarantee that banks would not ask for more records. This has made the process of obtaining loans prone to delays. Moreover, it has indirectly contributed to a thriving moneylending business causing severe financial hardships to the farmers.
- *Increase in land-related civil litigations:* Due to poor preparation, upkeep and updation mechanism of land records, there has been tremendous increase in the number of land-related civil litigations, as the issue of land has traditionally been central to a rural set-up. Land-based civil litigations constitute more than 70 per cent of total litigations. The courts often require various land records for disposal of such litigations. Records are not forthcoming from revenue officials in time, resulting in delay in disposal of such cases.

- *Loopholes in the existing khatian:* The khatian does not always give clear and unambiguous details about the landholder and the person(s) in possession.
- *Non-updation of khatian and village maps:* Another important issue is the non-updation of the khatian and village maps on a continuous basis. These two vital records are usually updated only in the next survey. The genesis of preparation of documents showing conflicting details about land ownership/transfer/possession has been the relative isolation of registry (where sale deed is registered), office of the CO (where mutation is effected and land revenue paid) and survey office (which does the job of updating khatian and village maps). The following example will help clarify the issue. Let us say, in khatian (finalisation year 1971) there is a plot, say khasra number 21 (area 51 decimal), owned by person A. In 1975 A dies leaving behind his widow(W) and two sons (B and C), the share of each of them being 17 decimal. In 1980, B sells 15 decimal to another person D.

Now there is no mechanism in place which prohibits further sale of the same piece of land. The 15 decimal does not have a unique khasra number and that sale deed does not include graphical identification—of the piece of land sold—on the map. It is quite possible that subsequently C may sell the same 15 decimal of land to another buyer. This lacuna has been cause of litigation and thus there is a serious need to overhaul this system.

## RESTRUCTURING THE PRESENT SYSTEM

As is evident from the above analysis there is a serious need to restructure the present system of preparation, upkeep, updation and retrieval of land records. Three core components to the land administration process are relevant to a reform programme:

- The physical form of the ownership record.
- The institutional and physical method of record-keeping.
- The method of updating ownership information including updating the village maps and changes in use and plot size.

In the context of restructuring the present system of land records, two options are available: to strengthen the present manual system or switch-over to a computerised system. The first option would need a procedural overhaul and increased manpower. Even then the drawbacks associated with a manual system would continue. On the other hand, the success of computer-based Land Information System (LIS) in states like Karnataka and Tamil Nadu does indicate that a computerised system can be a credible and worthy alternative to the existing system.

An LIS is a computer-based solution for addressing the requirements of land records management system. It attempts to preserve, maintain, up-date, retrieve and analyse records in electronic form, resulting in numerous benefits associated with this technology. The benefits of the computerised system include uniqueness of ownership, security of data, reduction in land disputes, facilitating implementation of land reforms programmes, improvements in planning land-related development programmes, facili-tating issue of copy of record of rights to the owner and making data avail-able in a compact and readable form at any time. Other benefits include reducing the time lag in effecting mutations in the field and registers to permissible limits, facilitating concurrent updation of data in records and village maps as the maps can be plotted instantaneously through high-speed plotters. Also the integration of land records data and the associated map data is possible. For instance, if a plot is identified in a village map, the computer can give the data relating to that plot by accessing the data-base instantaneously. Similarly aggregation of land records data and associated map data to produce higher-level data is possible. For example, using the basic data on plots, it is possible to produce village data and village maps. Sensitivity analysis of the data (wherever applicable) is possible. For example, using the data on type of land, area and rate of re-venue, it is possible to know the net effect of change of rate of revenue of any type of land on the total revenue. This feature can be useful for taking policy decisions.

Provision of timely and cost-effective service to people is the key factor in the success of any system. In this context, providing online access to people regarding the relevant land-related information is the key. Down-loading of any document can be allowed for a nominal fee. Service centres can be set up at the circle and the district levels. In this context a step forward can be the provision of certificate of land ownership (CLO) to the raiyats as a replacement for the existing form of owner-based land record, that is the khatian. The CLO is essentially the hard copy of infor-mation stored in the LIS. It should include the boundary map and area of

188 • RAJESH KUMAR

the plot, name, address and photograph of the owner. In case of change in ownership or alteration in the plot boundaries, the new information is first fed into the LIS and fresh CLO would be issued to the concerned raiyats. However, the real challenge lies in actual implementation of the programme and creating a system of immediate and continuous updating of the CLO with every change in ownership. For this to start, provision of a legal cover for CLO is essential first step. The CLO, to succeed, must be provided with the force of legal finality as distinct from the current situation wherein there is no specific finality except in the uncertain and very lengthy process of court judgements.

Any computerised system should be preceded with a fresh revisional survey and procedural restructuring or else the deficiencies existent in the prevailing system would get internalised in the computerised system as well. There are a number of deficiencies in the existing khatians. If the same khatian were to act as basis of the proposed LIS then the very purpose of restructuring the system would get defeated. Similar is the case with village maps. Thus, before embarking on the path of computerisation of land records, a fresh survey needs to be undertaken. Next, there is a need to simplify the procedure undertaken to maintain and update land documents at the circle level. A number of state legislations need to be amended to facilitate online operations. For example, to allow online mutations the Mutations Act needs to be amended.

Having discussed the issue of restructuring the present system, let us now dwell upon the present status of land records computerisation in Bhojpur.

## PRESENT STATUS OF BHU-ABHILEKH IN BHOJPUR

The evaluation was carried out in 2002. A beginning towards computerisation of land records has been made in almost all the districts of Bihar. National Informatics Centre (NIC) developed Bhu-Abhilekh software which is being presently implemented in Bhojpur to create database for the district LIS. Under the first phase of this programme the two primary land records, i.e., khatian and Register II are being computerised. The data-entry work is in progress at the collectorate NIC centre. The aim of the first phase is to have electronic copies of the land record documents. The database screens to feed in data are reproduced in Figure 10.1.

In the database screen number 1 (Figure 10.1) details of the landholder are entered.

**Figure 10.1**

*Database Screen No. 1*

| | |
|---|---|
| NIC BSU | Land Holder's Details |
| District Bhojpur | Mauza _____ |
| Sub-Div. _____ | |
| Block _____ | |
| Anchal _____ | |
| Mauza _____ | Halka _____ |
| Mahal _____ | |
| Land Holder's Name _____ | More Holder [Y/N] |
| Father/Husband Name _____ | |
| Caste _____ | |
| Residential Address _____ | |
| Share _____ | Father's Share _____ |

Store [0-Quit 1-Save] 1

Once relevant data (from khatian) gets stored, the system automatically generates unique *khata pustika* number and holder ID for each landholder.

In case more than one landholder co-shares plot(s) included in a particular khata number, database screen number 2 (Figure 10.2) needs to be filled in and share of each of the holders gets entered. But all such co-sharers would have the common holder ID. Thus it is evident that the deficiencies of the existing khatian are getting internalised in the computerised system as well. (Ideally one holder ID should pertain to one landholder only.)

Next in database screen number 3, (Figure 10.3) land details available in the khatian, that is khasra number of the plot(s), land type, boundary details and *hakim lagan*, that is annual payable land revenue as mentioned in Register II are filled up.

Once all the above data gets entered, the system calculates different values for cess, that is road cess, education cess, health cess, agriculture cess and other cess based on the standard calculation formula. The database screen (Figure 10.3) depicts the data related to above parameters.

**Figure 10.2**

*Database Screen No. 2*

```
┌─────────────────────────────────────────────────────────────────┐
│ NIC BSU                            Land Holder's Details          │
│                                                                   │
│ District Bhojpur                          Mauza _____       │
│                                ┌─────────────────────────────────┐│
│ Sub-Div. _____   │   Other Land Holder Detail      ││
│ Block _____   │                                 ││
│ Anchal _____   │ Holder No. _____   ││
│                                │ Khata Pustika No. _____  ││
│ Mauza_____   │ Holder ID _____   ││
│                                │ Land Holder's Name _____   ││
│                                │ Father/Husband Name _____   ││
│ Mahal _____   │ Caste _____   ││
│                                │ Residential Address _____   ││
│ Land Holder's Name _____  │                                 ││
│ Father/Husband Name _____   │ Holder's Share _____   ││
│ Caste _____   │ Father's Share _____   ││
│ Residential Address _____   │                                 ││
│                                └─────────────────────────────────┘│
│                                                                   │
│                       Share _____ Father's Share_____     │
│                  Store [0-Quit 1-Save] 1                          │
└─────────────────────────────────────────────────────────────────┘
```

**Figure 10.3**

*Database Screen No. 3*

```
┌─────────────────────────────────────────────────────────────────┐
│ NIC BSU                         Land Details                      │
│                                                                   │
│ Holder's ID        Khata _____     Mauza ID _____         │
│                    Khasra _____                                  │
│                              ┌────────────────────────────────────┤
│                              │ Hakim Lagan        Reasonable Lagan │
│ Khata Recorded in C.S. _____   _____      _____ │
│ Khata Recorded in R.S. _____   Cess (Breakup) _____             │
│ Raqba: Acre _____Decimal ___   Road _____                │
│ Type of Land _____    Education _____             │
│ East _____   Health _____             │
│ West _____   Agriculture_____            │
│ North _____   Other _____    Total _____  │
│ South _____   Current Demand _____             │
│                                                                   │
│ Tot. Arrear Year_____ Arrear Due_____ Jamabandi No._____   │
│ Fin. Year                              Navayat                    │
│ Remarks _____                                 │
└─────────────────────────────────────────────────────────────────┘
```

Total value for all cess automatically appears on the screen. Further, the screen shows a parameter as current demand which is just the sum of the *lagan* and cess. Next, the system asks for entry of the arrears due (to be entered from Register II) which is the sum total of all the arrears due to a particular landholder having the concerned landholder ID. This parameter is very important for consideration of a cut-off date from which accounting of collection and demand will be operated online on the computerised system. The last parameter is financial year which has to be entered correctly as based upon the financial year entry, the system opens a ledger for collection and demand incorporating details of khata, khasra wise land details vis-à-vis their lagan, cess, arrear due, etc.

Next the system asks for *dakhal* entry. As is evident from the database screen number 4, (Figure 10.4) the details of possession over the land as has been recorded in the khatian is fed into the system and therefore it would not reflect the current possession details unless it is updated annually.

CoLR has not succeeded in many states since the present manual data does not reflect the current position of ownership possession.

**Figure 10.4**

*Database Screen No. 4*

| Dakhal Detail Entry Screen |
|---|

Holder's ID _____     Khata _____
_____     Khasra _____

Holder No. _____        Procedure of Rent Fixation
Holder's Name _____
Father/Husband Name _____        Special Condition _____
Caste _____
Res. Address _____
                                     Let. No. _____
                                     Date _____

From Year _____          Period of Poss. _____ Order Given By
Dakhal Type _____          _____
Share _____          Father's Share _____ Substance of Order

Store[0-Quit 1-Save] 1

## CRITICAL EVALUATION

- The aim of the phase-I of the ongoing computerisation programme is to generate electronic copies of the existing khatian and Register II. But the lacunae existing in these two vital land documents get internalised in the computerised records as well. There is a strong need for conducting a comprehensive survey, which should precede any computerisation move, because only after such an exercise the actual position can be captured into the records. The issue of sustainability needs to be addressed before embarking on any computerisation process. Having said that, there is no denying the fact that a beginning has definitely being made in the form of implementation of Bhu-Abhilekh in the district. The immediate benefits that would accrue after the completion of phase-I is enumerated below:

  1. any further manipulations in the khatian or Register II would not occur;
  2. timely updation of Register II can be monitored at the district level; and
  3. hard copies of khatian and Register II can be made available to the concerned raiyats without any unreasonable delay.

- The system at present does not have a workflow automation system to handle mutations online. Unless this is implemented, the databases for generating land records will not give the real time information and hence cannot be used with 100 per cent certainty. The system of updation at present would imply that changes in databases would have to be made manually after specific time periods.
- The programme as it is being implemented in Bhojpur is still in the infancy stage and concerted efforts need to be made for the implementation of this programme to be successful. One could learn from the experience of other states notably Karnataka.

## CONCLUSION

In a predominantly rural set-up where agriculture is the prime mover of the economy, issue of land has traditionally been the prime concern of one and all. Moreover, with an ever-escalating population and lack of growth of secondary and tertiary sector of economy, pressure on land is bound to increase in future. Therefore, there is even greater need to re-structure the present system.

Any land record management system should be systematic, sustainable and sensitive to local requirements, culture and needs. The key to the success of the system lies in how it protects the land rights and permits those rights to be traded in a transparent manner. In computerising the existing records without matching them with the existing ground realities, the error will keep on getting magnified with the processing of incorrect data. Worse, there is neither trained manpower nor the required infrastructure to accommodate the technology. A mismanaged and mishandled technology can lead to incorrect diagnosis of the problem that, in turn, will result in policy prescriptions that may aggravate the problem further. Hence, before embarking on the path of computerisation of land records, procedural simplification of the existent system needs to be undertaken. Moreover existing manpower entrusted with the job to preserve, maintain, update and retrieve the land records need to be trained accordingly. Computer-isation process should not be limited only to the land record maintenance wing of the revenue department but should encompass registry wing and the civil courts as well.

There is no denying the fact that a computer-based LIS would take care of the preservation, updation and retrieval problems being faced by the existing system but to put in place a comprehensively sustainable system correctness of data, trained manpower, process and adequate financial resources need to be ensured.

# GLOSSARY

Circle or *Anchal* : the geographical unit of revenue administration in the district

Circle Officer : revenue officer in charge of a circle

Cadastral Survey : survey process to estimate land revenue; the first survey undertaken during the British rule to prepare record of rights (khatian) and village map

Revisional Survey : any survey undertaken after the cadastral survey (the difference lies only in the detailed procedure for the preparation of the maps and record of rights)

*Mauza* : revenue village
*Halka* : a number of revenue villages
*Lagan* : annual land revenue payable by a landholder
Cess : surcharge on the land revenue

## SELECT BIBLIOGRAPHY

**Bihar Tenancy Act 1885.** (1981). Patna: Malhotra Publication.
**Khatian for Revenue Village.** Shuklapura; Circle, Ara Sadar; District, Bhojpur; Bihar.
**Manual of Bhu-Abhilekh Software.** (2002). NIC Bihar, Patna.
**Register II for Revenue Village.** Shuklapura, Circle-Ara Sadar, District-Bhojpur, Bihar.

# 11

# An Experience of Application of IT to Land Records Management

## BACKGROUND

### Patwari Information System (PATIS)

The importance of land is increasing day by day, as is also the case with information technology (IT). There are litigations with regards to land and getting information to solve the cases is a problem area. *Patwaris*, who are the lowest, but most important, functionaries of revenue department of the state government, are overloaded with different kinds of jobs. They are the ones whom the general public approaches whenever a copy or updation of any land record is required.

The Government of India looked at IT as a solution way back in 1987–88 and introduced a 100 per cent centrally sponsored scheme of land records computerisation.

The following objectives were set:

1. to facilitate easy maintenance and updating of the changes which occur in the land database, such as changes due to availability of irrigation, natural calamities, consolidation, or on account of legal changes like transfer of ownership, partition, land acquisition, lease, etc.;
2. to provide for comprehensive scrutiny to make the land records tamper-proof, which should reduce the menace of litigation and social conflicts associated with land disputes;
3. to provide required support for implementation of rural development programme, for which data about distribution of landholdings is vital;
4. to facilitate detailed planning in the area of infrastructure development as well as environmental development;
5. to facilitate preparation of annual set of records in the mechanised process, thereby producing accurate documents for recording details such as collection of land revenue, cropping patterns, etc.;
6. to facilitate collection/compilation/supply of all information in response to a variety of standards and ad hoc queries on land data;
7. to provide database for agriculture census; and
8. issue of updated copy of record of rights (RoR) to landholders quickly and inexpensively.

At Rewari in Haryana, Computerisation of land records was taken up on pilot basis in 1990–91. NIC, Haryana was assigned the responsibility of conducting system study, design and development of application software. Initially the scope of the pilot project was only *jamabandi* (RoR). Detailed discussions were held with revenue staff and software was developed for data entry, editing and jamabandi printing. The platform was UnixWare as operating system and FoxBASE+ as data base management system (DBMS). Graphical Intelligent Script Terminals (GIST) were used for data entry in Hindi. The initial problems were:

- The complete cases were not explained during study/development phase. This called for applying of software patches from time to time.
- Each patwari had his/her own way of writing jamabandi, conveying the same meaning. This led to difficulty in data entry. The involvement of patwari in data entry was essential.

- The volume of data was huge; its management was a challenge during the pilot project.
- Non-availability of Hindi data-entry operators, especially on GIST keyboard, was one of the constraints.
- Errors in totals, especially in area figures, were found between computerised and manual jamabandis.

The problems were eventually resolved. The Government of India reviewed the progress and was satisfied with the progress and basic objectives of the project like *Nakal* Generation, database for planning. The software developed was able to generate nakal (copy) of the jamabandi. The scope was extended to *intkal* (mutation), *khasra girdawari* (crop inspection) and *shajra nasb* (pedigree table). During the pilot, it was felt that codification of every landowner and cultivator was a must. There could be two or three persons with the same name, and, in such a situation if there was a land transaction, it would be very difficult for the computer to identify the exact person, whereas it was possible with unique codification of every landowner and cultivator in the village first, then in the *tehsil*, district and lastly in the state. The software for shajra nasb was developed and implemented in some districts. It was found that data for the same was not available so it was dropped. The software for mutation and khasra girdawari was developed and implemented in a couple of districts. Based on considerable success of the pilot project, the project was sanctioned for Sirsa, Rohtak and Ambala. More cases emerged and the software became more robust and was replicated in other districts after incorporating the necessary changes. PATIS, as a product, was bundled in the form of jamabandi, mutation and khasra girdawari. Now users demanded the new jamabandi creation software. A study was carried out and it was felt that without codification of landowners and cultivators, it was not possible to have a fully automatic jamabandi creation software. After analysis, it was found that there were 10–30 per cent changes during the five years when the process of new jamabandi took place. It was also felt that new ownership numbers are created or merged or remain the same. This led to the concept of semi-automatic jamabandi creation. This software has the facility of copying the data from the previous database to the new database in a selective way, re-organising the *khewat* or *khatoni* numbers as per the requirements of the new jamabandi. This way the manual preparation of jamabandis has been reduced to a minimum. In the meantime, the project was sanctioned for remaining districts of Haryana. The older districts started giving nakal to the public. Now 98 per cent data entry is complete in Haryana. A few years back technology also took a turn for the better and everybody started shifting to Windows platform. This happened with land records' computerisation too. NIC, Haryana also started converting software from Unix platform to Windows platform. Data porting posed a challenge but it was achieved, and software to generate nakal at tehsil level was developed on Windows. The same is being implemented at tehsil level. The PATIS modules are:

1. jamabandi data entry and editing module;
2. jamabandi nakal generation module;
3. mutation data entry and printing module;
4. khasra girdawari data entry and printing module;
5. statistical data reports generation module; and
6. land records query module.

## Haryana Registration Information System (HARIS)

In March 2000, the Haryana government decided to take up computerisation of registration of deeds with the technical support of NIC, Haryana. The objective was to facilitate the land registration services and correct calculation of stamp duty and registration fee. Hence software was developed for major deeds like sale, mortgage, lease and conveyance. The software so developed was stand-alone, using Windows platform. The software was implemented at six tehsils on a pilot basis. The following observations are noteworthy:

- The software should cover all the deeds, if manual system is to be dispensed with.
- Stand-alone system can serve the tehsils where number of transactions is less than 35.
- The project should be modelled as self-financing so that it can become sustainable in the long run.
- Training and involvement of staff can make the project more successful.
- Backup power and computer operator should become important components of the project.

The Haryana government decided to replicate HARIS in all tehsils and sub-tehsils of Haryana. The district Red Cross was named as the financing agency and NIC, Haryana as technical agency for the execution of the project. Deeds-based service charges were fixed and the district Red Cross is maintaining the amount collected. The district Red Cross has recovered the initial investment. Recurring expenditure in terms of printer cartridges, CD for backup, diesel/petrol for generator and annual maintenance is being met by the Red Cross. The software was enhanced to multi-user (client-server-based), which covers all the 65 types of deeds. The software was made more secure by means of role-based operations and password on SQL Server-2000.

## Cadastral Maps (Musavis)

*Musavi* is an important document of record of rights. It depicts the physical location of a plot in a village. In Haryana, the unit of land measurement for mapping purposes is *karam*, which is equivalent to 5.5 feet. After consolidation, the total land of a village is divided into chunks called *murabbas*. One murabba is divided into 25 *kilas* and each kila is equal to 40×36 karam. One musavi contains map of 16 murabbas meaning thereby an area of 800×720 karam. Figure 11.1 shows a sample musavi.

**Figure 11.1**

*A Sample Musavi*

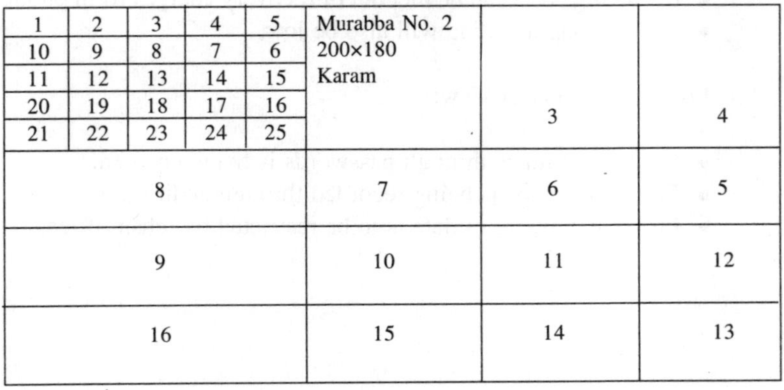

| 1 | 2 | 3 | 4 | 5 | Murabba No. 2 | | |
|---|---|---|---|---|---|---|---|
| 10 | 9 | 8 | 7 | 6 | 200×180 | | |
| 11 | 12 | 13 | 14 | 15 | Karam | | |
| 20 | 19 | 18 | 17 | 16 | | 3 | 4 |
| 21 | 22 | 23 | 24 | 25 | | | |
| 8 | | | | | 7 | 6 | 5 |
| 9 | | | | | 10 | 11 | 12 |
| 16 | | | | | 15 | 14 | 13 |

## The Objectives

The objectives of the project are:

1. to preserve the old record of the settlement time;
2. to update the record in fast mode in future;
3. to provide land map related services to the public;
4. to bring transparency in the land records maintenance; and
5. to bring accuracy and quality in the land records maintenance.

## Utility of Project

1. For the public:

   • Maps will be available without any delay.
   • Quality of maps will be better.
   • More information will be available, and on time.

2. From financial point of view:

   • This project will be more economical in the long run.
   • Recurring costs can be met out of recovery charges from public.
   • Cost of map updating will also be low.

3. From legal point of view:

   • Security of maps through passwords is being ensured.
   • Editing of maps is being recorded through audit trails.
   • Physical copying of data is to be restricted by tehsil office.

4. From administrative point of view:

- Duplicate records can be maintained at different sites for data protection.
- Data analysis will be possible, which otherwise was not possible.
- Database linkage with other documents of record of rights can be maintained.

5. From operational point of view:

- The application software with easy user interface is being developed.
- Operations will be much faster and more easy as compared to manual one.
- Lowest revenue functionaries are involved right from day one in the project development and implementation.

## Land Records Management Process Overview

Land records updating starts whenever there is land transaction between two parties. Registration of the transaction is done with the sub-registrar. Rural land transactions registered with sub-registrar are sent to the patwari for carrying out necessary changes in the land records. Mutation register is then written and a pencil entry is made in the remarks column of the jamabandi. The mutation is placed before the *tehsildar* for sanctioning. The tehsildar may sanction or reject the mutation. The concerned remarks of the tehsildar are recorded in the remarks column of the jamabandi in brief using red ink. In case mutation divides the plot, the village map is updated accordingly. After five years, the sanctioned mutations are incorporated at the time of generation of new jamabandi. Once it is incorporated, it still remains in the remarks column in black ink (Figure 11.2).

Figure 11.2

*Land Records Updating Process Overview*

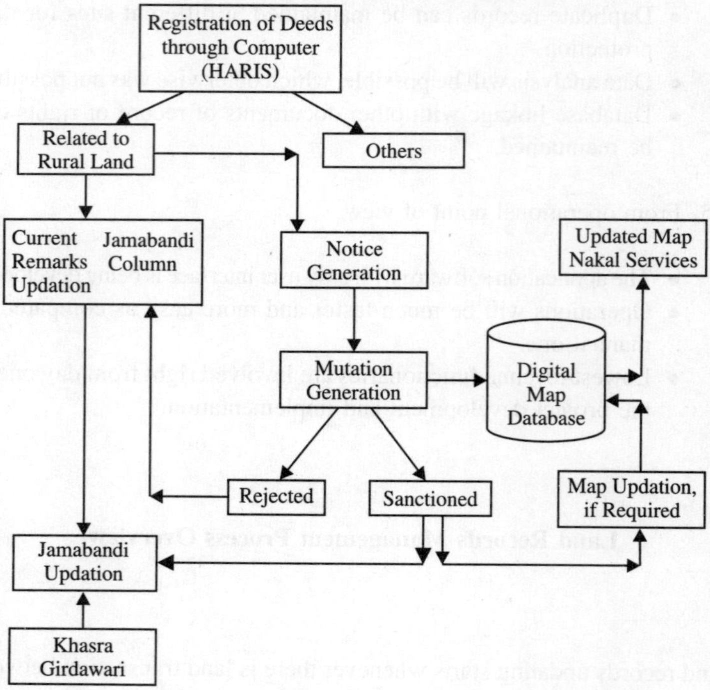

## IMPLEMENTATION ISSUES

### Patwari Information System (PATIS)

1. *Village directory:* This is the base of PATIS software. Without finalisation of revenue village directory, it is not possible to implement
this project. Village type (habitat/non-habitat), overview of the
village, attributes of the village like land tax criteria, etc., need to
be defined. Issues like re-organisation of districts, tehsils and village

boundaries and their effect on the databases need to be taken care of. A unique code for every village in the state and its linkages with the tehsil, district, etc., would be helpful.

2. *Availability of land records:* The volume of data is very big. Data is available in Hindi but the terminology is difficult to understand, so making it available for data entry is another problem. Data is available at tehsil level (*parat sarkar*) and at patwari level (*parat patwar*). Parat patwar is the updated copy of record of rights. In case of non-availability of parat patwar, data entry is done from parat sarkar leading to data inconsistency. Non-availability of records leads to other problems like underutilisation of data-entry staff, etc.

3. *Deputing revenue staff:* The involvement of revenue staff from the start brings higher success rate. Since readability of document is not good, therefore availability of revenue official, preferably the one directly concerned, is required. Supervision is also required at revenue department level.

4. *Data entry:* For data entry in Hindi, Hindi data-entry operators are required. Once they are available they should be retained for timely availability of records. Payment to the operators can be linked to the performance. Rates per khewat number/khatoni number need to be fixed rather than fixed monthly rates. Data entry needs to be done in-house due to security reasons of the land records. Availability of sufficient number of GIST terminals also needs to be ensured.

5. *Printing:* Since data volumes are very high in Hindi, printing is also an issue. Initially, printing was done on normal Dot Matrix printers but a lot of printing backlog accumulated at the district level. High-speed bilingual printer is the solution which has been implemented in Haryana. Every district of Haryana has these printers now.

6. *Data checking:* Once initial data entry is done and printout is generated, it needs to be checked for 100 per cent accuracy of data. This exercise is carried out by revenue officials. The usual errors made are mismatch of totals and non-standard way of writing jamabandi.

7. *Data editing:* Error reporting during the data checking is made effective in computers. There are 12 columns in the jamabandi. Errors are reported in all of the columns. A separate piece of software supporting columnar editing has been developed for this purpose.

8. *Data finalisation:* Final printouts are taken. Jamabandi is finalised once it is verified, validated and duly signed by the concerned revenue official. The data for the same is made read-only, once it is finally accepted.

9. *Data management:* Data is huge and need to be managed for easy retrieval. Data backup and its management need to be ensured. Data availability from computer has become a necessity, as it is the source of final data for revenue officials also.

10. *Nakal services:* Once data is finalised and in read-only mode except remarks column where updating is done when there are mutations, items like date of mutation, type of mutation, mutation number and remarks are recorded, nakal services to the public have been started.

11. *Monitoring:* Monitoring starts from district revenue officer (DRO) level and reaches up to financial commissioner, revenue level. The DRO is responsible for day-to-day operations. The deputy commissioner reviews the progress on monthly basis and director, land records and financial commissioner, revenue review it whenever it is required. For regular reviews at state level there is a technical committee.

12. *Training:* Training is a very important component of the project. General awareness training has to be given to all the revenue staff at district and state levels. Application training has been imparted to concerned revenue staff at district and state level.

13. *Public awareness:* The public should be made aware of the facility of computerised nakal services and leaflets in the local language should be distributed in the villages. Modes like cinema slides, seminars, boards, publications, etc., need to be adopted for wide publicity.

14. *Process re-engineering:* The software has been developed without changing the procedures and rule. The age-old system need to be simplified and re-engineering of processes be carried out. Some efforts in Haryana have already been initiated in this regard.

15. *Change management:* Software implementation in 19 districts and 67 tehsils is a tough task. Requirements differ from one place to another. Standardisation is the key here and software is also to be changed as per the requirements of the user. Here, changes need to be recorded and versioning done. Controlling changes at multiple location need a sense of management.

16. *Documentation:* Staff transfers and resignations are common in the field of IT. Therefore, documentation is a must. At least a user manual, technical manual and software requirement specification are needed to facilitate change management.

17. *Data security:* Land records data is very important. It needs to be secure from unwanted changes. Biometrics and other security tools need to be applied for recording of personal information about the officials responsible for the updating of record. Information auditing services need to be enabled for recording the facilities to be availed of while using software.

18. *Change of technology:* Earlier, the work was done in Unix/ FoxBASE+, now Windows is used. We need to manage technology, arrange funds for it and arrange software development resources.

19. *Data porting:* Porting of data from FoxBASE+ to SQL Server is a mammoth exercise. Apart from technological issues, managerial issues become more important in the implementation of new technology.

20. *Information architecture:* A global picture of the project, with clarity of integration in the form of information architecture, is needed. Standardisation needs to be done in terms of software, operations and procedures and implementation throughout the state need to be ensured. It facilitates controlling of overall project technically and managerially.

## Haryana Registration Information System (HARIS)

1. *Application software:* An application software, which is simple, easy to use, facilitates every feature using software like photo session, backup, etc., was developed by NIC, Haryana free of cost.

2. *Financing agency:* The Red Cross was the financing agency in Haryana. They invested initially in the hardware, system software, generator and UPS, etc. The investment was recovered by taking service charges from public.

3. *Hardware procurement:* Deputy Commissioners, who are chairpersons of the district Red Cross societies, were given freedom for hardware procurement at their level and this was very helpful.

4. *Availability of consumables:* Consumables like CDs for backup, paper for printing, toner cartridges for printers, diesel/petrol for generator are required for day-to-day functioning of project.

Hardware maintenance is also required for proper functioning of the project. The district Red Cross agency was made responsible for procurement of these items from service charges collected.

5. *Operator availability:* Even if there is a trained registration clerk, an operator for execution of this project has been engaged. He is being paid on a per deed basis from the service charges collected by Red Cross.

6. *Handling large sites:* Using a single PC, up to 35 transactions per day can be handled easily. Since HARIS is multi-user software, it supports multiple operators simultaneously. Photo session and data entry have been separated out to manage the public. In Haryana, we have about five such sites where transactions from 100 to 200 per day take place.

7. *Training:* General awareness training to the staff of sub-registrar office has been imparted. Application training has been imparted to concerned staff at tehsil level.

8. *Changes in act/rules:* Steps in this direction have already been initiated. Changes have been sent to government for approval. Government of India also has approved the bill in this regard.

9. *Data security:* Photos of seller, buyer and witness are being recorded in the computer as permanent record. Data security is an issue. Photos are being kept in database, which is secure.

10. *Data management:* Data backups are being maintained and serialisation of CDs have been advised at lowest level for future retrievals. Daily, weekly and monthly backups have been planned.

## Digitisation of Cadastral Maps (Digital Musavis)

1. *Availability of maps:* One of the objectives was to retain the musavis prepared at the time of consolidation. Then the changes are to be carried out in the digital maps to update them. The state of Haryana has retained these maps in most of the cases. Their complete availability for digitisation needs to be ensured.

2. *The process:* Manual maps are scanned and then converted into vector form using software so that they can be updated at a latter stage.

3. *Digital maps verification:* The criteria for acceptance of digital maps need to be finalised. The continuous involvement of revenue staff is crucial for manual verification and modification in computer.

4. *Application software:* Application of software for map retrieval at different levels (plot/musavi/village) and its updation for splitting and merging need to be done.

5. *Data integration:* First, data consistency between maps and record of rights need to be established and then its integration with record of rights is to be ensured. Khasra number is the key for both the databases.

6. *Training:* Since it is a new area and different from the normal computerisation, therefore operational and technical training is essential.

7. *Verification of digital data with ground reality:* Once data is in digital form, it is to be verified with ground realities and necessary updating in the data needs to be carried out.

8. *Nakal services:* Once the data is fully updated and matching the ground realities, nakal services can be initiated and the data can also be used for administrative purposes.

9. *Data updation:* Whenever there is mutation with changes in plot dimensions, this module on digitisation of cadastral maps will be activated for updating the digital map database.

10. *Data security and management:* That data changes are carried out by the right person needs to be ensured, for which application software should have the information auditing services enabled. This should record the activities carried out with the time stamp and person's identification.

## What Next?

### Top on the Agenda

1. *Integration of HARIS and PATIS:* Software is being developed for this purpose. This will lead to automatic generation of notices and mutation and their incorporation in the jamabandis.

2. *Integration of PATIS and digital musavis:* The software has been tested on an experimental basis and found to be successful. Now linkages need to be established at mass level for six tehsils.
3. *Online land records services to public:* The complete processes of the jamabandi creation need to be made automatic. Only for those activities where processes cannot be automated, data will be captured manually. Software needs to be developed for the same.
4. *Web-HARIS:* The Stamp Act, Registration Act, registration fee, and collector rates for all locations in Haryana will be placed on the Web so that greater transparency can be brought into the system.
5. *E-learning for the revenue staff:* Without the involvement of staff, no project can be a success. Full training of the Revenue Staff is to be ensured so that IT projects can be made a success.

## Next on the Agenda

1. *Connecting tehsils:* Data transfer between tehsils and district is required. At least *dial-up* connectivity is required. The Haryana government has planned HARNET; last mile connectivity will be achieved in the future.
2. *Digital deeds:* Deed-writing software has been developed and digital signature solution has been in place to maintain the consistency of deed contents. This has been launched after successful testing.
3. *Processes re-engineering:* Many processes need re-engineering for providing effective service and simple interface with the public, and suitable efforts are being made.
4. *Land-related information on Web:* Land records manual, land records administration manual, settlement manual and other related notifications, rules and acts will be placed on the web to bring more transparency in the system.
5. *Land records on the Web:* Anyone will be able to see the contents of his/her land records once it is available on the web.
6. *Integrated query system:* Once all the databases are integrated, a powerful integrated query system needs to be developed for administrators and planners.

## LAST WORDS

Based on the experience of working with e-HARLAND project, the following are the words from the heart:

- Let us re-engineer our thinking process before implementing IT projects.
- Let us build trust in the e-systems.
- Let administrators own the IT projects.
- Let there be continuous efforts till we achieve complete success.
- Let us join hands to make India a real IT destination.

# 12

# Computerisation of Land Records in Punjab: Need to Rethink

## MANOJ AHUJA AND A.P. SINGH

## INTRODUCTION

The nature of land records in India makes the system amenable to computerisation. Although a large staff is engaged at the village level, the process of land records management in India suffers from a lot of inefficiencies. In the manual system, a *patwari* has to manage four to five villages and numerous different records. In other words, despite the existing large manpower at the village level, we have a non-transparent archaic method which does not help to build efficiency. Therefore, in 1991–92, the Ministry of Rural Development, Government of India sanctioned a pilot project for computerisation of land records in Rupnagar district of this state. Later, in 1994–95, this scheme was extended to Jalandhar, Bathinda, Kapurthala and Sangrur districts. In 1997–98 it was further extended to the remaining districts.

---

For all figures in lakhs and crores, please note that 1 lakh = 100,000 and 1 crore = 10,000,000.

Twelve years after the sanctioning of the pilot project the process of computerisation of land records has not achieved any remarkable progress in the state. The central government has released Rs 2.83 crore to the state since the inception of the scheme but till 31 January 2003 the state government could utilise only 19 per cent of the total funds released.

## ORGANISATIONAL OVERVIEW

The deputy commissioner of the respective district is responsible for maintenance of land records. To do this, he has an organisation consisting of sub-divisional magistrates, *tehsildars*, *naib* (deputy) *tehsildars*, *kanungos* and patwaris. Each patwari is responsible for two to four villages, depending on the village size, and maintains the following records:

1. *jamabandi* (record of rights);
2. register *intkaal* (mutations register);
3. *khasra girdawari* (harvest inspection register);
4. *shajra nasb* (genealogy table);
5. field maps;
6. field measurement book; and
7. *roznaamcha waqiati* (daily journal).

The jamabandi contains the list of all landowners; whenever changes to this happen, the changes are recorded in the mutations register. At the end of five years, all the changes in ownership are incorporated into the jamabandi and a new jamabandi is written. Since a patwari is responsible for more than one village, almost every year he has the work of preparing the jamabandi.

## PRESENT SCENARIO

In the beginning of the scheme, data entry for some of the districts was started by National Informatics Centre (NIC), but it contained a lot of mistakes. Therefore, it was felt that the job of data entry should be stopped and given a fresh look. After this decision, no work relating to computerisation of land records was undertaken for a long time. The director of land records in Punjab is reviewing the reasons for the failure of CoLR in Punjab. The state government is in the process of implementing three pilot projects in Jalandhar, Kapurthala and Fatehgarh Sahib districts through private agencies. These agencies are: (*a*) Pioneer E-Labs in Jalandhar; (*b*) SCL Limited in Fatehgarh Sahib; and (*c*) Ramtech Limited in Kapurthala. These projects have been covering only one kanungo circle from each district. The following guidelines have been set for these pilot projects:

- The record of rights must be up-to-date at all times.
- The accompanying cadastral maps must also be updated automatically.
- The availability of the data and maps must be ensured on the Internet.
- The revenue department must be integrated with registration department.
- The interface must be in Punjabi, even over the Internet.

The pilot project for Jalandhar district can presently be viewed on the Internet. This project has been implemented in Pholliwal kanungo circle of Jalandhar-I *tehsil* of Jalandhar district and the name of the software is Integrated Software for Punjab Land Records (ISPLR). The salient feature of this software is an integrated approach to computerisation of land records. The sub-registrar's office is closely linked (90 per cent of all mutations originate in the sub-registrar's office); and has been fully integrated with the solution. To integrate the cadastral maps Geographical Information System (GIS) software components have been used, so that the main interface between users and the system is based on maps. If they click on any land parcel, they get to see the details of ownership and the land. If any changes are required, like partitioning of land parcels, they can be made on the map itself.

To enable patwaris to do this, a user-friendly interface has been developed. All the notations and conventions have been captured in the data structures so that the existing practice can be implemented without major changes. The other features of the system are native language support in the Punjabi language and the application is totally web-enabled, including the maps (see Figure 12.1).

**Figure 12.1**

*Components of Pilot Study of Jalandhar-I*

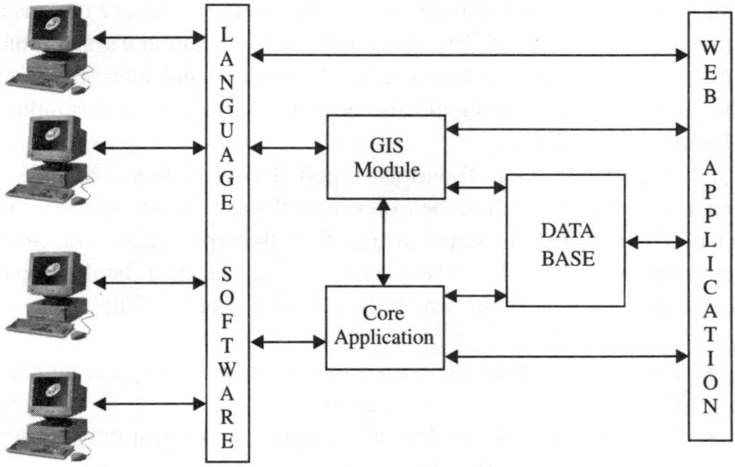

## PROPOSED MODEL

A state committee has been formed on the computerisation of land records to present a future model in this field. The report entitled 'Todarmal' has been submitted to the Government of India. According to the report, CoLR project can best be implemented by an autonomous agency. In our opinion, NIC has built up expertise in the field and successfully implemented land computerisation projects in some states, especially in Karnataka. The major issue here is a proper system study, re-engineering of processes and project management issues, which need to be taken by the state government. The software provider is not a major issue. However, given the organisational experience and capability of NIC, we feel they may fit the bill better. The state government may have to take help of the private sector in data entry, site preparation, supply of hardware and software. Previously, the coordination between the NIC state unit and the Directorate of Land Records was not of the nature and extent as required for the successful implementation of this scheme. This was the main reason for the failure of the CoLR scheme. Since the application software would be same for the whole state, it becomes necessary that a single software agency should develop application software in consultation with the directorate. This programme needs a thorough system study, which generally takes a lot of time, discussions and interactions and therefore the directorate should also be involved fully in the development of application software.

After going through 'Todarmal' report it is clear that even after 12 years, the project is still at the experimental stage. In our opinion, there is a need to re-think. The state can learn from the experiences of successful states like Karnataka, Tamil Nadu and Gujarat. The state should keep the following factors in mind, which the software should fulfil:

- The software should have an online module to carry out mutation. This will ensure dynamic updation.
- It should be built-in workflow automation, where transactions move from one personnel to another on the system.
- The process of mutation should be synchronised with the existing fieldwork done by the revenue officials.
- It should be integrated with Fingerprint (Bio-metrics) Technology to ensure foolproof authentication system instead of a traditional password system. This enforces the concept of non-repudiation.
- The software should be in local language (Punjabi).
- Various analytical reports should be generated in text format and also viewed in graphical form.
- The project may be taken up in phases. Computerisation of non-spatial data may be taken up first. After the completion of the computerisation of non-spatial data of land records, it is necessary that in the next phase, digitisation of maps is taken up either by scanning and digitising the existing maps or by re-survey/fresh survey through modern survey equipment like total stations, etc., for the generation of new maps.
- Adequate attention has to be paid to the security of databases and preventing tampering/manipulation of data. Backups of data should be ensured.
- There will be a need for placing of a trained resource person at each district to look into hardware-and software-related problems.
- The project would need a champion, who would be the overall project

incharge and would look after technology, change management and project management issues.

• It should have two modules for public interface:

    i. one module should be used by the revenue official at Land Records Centre to issue the land records documents on demand from public and accept the request application for mutation from the public; and

   ii. the other module of Touch Screen Kiosk, should be established at tehsil office. This module should be easily operable by even the person/farmer having little knowledge of computers.

## EXECUTION POLICY

The implementation process of computerisation of land records should be started with digitising the legacy data. The patwari should ensure the correctness of the data fed from the old land record books. This would be an iterative process. The checklist of documents should be printed by the data-entry agency and should be submitted to the patwari. The patwari should verify the printed checklist with the original record and correct the checklist accordingly. The correction of wrongly entered data should be carried out by the data-entry agency. Once the data is corrected, the agency will take the final print of the land records documents. Thereafter the patwari should verify the printed data for correctness. The process should be repeated till all the data-entry errors are eliminated. The data-entry agency should hand over the digitised data in CD form to the revenue authority. The revenue officers/officials should cross-check the final printed land records documents with the manual documents on random basis.

Once revenue officials certify the correctness of the digitised data, the CD data should be ported into databases for online operations. During this stage all errors such as duplicate records and RoR data not conforming to validation criteria should either be eliminated or should clearly be marked for possible corrections. Records marked for correction will not be allowed for transaction processing till they are cleared and properly certified. The system should maintain the log of corrections and the authority that approves their correctness along with dates.

The online mutation process will be started after porting the data provided by the data-entry agency into the computerised land records system. Meanwhile, the revenue department should issue tehsilwise circulars saying that only computerised land records documents will be valid for all legal purposes. This will put pressure on the revenue staff to carry out the mutation on computerised land records system only, and as a result the computerised land records system will always have live and up-to-date data. As computerised land records system work on client/server architecture, all the clients and kiosk interact with the server through an ethernet-based local area network (LAN) implementing TCP/IP.

Every district should be provided with a consultant to act as a bridge between the data-entry agency and the district administration. Operators should be provided for one year to handle online data entry at the kiosks and thereafter the patwari should take over the work from these operators. A comprehensive training module should be designed jointly by the revenue department and NIC (software development agency) to train the patwari.

After the completion of the computerisation of non-spatial data of land records, it is necessary that in the next phase, digitisation of maps is taken up either by scanning and digitising the existing maps or by re-survey/fresh survey through modern survey equipment like total stations, etc., for generation of new maps.

## CONCLUSION

In Punjab, the work of computerisation of land records started in 1991–92 as a pilot project in Rupnagar district. After 12 years, even the data-entry work was completed only for 8 per cent of the villages of the district. Therefore we may say that progress of the pilot district is highly disappointing. This scheme was later extended to remaining districts without assessing the performance of the pilot district. In terms of utilisation of funds, the Directorate of Land Records utilised only 19 per cent of the total fund released by the Ministry of Rural Development, Government of India.

According to the officials of the Directorate of Land Records not much progress has been made till now with regard to computerisation of land records. In the primary stage, some work of data entry in some of the districts had been started with the help of NIC but failed to achieve the desired accuracy. Therefore, it was felt that this data-entry work should be stopped immediately since the NIC had not done the work satisfactorily. After the failure of this scheme, the director of land records is in the process of implementing three pilot projects with the help of private agencies. These districts are Jalandhar, Fatehgarh Sahib and Kapurthala. These projects are covering only one kanungo circle from each district. The state government is of the view that CoLR project can best be implemented by an autonomous agency. This in our opinion, is not the major issue; in fact we feel that NIC with its experience and organisational strength may be in a better position to prepare the required software. It appears that one of the major reasons of the failure of this scheme in the past was the lack of coordination between the directorate and NIC state unit.

The directorate needs to carry out the implementation of the scheme in a systematic manner. This would require a

1. thorough study of the system;
2. regular interface with the software provider;
3. re-engineering of processes; and
4. envisaging a computerised system which takes into consideration the manual system and ensuring that the implemented system will be adopted by the revenue personnel.

The best way would perhaps be if a separate project structure was created for the implementation of the programme. The project would only be an organisational set-up and should use existing human and other resources, and thus no additional finances would be required. However, this approach will result in proper focus being given to the issue as well as ensuring time-bound implementation and accountability.

## REFERENCES

**Todarmal.** Project on Land and Revenue Information System, Version 8, Submitted by State Committee on Computerisation of Land Records Project, Punjab.
**URL:** *http://www. jamabandi.com*

# 13

# Computerisation of Land Records in Rajasthan

## INDU GUPTA

## INTRODUCTION

Given the background of allotment, increasing number of title disputes, land reforms, collection of land use and agriculture data and introduction of micro-level planning, it is being increasingly felt that the traditional methods of land records management should be upgraded so that gathering of data, analysis and disseminating becomes speeder, simpler and, at the same time, reliable. Keeping this in view the necessity for computerisation of land records gained acceptance.

The Ministry of Rural Development, Government of India felt the need to work out a practical modality for improving management of land records on a nationwide scale utilising tools of information technology. Therefore, computerisation of land records in Rajasthan was started in 1994–95. Initially, it was started in two pilot districts, that is Jaipur and

For all figures in lakhs and crores, please note that 1 lakh = 100,000 and 1 crore = 10,000,000.

Barmer. Later on computerisation of land records was taken up in all 32 districts of the state in 1996–97. The project is being implemented with the complete technical assistance of NIC on turnkey basis which includes feasibility study, design, development, implementation of software and consistent technical support at state, district and field level in all respects.

In Rajasthan, there was no uniformity in writing and maintaining land records registers. There was much diversity between districts and even among *tehsils* in the same district in maintaining land records. It was therefore imperative to find out a unified and common system of writing land records for the whole state as per land revenue rules and acts, for preparation of software. Several conferences of collectors were organised at the state level to document and understand the diversities in existing system. A study was also made through interactions with grassroots level and field officials. The first successful milestone was achieved in 2001 when common software was launched for all the 241 tehsils. The software was rolled out throughout the state in February–March 2004.

## OBJECTIVES

The prime goal of land records computerisation is to store all information regarding land in a systematic and logical way so that information is easily retrievable according to the requirement of the farmers and administration. At the same time it is important that records of tehsils/districts are stored in CD-ROMs, so that data becomes portable.

## ORIENTATION PROGRAMME

Regular training programmes for revenue officials on computer awareness and software features have resulted in significant gains for the project. Different types of training programmes are being carried out throughout the state. Three major training programmes for a total of 1,070 revenue officials for 12 days, refresher training programmes for four days and many exclusive application-related training programmes have been conducted so far. It has spread awareness and motivated a majority of revenue officials to work with new zeal for the project. In the similar manner all district units of NIC are providing day-to-day support for the computerisation project at tehsil and district levels. The software helps the revenue officials in their day-to-day activities, namely writing of new *chausala*, summary report, *khasra* index, in *goswara* and land utilisation reports. The operational manual has been provided in Hindi for smooth operation. Till now, 235 out of 241 tehsils have been operationalised.

## RAJASTHAN'S LAND RECORDS ON WEBSITE

Rajasthan is one of the first states to host the entire state land records data on the Web for public use. The details of land can be viewed on *apnakhata. raj.nic.in* website. The certified copy of RoR can be obtained from the authorised centres. The Government of Rajasthan has authorised kioskholders to obtain the land records copy from the Internet on payment basis as prescribed, which is valid and legal for all purposes. At present the project has been successfully launched in all 32 districts of Rajasthan at tehsil level. The data is available in Hindi. Anyone can retrieve his/her land details by just providing the tehsil name, village and *khata* number. The data is being updated in a decentralised manner on regular basis.

## STATUS OF COMPUTERISATION OF LAND RECORDS

Rajasthan has 7 million land records ( RoRs) and 34 million plots in nearly 42,000 villages. A computerised printed copy of RoR can be obtained from Apna Khata Centre in 235 tehsils after paying Rs 10 for up to 10 plots and Rs 5 per 10 plots thereafter. The state government has provided a validity and legality for the computerised RoRs, but there is still a need to abolish handwritten RoRs. The chausala (four year) updation process can be accomplished through computer. Unavailability of regular power supply, lack of trained personnel in remote tehsils, the unfamiliarity of revenue officers with computer application, etc., have been some major teething problems in the computerisation process.

New computer centres have been constructed in 240 tehsils and they have been equipped with necessary hardware and software. About 1,000 *patwaris* and other field functionaries have been trained to run them and already more than 2.5 lakh tenants have been provided with copies of land record in computer printouts.

The future plans of Rajasthan government include digitisation of revenue maps, computerisation of the data relating to crop survey, revenue collection and court work.

## CHARACTERISTICS OF APNA KHATA SOFTWARE

In order to prepare computerised land records data in local language, GIST technology was used as hardware solution in Unix/Oracle platform. In this project 10–20 terminals along with one server were used at all the district NIC centres. After the verification of data at the district level, data were normalised and converted from seven bit data to eight bit data at the state centre for all tehsils. It took around two to three years for the data entry and verification processes. The software was developed in-house in NIC state unit, Jaipur.

The application is user-friendly and GUI-based. It operates in Windows 2000 operating systems. The front-end uses VB 6.0 and database is managed in SQL server 2000. The security aspect for the smooth operation is well taken care of. The software also takes care of automatic backup.

The report generation section has been made more powerful and one can generate the report of the whole block/village at a time within a few seconds. The general features of Apna Khata are as follows:

- The software is in Hindi language.
- Various analytical reports can be generated in text format.

The software at present does not have in-built workflow automation, where transactions move from one personnel to another revenue personnel on the system itself. In January 2004, the International Organisation for Standardisation certified the existing software of land records.

# MUTATIONS

In 1957, it was decided that the powers under Section 135 of Rajasthan Land Revenue Act should be exercised by the *panchayat* concerned instead of *tehsildars*.

The process of mutation is as follows: The applicant may report for mutation directly to patwari or through tehsildar. The patwari writes the report in mutation register as per para 121 of the Rajasthan Land Revenue (Land Records) Rules, 1957. After that the inspector of land records verifies the mutation and puts it forward to the *sarpanch* (instead of tehsildar) for necessary orders. The panchayat decides mutations in accordance with the provisions of Section 135 of the Rajasthan Land Revenue Act, 1956 and Rajasthan Land Revenue (Land Records) Rules, 1957.

In case the panchayat fails to give any decision on the mutation cases as per the rules the matter may be reported to the tehsildar. He may order within 30 days for the disposal of mutation.

The tehsildar has no power to review the orders of the panchayat. The panchayat has also the power to sanction the mutation under Section 19 of the Rajasthan Tenancy Act. The tehsildar cannot exercise these powers. An appeal against the orders of the panchayat would lie with the collector.

After the computerisation of land records the same process is continuing. After completion of mutation, as per above-mentioned procedure, the mutation entry is entered in the computer. The mutation does not work like an online module to carry out mutation on the database for dynamic updating of database. Another flaw of the present mutation system is that it does not have a built-in workflow automation system which moves transactions from one personnel to another on the system with specific roles and responsibility of the revenue personnel. According to the revenue personnel, online mutation as has been done in Karnataka may not possible in Rajasthan due to involvement of *gram panchayat* in the mutation procedure. Therefore, either an amendment should be made in this regard for the success of computerisation of land records programme or the activities being carried out at the panchayat level have to be incorporated in the workflow system either in an online manner or, if this is not feasible, in an offline manner. The latter would involve batch updation of data on a periodic basis.

# CONCLUSION

It is true that the International Organisation of Standardisation has certified the existing software; however, this software still contains many glitches. The computerised mutation does not reflect the real benefits of computerisation as it does not ensure automatic updation of land records. It needs real online mutation, which can work only in a workflow automation system. The real online mutation may not perhaps be possible without amendment in the present mutation procedure. Presently, the Rajasthan government has computerised only the RoR (*khatauni*). The *khasra* (crop details document) still remains to be computerised. The people of Rajasthan will be able to get full benefits from computerisation of land records only after the computerisation of khasra and implementation of online mutation.

**Figure 13.1**

*Existing Mutation Process in Rajasthan*

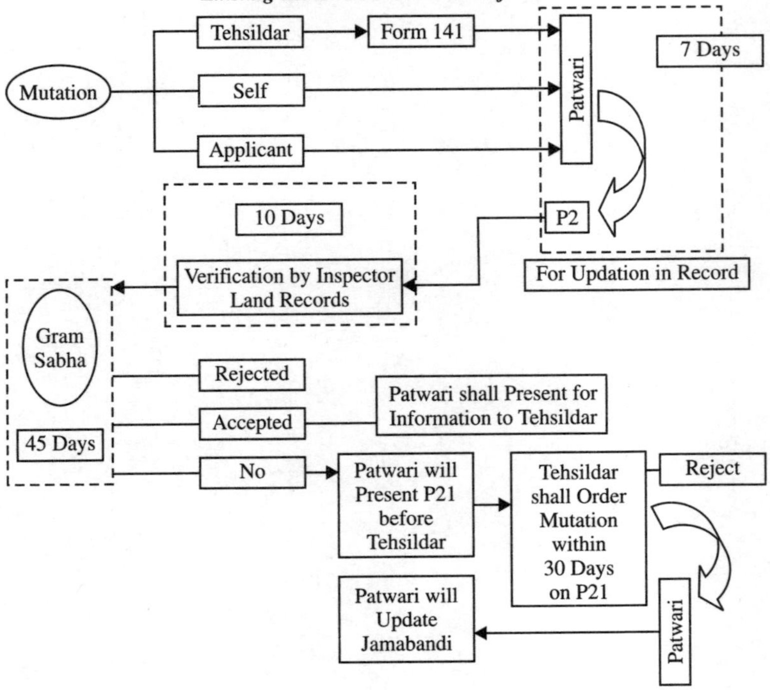

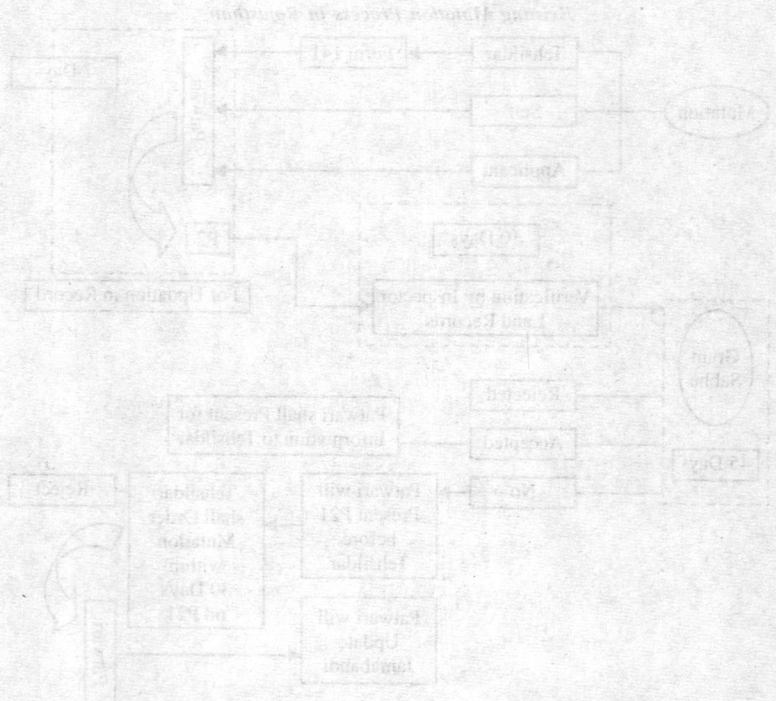

# Part II: Digitisation of Cadastral Maps

# 14

# Cadastral Surveys: Problems and Solutions

N.K. AGRAWAL

## INTRODUCTION

The first and foremost task is to survey the land which consists of data capture relating to individual landholdings, natural and man-made features of land, boundaries, etc., in their correct relative positions and to present these in the form of a map on a desired scale. The following steps should be considered:

1. reference surface/datum;
2. projection/grid system;
3. methods of survey: control survey, photogrammetric survey, field data capture/ field survey, scale of survey;
4. accuracy;
5. cartographic design/ mapping and digitisation of documents;
6. integration of data and creation of LIS/ GIS; and
7. training.

## REFERENCE SURFACE/DATUM

Reference surface/datum for India is Everest Spheroid which is a local system given by Sir George Everest who was Surveyor General of India from 1830 to 1843. All mapping in India is carried out on this datum.All our cadastral survey maps are supposed to be on this datum. Cadastral survey maps of some of the states, namely Tamil Nadu, Kerala, etc., refer to this datum, whereas no datum is taken in respect of a number of states. Vertical datum for heights is however Indian mean sea level or Indian geoid which is supposed to be an equipotential surface of earth's attraction and rotation. GPS, however gives coordinates in WGS 84 system which is a global geocentric system. The two systems differ and the coordinates will have to be converted into Everest through transformation parameters. It is, however, of paramount importance that all cadastral surveys and mapping is done on one datum, which is Everest Spheroid for India. All the states which have not adopted any datum or are surveying arbitrarily, will have to adopt the datum for uniformity and proper integration of surveys/data.

## PROJECTION/GRID SYSTEM

Mapping is carried out on a three-dimensional earth's surface/reference surface whereas maps are produced on a two-dimensional plane surface. This is done through map projections. Some distortions in angles, distances, shapes or area take place which are taken into consideration for choice of a projection system. The projection system is also necessary for digitisation and computerisation of land records (CoLR).

Some of the states, for example, Tamil Nadu, Andhra Pradesh, etc., have adopted a projection known as cassini projection. This projection is suitable for small areas, that is, nearly 60 to 70 km on either side of central meridian. Each district, therefore, had a different origin thus having a number of coordinate systems in one state. It is therefore, advisable to adopt transverse mercator/UTM or lambert conformal conic projection. These two projections are excellent projections used extensively all over the world and suitable for large areas covering any one full state of India. These are conformal (shapes are preserved) and have minimal scale distortion. It is therefore recommended that one of these two projections be adopted by each state. There will be only one origin, one coordinate system and one type of seamless data for each state so as to have easy integration of data for LIS/GIS. A regulation will be necessary that not only cadastral survey but all types of surveys to be carried out in that particular plane coordinate system of the state.

We have designed a number of grids for various states in Lambert conformal conic projection, namely Tamil Nadu grid, Andhra Pradesh grid, Karnataka grid, Maharashtra grid, Gujarat grid.[1]

Various cadastral survey conferences have deliberated on the projection to be used for cadastral surveys. The 12th All India Cadastral Survey Conference constituted a committee headed by the additional surveyor general of Survey of India, with some Directors, Land Records as members, to standardise framework, projection, scale, contents, symbols and accuracy in respect of cadastral surveys and mapping. Unfortunately, nothing has come out of the same. It is recommended that transverse mercator or Lambert conformal conic be adopted by various states depending upon whether their extent is North-South or East-West. It is not difficult to decide on other matters, e.g., framework, scale, accuracy, etc.

## METHODS OF SURVEY

Conventional as well as modern methods are being used. At present we will discuss modern methods. Photogrammetric survey has been adopted by some states, for example, Madhya Pradesh and Orissa(Angul Nalco project). It appears that Andhra Pradesh is not happy with photogrammetric survey. Orissa has tried Angul Nalco in association with R&D Directorate of Survey of India.

### GPS and Total Station

GPS and Total stations are modern surveying tools, capable of surveys of required accuracy, economically, efficiently and speedily. GPS is space-based method whereas total station is a combination of EDM and

Theodolite. Both are user-friendly for creation of LIS and GIS. GPS can be used as a total station also. GPS in relative mode should be used for providing main control up to village boundary. Total stations can then be used for survey land parcels and other details. This has been tried in Survey Training Institute during training of officer trainees. One should, however, have sufficient knowledge and training in GPS to know its utility as well as drawbacks. Conventional instruments and methods can also be used in combination with modern methods in order to get the best results depending upon various situations and availability of instruments, manpower and funds. One should first define the aim, and plan to achieve the same with minimum expenditure of time and money.

## ACCURACY

Accuracy (relative) of the present cadastral survey maps varies from 1:100 to 1:1000 at the most which is insufficient. International standards for cadastral survey is from 1:20000 to 1:100000 . In India the main control for cadastral surveys should be 1:20000; subsidiary control 1:10000 and ordinary traverse control/survey with total station better than 1:1000. This will take care of surveys in towns also where cost of land is very high. All corner points in towns should be established with accuracy of 1–5 cm whereas in villages it could be up to 20 cm. State control on which main control is based, should be of the order of 1:100000. Instrumentation and methods of survey are based on the desired accuracy. It will greatly help if control in each state is provided with GPS or otherwise as given below with permanent monuments as control points:

| Distance | Accuracy |
|---|---|
| 50 km apart | 1: 100000 |
| 20 km apart | 1: 20000 |
| 5 km apart | 1: 10000 |
| 2 km apart | 1: 5000 |

# CARTOGRAPHIC DESIGN/MAPPING AND DIGITISATION OF DOCUMENTS

These are not being discussed here. Standard procedures are available. A technical committee can go into these to standardise the procedures in respect of cadastral surveys/maps.

# INTEGRATION OF DATA AND CREATION OF LIS/GIS

Digitisation and then integration of data for LIS pose problems if the data is not seamless. We have various types of data, for example, with or without datum, projection system, accuracy, quality, standards, etc. It will be a nightmare to integrate the data, as the metadata (data about data) is not available. The following data about data should always be asked for:

1. datum;
2. projection system;
3. date of survey/capture of data;
4. accuracy of survey/data;
5. parameters of datum and projection system ;
6. instruments used;
7. adjustment procedure; and
8. method of collection of data.

The requirement of cadastral survey for any one state is given below:

1. data in one datum;
2. data in one projection system ;
3. seamless digital data;
4. appropriate methodology; and
5. legal sanction with a mandate to carry out all surveys as per above regulations.

The creation of LIS or GIS will then not pose any difficulty.

## TRAINING

Lack of training is the greatest problem. We just go in for new technology and buy new instruments without proper preparation, planning, knowledge and training. This creates a lot of problems and loss/delay. It is therefore appropriate that manpower should be developed by proper training. Survey Training Institute of Survey of India can give training to instructors, who in turn can give training to others in State Survey Training Institutes. Short courses in GPS and modern technology should also be attended by executives and administrators, who are decision makers, so that they may be able to take correct decisions.

## CONCLUSION

We should adopt one grid/projection for each state; construct survey monuments 2 km apart; provide control by GPS all over the state; create data bank; recruit and train the required manpower in phases; standardise and adopt survey/mapping procedures; enact legal laws if necessary and create LIS/GIS for better decision making and development.

## NOTE

1. Details are available with the author, who can help in case any state wants to adopt a particular grid.

## SELECT BIBLIOGRAPHY

Agrawal, N.K. (1998a). 'Abandon Polyconic Projection', *GIS India* 7(1): 38–40.
———. (1998b). 'Andhra Pradesh Grid for Cadastral Surveys', *GIS India* 7(2): 18–20.
———. (2001). 'Data Capture', *GIS India* 10(5): 19–21.

# 15

# *Digitisation of Cadastral Maps in Madhya Pradesh*

M.K. AGARWAL

## BACKGROUND

Computerisation of land records in Madhya Pradesh commenced in 1988.The initial computerisation process encompassed the start-up use of modern administrative practices to facilitate and eventually replace the traditional system of land records management. Initially the process involved the use of computer to enter the land and related data from the *khasra*. The attributes related to all aspects of khasra and landholding are available with the *patwari* and the government. This was basically textual data and was entered through a programme made using Clipper and Dbase. Since all the information that was to be computerised had to be in the vernacular, GIST technology was used to enable the Hindi environment. The programme enabled all information as it is to be entered in the computer. The reporting and printing options enabled the printing and subsequent distribution of khasra copies. The programme was installed and made available at the *tehsil* and the updated data was consistent with the manual records of the patwari. The copies of the map were still distributed by making a manual copy of the selected plot/polygon.

The next logical step in computerisation of land records is this enabling of spatial component of the data to digitised from the cadastral maps and put on the computer. Various guidelines/directions have been issued by the Ministry of Rural Development in this regard for overall computerisation of land records. The ultimate aim, as envisaged in various documents, is the creation and successful implementation of a 'Online Land Information System'. The structure and record-keeping of land records is different in each of the states and varies as per the way the local records of rights are kept. The state of Madhya Pradesh also follows a unique system of the maintenance of land records and related cadastral maps.

These cadastral maps available with the patwari are the only source of information for the spatial component/visual component of the landholding information. These cadastral maps have been made after a detailed survey and subsequent updating based on transfer or division of landholding. Subsequent updating of these records is also made whenever survey of the land is done. These cadastral maps and their copies also find acceptance in a Court of Law for all matters of dispute pertaining to location and position on ground. The corresponding information about ownership and other details is made available from the khasra copies.

## PILOT PROJECT

In continuation of the centrally sponsored drive for the computerisation of land records in 1999 pilot projects were sanctioned by the Ministry of Rural Development, Government of India for digitisation of village-level cadastral maps on experimental basis in selected states. In Madhya Pradesh the same was taken up for Raghogarh tehsil of Guna district and Shivpuri tehsil of Shivpuri district. Initially, four vendors were identified for sample digitisation covering these two tehsils. The four vendors worked on four different platforms, namely, ArcInfo, AutoCAD Map, MapInfo and Microsation.

# OBJECTIVES

Although the project was financed by the Ministry of Rural Development no specific objectives were set at the national level. In Madhya Pradesh it was started keeping in mind the following objectives:

- Valuable ancient land records which form the backbone for land revenue administration can be preserved for longer period.
- Creation of computerised LIS for efficient storage, easy retrieval and prompt updating of cadastral information.
- Quicker response for meeting public demand for maps and providing accurate and updated records.
- Transparency in records to minimise the evils of interpolation.
- To develop an LIS to enable the optimum use of land resources, and facilitate better decision making in the planning process.
- A system easy to integrate with other computerised systems like registration, forests, electricity, education, health, etc.

# PROCESS/METHODOLOGY

The overall process was divided into the following steps:

1. scanning of cadastral maps
2. digitisation of cadastral maps in a number of layers such as:

   - village boundary, railway line and road network (all types)
   - rivers, canals and water bodies
   - plot boundaries
   - plot (khasra numbers) etc.

3. edge-matching and verification of the cadastral maps
4. acquisition of DOS-based GIST textual data

- plot number, ownership, area, crop, revenue, land type, irrigation pattern, etc.
5. linking of textual data to digitised data
6. application software for queries and printout of the cadastral maps as per requirements

Since this was the first such process in the state, to facilitate the identified four vendors provided working space for scanning and photocopy of the cadastral maps within the premise of the Office of the Commissioner Land Records. Textual DOS GIST format data was provided to them for attachment to the digitised cadastral maps.The maximum error permissible for the process of digitisation of the cadastral maps from those of the original maps is 0.01mm. No error was permitted for the linking of the DOS GIST textual data to the digitised cadastral maps.Entire work was completed in one year's time and data were finally handed over to the *tehsildar* of respective tehsils. The flowchart of map digitisation process can be seen in Figure 15.1.

**Figure 15.1**

*Flowchart of Map Digitisation Process*

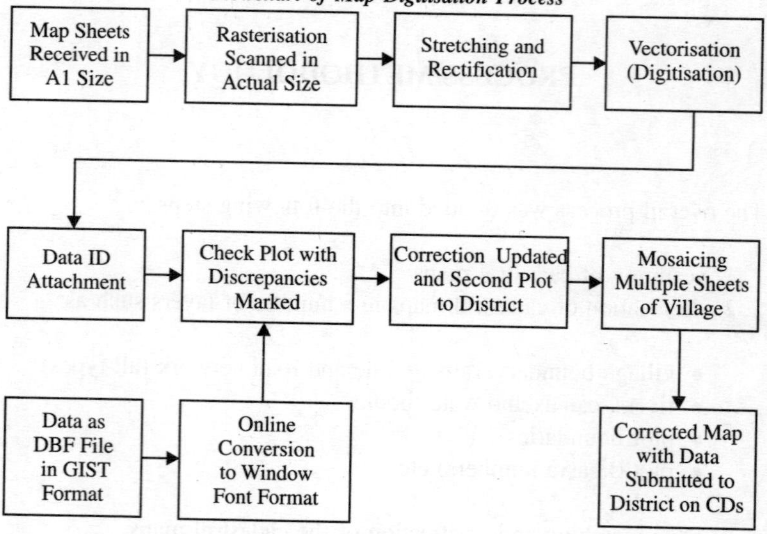

## RESULT: IMMENSELY BENEFICIAL TO LANDHOLDER

Although the computerised RoR system was implemented in Madhya Pradesh in 1988, copies of map were being distributed by making a manual copy of the selected area/plot. After the digitisation of maps in Raghogarh and Shivpuri tehsils any selected khasra (plot) map can at random be printed alongwith the adjoining khasras on an A4 size paper. This A4 size printout also contains the details of district/tehsil/village name, khasra number, owner's and father's name, area, scale of the map, etc. Separate format has been devised for the government land. Government of Madhya Pradesh has given legal sanctity to it by amending the copying rules in the year 2000.

## A POWERFUL TOOL FOR DECISION MAKERS

The spatial and non-spatial data, together with the developed application tool with GIS interface, is helping tehsil and district administration in various useful aspects of land management.These are:

1. locating plot(s) belonging to person(s) on the basis of name, father's name, caste, etc.;
2. locating multiple plots of a person;
3. division of plot based on various criteria;
4. faster updating and presentation of data (spatial and non-spatial);
5. planning of crop pattern;
6. planning of irrigation pattern;
7. planning of revenue generation;
8. land acquisition;
9. development of existing and planning of new structures;
10. finding of land use like, residential, commercial, industrial, water bodies etc.;

11. generating of reports for higher officials/management with adequate maps; and
12. generating a component for MIS at state/national level.

Sample screen of the customised software is shown in Figure 15.2.

**Figure 15.2**

*Sample Screen of Customised Software*

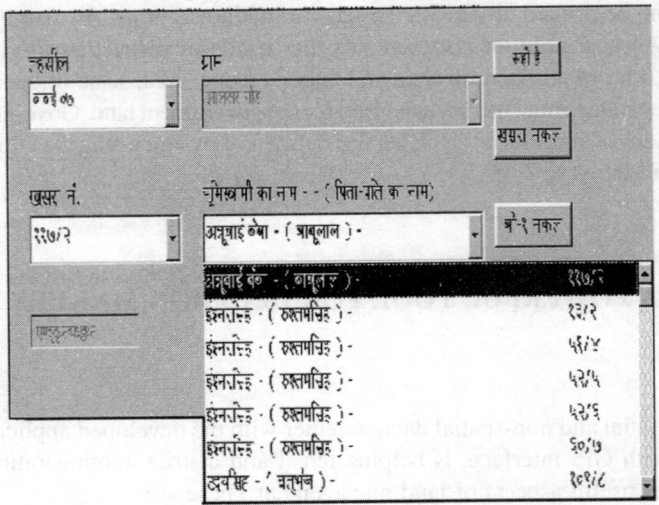

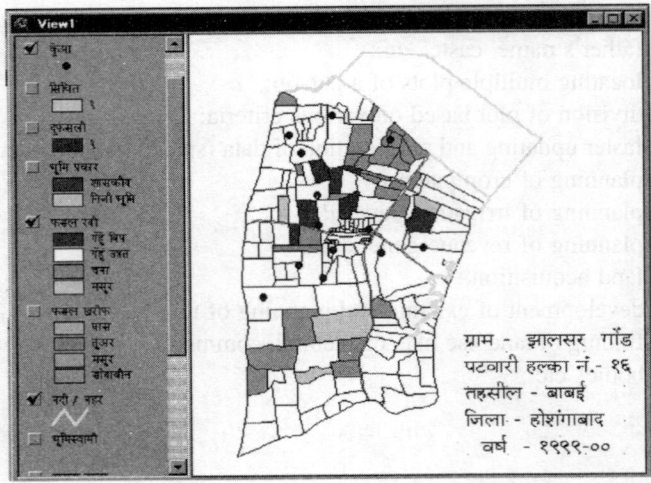

## COMPARATIVE STUDY OF GIS PLATFORM USED AND SUITABILITY OF PLATFORM FOR FUTURE

It may be noted that the Geographical Information System field is evolving and there is a great need to evaluate and ascertain true needs and finances before making a decision. The various GIS platforms available in the market offer functionality and features which are far greater than the need of the department.

Our requirements primarily relate to:

1. digitisation of land records from base khasra maps;
2. correlation of these components with non-spatial(text) data;
3. generation of khasra maps as per requirements; and
4. GIS-related analysis for the purpose of better administration.

The top two requirements, namely, digitisation of land records and correlation of the spatial data with non-spatial data are very generic in nature and nearly all GIS platforms will suit our needs. The other two requirements are very specific in nature and have to be specially designed and developed as an application for land records and cannot be extracted directly from any existing GIS platform, whether those evaluated or those not evaluated but available in the market. The GIS platform and the application surrounding it has to be customised and developed as per needs and requirements.

The second most important issue is to evaluate and give a detailed thought on the number of instances ( copies ) of the software of such applications which will run in the whole state and their compatibility issues. The replicability of the system and solution within the parameters of cost, ease of use, time of development, time of deployment, ease of installation, etc., have to be kept in mind before making any decision. Any single solution which involves purchase of a full and complete GIS may be very complex and would also involve factors wherein the cost–usage parameters may not be justifiable.

All good GIS platforms come in basically three variants. These are:

1. full software version with a possibility of add-on modules;
2. run-time version with nearly all functionality; and
3. components which can be integrated into other third party front-end development tools.

After evaluation of the ongoing projects, it is recommended that *a component-based model is best suited for our requirements*. This model will also be the best in terms of the future use of the department. The objects can be integrated in the single application and can be easily deployed by a single installation, obviating the need to deploy, configure and maintain more than one software environment for the single usage and application.

# CONCLUSION

The generation of the base map and attachment of attribute data not only help revenue administration but also the landholder and other government organisations, providing multiple usage of one-time effort. Looking at the result of the pilot project, the state government is very enthusiastic and has made a detailed plan for the digitisation of all the available cadastral maps in the state. The time has come when all the land records information in Madhya Pradesh will be available at the click of a mouse. Land records information management will be easier and faster.

# 16

## Do We Need a Digital Cadastre?

S. SURESH KUMAR

## HISTORICAL BACKGROUND

Cadastral surveys are as old as the start of civilisation when people gave up shifting cultivation and started settling in river valleys for the purposes of cultivation. The *Arthashastra* mentions the system of land administration through a specialised class of officers. The earliest land surveys undertaken by the state were principally for revenue assessment. The earliest known land survey was carried out 1,000 years ago by the Chola king Raja-Raja the Great. Attempt to reform the system was first made by Sher Shah through the classification of land and fixing of schedule of rates for the land according to types of crops. This revenue survey was further refined in the reign of Akbar with the assistance of Raja Todar Mal. The monetisation of revenue, hitherto in the form of share of produce, took root. Elaborate methods were devised for determining the average produce of each class of land and for commuting grain rates into money rates. This rational and scientific basis incidentally resembles the British system closely. The British started the Ryotwari Settlement surveys in

For all figures in lakhs and crores, please note that 1 lakh = 100,000 and 1 crore = 10,000,000.

Salem district of the then Madras Presidency during 1793–98. Subsequently in 1822, regulations were introduced for detailed surveys and regulations, revenue surveys initiated by the East India Company continued in its domains even after the Crown took over the domain after the 1857 Mutiny but with some further legislation regarding land tenancy. The Survey of India (SOI) which was established in 1767 was involved in the process of preparation of all maps necessary for administration of the sub-continent until 1904 when the cadastral surveys were delegated to the states on the recommendations of a committee of the Government of India. This led to the evolution of various revenue surveys but the initial inputs were given by SOI officials on deputation.

Distinctly, this led to the evolution of two systems of survey: (a) the village-map-based system; and (b) the field-management book (FMB)-based system. The village-map-based system prevailed in the northern states of UP, MP, West Bengal, Orissa, Rajasthan and Punjab where the Mahalwari and Zamindari revenue settlement systems were prevalent while the southern ryotwari states of Andhra Pradesh, Tamil Nadu, Karnataka, Kerala and Maharashtra followed the FMB system. There were variants in the FMB system, namely the Bombay Survey System and the Madras Survey System. Both systems of revenue settlement have advantages and disadvantages.

The village map in the first system is actually a pictographical representation of the parcels of lands within a well-defined village boundary to a scale. The village boundaries are established through control points by theodolite and the patch work of the fields is generated by surveys by restricting any error within the village boundary by distributing it equally. The map serves as an index to the individual *raiyat*-wise records and there is an organic link between the map and the raiyat-wise records. Distances may be calculated directly from the maps to the required accuracy. Here both the map as well as the records are of equal legal sanctity.

## IMPORTANT TERMS AND THEIR MEANING

*Cadastre:* The International Federation of Surveyors (FIG) defines a cadastre as a parcel-based and up-to-date land information system containing a record of interests in land (for example, rights, restrictions and responsibilities). It usually includes a geometric description of land parcels linked to other records describing the nature of the interests, the ownership or control of those interests, and often value of the parcel and its improvements.

*Digital Cadastral Data Base (DCDB):* This is the complete cadastral framework of parcel/plots shown graphically on a cadastral map, and when computerised is often termed as a digital cadastral data base (DCDB). The coordinates of each parcel corner mirror the true co-ordinates. The DCDB will show all the parcels, that the topology is correct and that the parcel is kept up-to-date.

*Data Digitisation:* Digitisation refers to the conversion of non-digital material into digital form. A wide variety of materials as diverse as maps, manuscripts, images and sound can be digitised.

*Raster Data:* This mainly consists of pixels or a series of black and white dots to represent any object obtained after scanning of an image. The computer cannot recognise what these dots are supposed to represent and hence raster data is normally known as unintelligent data. The advantage and disadvantages are:

1. fastest and most cost-effective method of capturing drawings, minimum initial capture costs;
2. suitable for minor modifications;
3. good for drawing restoration, viewing applications, archiving;
4. as accurate as the original drawing/map;
5. large storage requirements; and
6. poor image quality.

*Vector Data:* This is generated through a process of vectorisation of digit-ising whereby the computer knows the start and end point coordinates of each piece of geometry. Once this is known, the length, angle, line style, colour, etc., drawn in will be known. Attribute data can also be attached to the geometry for further analysis. The process can be done manually by inputting coordinates or electronically by a digitiser whereby the scanned raster image is vectorised. The advantages are:

1. vector data (which is the base data) compatible with all software CAD solutions;
2. easy to edit;
3. more compact storage;
4. better quality than original drawing; and
5. provides seamless integration with other applications like modelling, databases, GIS, etc., for adding attribute data.

*Geographic Information System (GIS):* It is a computer-based tool for the input, storage, management, retrieval, analysis and output of information with relation to their spatial distribution at various stages of information handling. It is a computer-based representation of the real world and provides tools for organising information about spatially defined features. The basic organising principle of a GIS is the data layer. Rather than storing all spatial features in one place, as on a topographic map, groups of similar features are combined in one or a number of these data layers. In addition, GIS software allows us to create new data layers based on existing ones. Hence, it also allows for the integration of fresh data layers within a common reference framework. This ability to integrate data from heterogeneous sources is indeed one of the most important benefits of GIS.

*Land Information System (LIS):* This is defined as the combination of human and technical resources, together with a set of organising procedures, that produces information on land in support of a broad range of managerial requirements. It is also called Land Records System, or Cadastral System. It is built upon the cadastre defined previously. Thus, when the data in the GIS is related to various quantitative and qualitative aspects of land resources, it is termed as computerised LIS.

*National Spatial Data Infrastructure (NSDI):* This means the technologies, policies, standards and human resources necessary to acquire, process, store, distribute and improve utilisation of geo-spatial data.

*Metadata:* Metadata is data about the data. The GIS or DBMS software creates a data dictionary internally to the system to tell the underlying software how to handle the data. Metadata is used to describe the characteristics of the database such as custodian, data description, geographic extent, unsurveyed storage format, data quality, contact information, etc. Metadata system is a form of catalogue which allows users to explore and determine whether the dataset is useful or not without having to go through the data in detail.

*Datasets:* There are abstracts of data replicated from the various databases of land-related agencies that can be made available to land information uses on request in an online real time system.

*Accuracy in Data Digitisation:* This is the most important aspect in digitisation of maps. Spatial accuracy of the features depicted on the map is very important for a good digitised output. The magnitude of error is such that a hairline error of 0.5 mm on a 1:4000 scale map would lead to a difference in the ground measurement of 2,000 mm or 2 m

which can mean a life and death difference for a raiyat. Different types
of errors are:

1. *Geodetic error:* This crops up because of the improper choice of a
   projection system which results in an inaccurate placement of
   features such as that the map and the digitised image do not overlap
   each other.
2. *Machine error:* This is an inherent error which cannot be removed
   but can only be minimised. This occurs at the stage of scanning
   process, during the digitisation process and the printing of the map
   itself.
3. *Cartographic errors:* There are errors which are present in the
   source map itself and which get transferred into the digital form of
   the map/image.
4. *Manuscript errors:* These are introduced due to the quality of the
   source maps. Paper maps and images are known to shrink with
   time. Any warping, stretching, folding or wrinkling of the original
   map/image will affect the digitisation process as proper coordinates
   of such map/image cannot be placed.
5. *Operator introduced errors:* The quality of digitisation greatly
   depends on the operator. An experienced digitisor can digitise the
   maps/images with more accuracy and speed as compared to a
   novice.

## PRESENT STATUS OF LAND RECORDS
## AND LIS IN INDIA

After the transfer of the responsibility of conducting cadastral surveys
was given to the Provinces of British India in 1905, survey and settlement
operations started in most cases which were more or less completed
around the time of Independence in 1947. Subsequently, very few states
carried out fresh survey and settlement operations and most states either
undertook revisional surveys or progressively updated the maps and
records. Recognising the importance of land records and realising the
deficiencies in the cadastral system, the planners advocated proper
maintenance of land records as the basis for good administration in the

First Five-Year Plan and subsequently in the Second and Third Five Year Plans also. The Sixth Plan laid down a target of five years from 1980–85 for completion and updating of land records. The Seventh Plan while re-emphasising the need for updated land records also advocated induction of the latest technology and scientific survey of unsurveyed land. Towards achieving these objectives, a few pilot projects were taken up using various technologies for generating cadastral maps. Computerisation of land records which was started under a centrally sponsored scheme in the Seventh Plan continued through the Eighth, Ninth and Tenth Plans. The programme of digitisation of cadastral maps was started in 1998–99.

The present-day land records have thus hardly undergone much change and are under severe strain to serve the planning and developmental requirements of the present economy. A few of the reasons are:

- The accuracy of the original cadastral surveys, which were carried out based on the technology and accuracy standards relevant at that time, are wholly inadequate now due to rapid fragmentation of land parcels coupled with rising land prices.
- The present-day land records were mostly framed with revenue mobilisation in mind by the British, and even though they are scientifically sound they are not in tune with the current planning and developmental imperatives.
- The land records at the most confirm the factum of possession but do not necessarily provide the guarantee to the title.
- They can be quite outdated at times and may not reflect the ground realities, namely correct title, correct boundary and correct area.
- The crop statistics related to it are only very rudimentary and do not provide the accurate inputs required for micro-level and macro-level developmental activities.
- The generation and maintenance of land records is quite cumber-some, requiring such an elaborate land administration and signifi-cant expenditure that state governments have found it difficult to conduct timely maintenance and updating.
- There has been a proliferation of land-related litigation due to the apathy of landowners for correct delimitation of plot boundaries and recording of their title, which in turn has not led to an effective maintenance of records.
- The lack of standardised practice has led to serious mismatch of maps prepared in various scales with different attributes and this is

a serious barrier to the creation of a national geo-spatial data infrastructure.

● The existing land records do not have any interrelation with the system of registration of title and both are absolutely independent of each other. This is partly due to the existing separation of the administration of land management and land registration.


## PROBLEMS FACED BY PILOT PROJECT ON DIGITISATION OF CADASTRAL MAPS


Presently, the pilot projects are running in the states of Andhra Pradesh, Kerala, Orissa, Bihar, Tamil Nadu, West Bengal, Maharashtra, Uttar Pradesh, Gujarat, Madhya Pradesh, Pondicherry, Karnataka, Goa, Punjab, Jammu & Kashmir, Manipur, Mizoram, Nagaland and Haryana. On an average Rs 30–40 lakh had been invested in these projects and they are in various stages of completion. There has been a persistent complaint that the projects have not lived up to their expectations since their initiation in the year 1998–99. Hence there has been a feeling that the process should even be abandoned. The many problems bedevilling these projects are listed below:

1. *The problem of excessive expectations:* There has been a perception that digitisation of maps would be a straightforward process which would take the least possible time and expense. However, the problem has become acute in a few cases due to a number of factors. Hence there is a wide gap between the expectations and the actual performance.

2. *The size and quality of maps available:* Most of the FMBs or the village-level maps are on paper which with time and exposure to the environment leads to significant deterioration and degeneration. The size of maps also is a significant factor in some of the states where the map is A0 or A1 in size and in other states it is A4 size. Hence the quality of scanning varies due to the manuscript errors as mentioned earlier. Scanning on A4 size map is far easier than an A0 or A1 size map due to the plethora of high resolution scanners available for the former size whereas the large format scanners do not support such high resolutions.

3. *Accuracy of digitisation:* Computer Aided Design (CAD) projects in the country are still in their infancy and mostly are involved in digitising engineering drawings which mostly involve straight lines unlike cadastral maps which involve a high degree of topology and topology building. The digitising operators upon whom digitisation depends have not yet reached optimum levels of competence and they are still learning. Accuracy features have been discussed previously and it can be re-iterated that under no circumstances the overall accuracy of the digitised output can be compromised.

4. *Quality of equipment:* Scanners are the primary source of error. Roller scanners introduce a skew factor in the digitised output due to any form of unevenness in the sheet being digitised. The best flat-bed scanners available give an accuracy of 0.5 per cent to 1 per cent against the minimum requirement of 0.25 per cent accuracy. The GIS software such as AutoCAD 2000 or SPANS or ARCInfo or MapInfo are built around engineering drawing and design applications and not with map digitisation in mind which requires some customisation through a trial and error process. Even the best large format HP printers available can introduce an error if not calibrated properly and inherently they do add an unavoidable error into the final printout used for physical inspection. The best equipment presently available in market are the VIDAR AO colour scanner at 400–800 DPI resolution and HP 1050 AO Plotter which support the required specifications. The price of the equipment itself is Rs 10 lakh for the scanner and Rs 4.5 lakh for the plotter which are too expensive to be purchased by any individual agency involved in the project.

5. *Length of the learning curve:* The apparently inordinate time taken in the process of implementation of the pilot project is a cause for concern. However, this is a virgin area which was not supported by adequate technology in the initial stages. Technology requiring such an accuracy was initially not in the mind of the manufacturers also. It was only after some technological breakthrough made in the basic equipment and after improvements made in the raster to vector (R2V) software that the specifications have become attainable. Moreover, even the process itself involved some understanding on the part of the institution and the agencies involved as to the exact scope of work. During this trial and error process without much

assistance from any specialised agency having previous experience in this field, the programme did meander a bit but has now stabilised all over. Hence the apprehension that the pilot project is not leading to a conceivable destination has not been proved yet.

6. *Costs involved:* The cost of digitisation involved was never clearly assessed at any point of time. This issue was handled without any previous experience as to the exact scope of work, the quantum of work involved and the other imponderable problems which cropped up from time to time. Hence often the estimated cost of digitisation of a unit map was far below the rate finalised towards the time of awarding the contract to the agencies. The variation in rates fluctuated widely from state to state depending on the quantum of work involved. Even the present rate offered has not led to any appreciable benefit to the agencies due to the high initial cost of investment, the energy and time involved in customising their knowledge for digitising cadastral maps. However, as the technology has reached a plateau of development there is a better chance of obtaining appreciable low rates in the near future even to the extent of half the existing rates!

## RATIONALE FOR THE DIGITISATION OF MAPS

The current paper-based or manual system involves the problems of preservation, updating, retrieval and creation.

### Preservation

The paper maps are in extremely poor shape and are falling apart in most cases. Duplication on similar media is again cumbersome and will lead to similar problems in the near future. Microfilming has a limited objective and can only preserve the image and no value addition or improvement can be effected further. Scanning of documents has also a similar limitation, the data is only graphically represented and cannot be queried as a structured data such as in a database and is also, therefore, essentially a paper-based system. Hence, the maintenance of vast amounts of paper documents is both costly and time-consuming.

## Updating

The updating of boundaries caused by mutation and other title information manually is an extremely tedious and cumbersome process. The maintenance of an infrastructure to continue with the process involves an extremely high cost. Moreover, the limitation of the paper-based system are such that continuous cross-verification of records is required over long periods of time to ensure absence of inconsistencies after updating.

## Retrieval

Sadly even after the expense of, and time spent on manually creating a system, the particular record may not be available when required. Frequent handling also has a deleterious effect on the records and could damage them.

## Creation

Use of efficient new technology is restricted and new data layers cannot be created with the same ease as is possible with digitisation of maps.

# APPLICATION OF MAPS

Maps are an extremely powerful medium for planning, analysis and monitoring of execution of large projects and the ease of their availability has a force multiplier effect in their utilisation in micro-level planning or in macro-level planning. In micro-level planning the analysis extends to the evaluation of data of a specific area of interest like in land management, land reforms, consolidation of land, urban planning, irrigation, groundwater development, rural development schemes, etc.; and in macro-level planning the evaluation of statewide policies regarding fiscal analysis, planning, agriculture projections, etc.

# MODUS OPERANDI FOR THE IMPLEMENTATION OF FUTURE PROJECTS IN DIGITISATION OF MAPS

Presently the Land Reforms Department in the Ministry of Rural Development is the sole authority to authorise and sanction projects. There is a limitation to this administrative arrangement as a mission mode approach cannot be taken up and is presently devoid of any technical personnel or specialist to authorise and then monitor the programme. There is an urgent necessity to bring about some form of standardisation in practices and to coordinate the activities of many agencies and departments. It is hence imperative that a national mission on the lines of the National Literacy Mission with multidisciplinary personnel is created for the pooling of expertise and optimal utilisation of resources. It is recommended that a digitisation sub-group is at least formed with the following terms of reference.

1. to exchange information on digitisation activities and initiatives within the various government and non-government institution;
2. to examine strategies and best practices in management across the institutions;
3. to explore possibilities for developing and adopting common standards and specification for digitisation, especially with a view to promoting inter-operability; and

4. to explore opportunities for shared business arrangements, including the potential for common service providers or provision of services between institutions.

The principles of digitisation to be followed by the sub-group are as follows:

- *Goal-directed:* The decisions regarding how and what to digitise will vary according to the goals of the project. Decisions about quality and quantity will be bounded by priorities, goals and available resources.
- *Institutional policy driver:* The programme should reflect the strategic and operational goals of the institutions and should reflect the internal policies regarding collections, access, preservation and marketing.
- *Long-term thinking:* Digitisation is a complex and expensive process. It should avoid cheap short-term solutions and avoid using formats of limited longevity.
- *Elimination of duplication:* Double handling and unnecessary duplications of products have to be eliminated.
- *Integration of digitisation into the institutional activities:* It is desirable that digitisation should be seen as a part of a larger routine process rather than an isolated separate activity.
- *Collaboration:* Collaboration with other institutions and commercial partners can contribute to minimising duplication of efforts, improving access and improving knowledge about the process of digitisation.

**Table 16.1**

*Specifications to be Adopted for Digitisation of Maps and Other Usual Media*

| Specification area | Suggested minimum specification and practices |
| --- | --- |
| File format | SHP/TIFF or any latest version |
| Resolution (in pixels) | Not less than 400 DPI |
| File naming | Each file should have a unique identifier |
| Cross-platform requirements | Content should be readable across AC Info, SPANS, etc. |
| Accuracy | Specify according best practices |
| Handling/Case of original | Specify according best practices |
| Non-map features | As per institutional requirement |
| Data layers | Can be any number such as plot, area, non-map features, etc., as per institutional requirement |

The existing pilot projects have been completed but these are still to be implemented. Future map digitisation projects should be closely scrutinised by the national mission or the constituted digitisation sub-group before the sanction of the proposal.

The international experience in financing this form of project has been contrary to expectations. In an economy where privatisation and commercialisation have acquired a deep significance, it is rather surprising that all the projects have been treated as infrastructure projects and have been totally funded by the government. It has always been felt that the new information service is a new and emerging infrastructure which is essential for the well-being of society and is dependent on the energy and transportation sectors. The USA, UK and Australia have pioneered work in digitisation and have three different models. In the USA it has been totally federally funded and in the UK partly by the Ordnance Survey and partly through some private participation.

In other countries such as Singapore, Malaysia, New Zealand and some European countries it has been a mixture of federal and state involvement. The funding model for India should be a centre–state equal sharing model which is already in operation under the SRAULR (Strengthening of Revenue Administration and Updating of Land Records) Scheme.

## INTERNATIONAL EXPERIENCE

The international experience is totally devoid of any Indian presence. There is neither an academic with knowledge of some statutes who is well used to the theory and practice of cadastral systems nor an expert on the latest applications involved in the cadastral system. The Declaration of the FIG (International Federation of Surveyors) at Melbourne in 1994 reflected a vision of the cadastre in 2014.

Cadastre 2014 will have the following features:

- It will show the complete legal situation of land, private or public; rights and restrictions on land will be systematically documented.
- The separation between maps and registers will be abolished.
- Cadastral mapping will be replaced by modelling through computers.

- Paper-and-pencil-derived cadastre will no longer exist.
- Cadastre 2014 will be highly privatised. The private sector will gain importance. The public sector will concentrate on supervision and control.
- Cadastre 2014 will be cost-recovering.

Efforts to create a digital cadastral database (DCDB) had been pioneered in USA and closely followed by the UK in the mid-1970s. In Australia and New Zealand the creation of the DCDB was started in early 1980s and was completed by the end of the 1980s. Malaysia and Singapore started on the development of DCDBs in mid-1980s. Other European states such as the Netherlands and Sweden have not only created DCDBs but are in the process of setting up NSDIs (National Spatial Data Infrastructures) throughout their countries. India in this respect has remained totally aloof from all developments and is yet to reach a position of competence.

## REFERENCES AND SELECT BIBLIOGRAPHY

**Bin Mohammed, Abdul Majid.** 'Case Study of NSDIs in Countries in Transition—Malaysia'. Paper presented at workshop on 'Policy and Organizational Frameworks for GSDI', GSDI Association, Canberra, Australia.

**Blakemore, Michael.** (2001). 'Financing the NGDI', paper submitted at workshop on NGDI, 5–6 February, New Delhi.

**Cadastre 2014.** Report of FIG Commission at *www.swisstopo.ch/fig-wg71/cad2014.htm*

**Dasgupta, A.R.** (2001). 'National Geo-Spatial Data Infrastructure: Theories and Technologies', paper submitted at workshop on NGDI, 5–6 February, New Delhi.

**Mathan, Rahul.** (2001). 'The Proposed Legislation Constituting the NGDI—Legal Issues, Concept Note', paper submitted at workshop on NGDI, 5–6 February, New Delhi.

**Mishra, Prabhakar.** (2000). 'Cadastral Surveys in India—A Critique', paper presented at National Conference on LIS, 18–19 October.

**Nori, Chandrasekhar.** (2000). 'Development Oriented Land Administration in India—A Case for National LIS', paper presented at National Conference on LIS, 18–19 October.

**Potdar, V.B.** (2000). 'Land Information System in the Present Day Context', paper presented at National Conference on LIS, 18–19 October.

**Raja Rao, T.** (2000). 'LIS—Issues, Technologies and Standardization', paper presented at National Conference on LIS, 18–19 October.

**Rajkhowa, P.K.** (2000). 'Policy Issues in a National LIS', paper presented at National Conference on LIS, 18–19 October.

**Rao, M. Gopal.** (2000). 'LIS in India—Perspective and Retrospective', paper presented at National Conference on LIS, 18–19 October.

**Rhind, David.** (2001). 'Lessons Learned from Local, National and Global Spatial Data Infrastructures', paper submitted at workshop on NGDI, 5–6 February, New Delhi.

**Siddiqui, Kamal.** (1997). *Land Management in South Asia.* New Delhi: Manohar.

**Vision Document for the Computerisation of Land Records.** (1999). Ministry of Rural Development, Government of India.

**Warn, W.Y.** and **Ian Williamson.** 'A review of the Digital Cadastral Databases in Australia and New Zealand', *at www.sli.Unimelb,edu.An/research/Publications/ipw/*

# 17

# Modern Technology in Survey and Settlement Operations in West Bengal

## C.R. DAS

## INTRODUCTION

The state of West Bengal has a rich history of cadastral mapping, which was conducted on the basis of scientific survey initiated in 1888. The method of surveying and scale of mapping was uniform throughout the state (the then undivided Bengal) and achieved a remarkable degree of accuracy. Bengal was one of the states in eastern India where land records were prepared as per Permanent Settlement regulations invoked by the British East India Company in 1793.

## BRIEF BACKGROUND OF SURVEY AND SETTLEMENT OPERATIONS IN WEST BENGAL

The first series of cadastral maps, covering the entire state, was prepared during the District Survey and Settlement Operations of 1888–1940 for implementing the provisions of the Bengal Tenancy Act, 1885. A revisional survey and settlement operation was conducted mainly during 1954–62, under the West Bengal Estate Acquisition Act, 1953 in which district settlement maps and records were revised and updated. Presently, the survey and settlement operation for land reforms, under the West Bengal Land Reforms Act, 1955, which has been going on since 1972 by updating revisional survey maps and records, is nearing completion. Due to rapid urbanisation and industrial development, fresh mapping is being carried out in many areas, mainly in towns, due to change of topography.

## METHODOLOGY FOR CADASTRAL MAPPING IN WEST BENGAL

The unit of survey for cadastral mapping and preparation of land records in West Bengal is a *mauza* (a revenue village). In the cadastral maps, the property boundaries of individual ownership, including depiction of separate plots for different classes of land with the same periphery of ownership are shown by ground survey in the mauza. *Distance and planimetric area of land are extracted from the map itself, as no dimension of the plots are mentioned in the cadastral maps. Separate map for individual plots or survey numbers, showing dimension of sides or diagonals given, are not prepared in the state.* As such, accuracy in survey and plotting are of prime importance in this form of cadastral mapping. The area of mauza varies from 100 acres to 12,000 acres and plot numbers vary from 20 to 20,000. The number of sheets covering one mauza depends upon the area of the mauza, the average area shown in a single sheet being 100 to 350 acres. There are 66,385 such cadastral sheets covering 42,301 mauzas of the state as per current settlement operation. All maps are of 30"×22" size or more (A1 to A0 size).

Following the survey principle of 'from whole to part', a mauza under survey is first subjected to theodolite traverse for establishing control points of high accuracy (normally 1: 1000) and then ground details are subsequently surveyed and plotted on the basis of those control points by plane table or chain survey ( accuracy 1:200). The main circuit of the theodolite traverse follows the boundary of the mauza, so that the periphery of the mauza is accurately surveyed and the area of the mauza

258 • C.R. DAS

correctly determined. Astronomical observations are taken at regular intervals for determination of azimuths of survey lines in respect of the true north and the traverse survey is connected with the local great triangulation survey (GTS) pillars for determination of accuracy of the survey. The main circuit is further divided into sub-circuits, sub-traverse (ST) and open ST lines to provide adequate number of control point on the ground for facilitating the survey and plotting of property boundaries (or plots) and other details to be surveyed inside the mauza for cadastral purposes. The total number of control points may range from 200 to 10,000, depending upon the area of the mauza and scale of survey.

The scales of cadastral mapping are 16"=1 mile (1:3960) for rural areas, 32"=1 mile (1:1980) for semi-urban areas, 64"=1 mile (1:990), 128"=1 mile (1:495) and 1"=50 feet (1:600) for urban areas.

## SURVEY SET-UP IN WEST BENGAL

Theodolite traverse survey is conducted in the mauzas in different districts, by the surveyors of the West Bengal Traverse Party under the Directorate of Land Records and Surveys, as per requisition of the district land and land reforms officers (erstwhile settlement officers). The surveyors, who are trained at Government Survey Training Institutes, do the field work and send the field data for computation of coordinates of the control stations and preparation of survey plot sheets by the computers at the directorate. The plot sheets are then sent to the district offices for detailed survey by chain survey method.

## INTRODUCTION OF MODERN SURVEY EQUIPMENTS

From the mid-1950s till 1990, traverse survey for cadastral mapping was conducted with conventional vernier theodolites with least count of 20" (made by the companies Stanley, Maughm, and Hilger & Watts) for angle measurements and steel band chains for distance measurement.

In 1990–91, the following modern survey equipment were inducted in the West Bengal cadastral surveys under the centrally sponsored schemes, for higher accuracy and speed.

1. eighteen micro-optic glass-arc T–2 precision theodolites with least count of 1" (of Wild Heerbrug make) for angular measurement;
2. eighteen NI–450 Electronic Distance Measurement (EDM) with 5mm+5 ppm accuracy for distance measurement, to work in tandem with the T–2 theodolites;
3. one T–2000 electronic total station theodolite (of Wild Heerbrug) of 1" accuracy; and
4. one DI–1000 EDM with 5 mm +5 ppm to work in tandem with the T–2000 total station.

During 1999–2001, additional equipment was procured as follows:

1. one TC–1800 electronic total station theodolite (of Leica-Wild) of 1" accuracy; and
2. four DI–1600 distomats (accuracy 2 mm+2 ppm) with GTS–5 attachments (of Leica-Wild) to work in tandem with the T–2 theodolites. The T–2 theodolite + DI–1600 + GTS combination works as a Total Station.

The above mentioned survey instruments became the standard equipment of the West Bengal Traverse Party immediately on acquisition, as the trained surveyors could adopt them easily.

## USE OF TOTAL STATION AND ITS UTILITY

Total Station is basically a combination of theodolite, EDM and a microprocessor, which computes rectangular coordinates of the survey stations on the field, with the data of angular measurements taken by the theodolite, distance measurements by the EDM and the initial bearing of the survey line. The coordinates may either be plotted on a mapping graph sheet manually to prepare a cadastral map or the data may be recorded in the PCMCIA (Personal Computer Memory Card International

Association) Card available with most brands of Total Stations, which may be taken from the field to a separate computer in office with a printer for graphical output of the coordinates, in the form of a map. Total Stations are also directly compatible with computers. It is a high-end survey equipment, which can be used properly by a trained surveyor only.

The T–2 theodolite + DI–1600 + GTS–5 combination works similar to that of a Total Station, except that it provides polar coordinates which are required to be reduced to rectangular coordinates separately. This combination upgrades an optical theodolite to the level of a Total Station.

Total Station has been in use in West Bengal since the early 1990s. As it can provide rectangular coordinates of control points right in the field, it was hoped that it would be able to cut short the time taken for the existing procedure of sending the theodolite field data of angle–distance–azimuth from the field to the Directorate for traverse computation to prepare survey plot sheets. However, it was found that the equipment has a limited error adjustment capability. Though it is a high precision equipment itself, yet it is difficult to adjust accumulated errors with it, in case of survey of large areas, involving hundreds of stations, as is the case in West Bengal. It did not prove to be a good control survey equipment but it was found to be very useful as a detailed survey equipment of very high accuracy in large-scale town survey.

For control survey, manual error adjustment in traverse computation from field provided by T–2 theodolite+EDM combination was found to be better.

## SALT LAKE CITY SURVEY USING TOTAL STATION—A CASE STUDY

Salt Lake City is a satellite township adjacent to Kolkata. It was decided to prepare cadastral map of Salt Lake city in 1:500 scale. The methodology involved was, (a) to provide traverse control by T–2 theodolite + EDM; and (b) to conduct detailed survey by Total Station instead of chain survey of plotting of property boundaries and other details. It would also provide a good opportunity for surveyors to develop and practise the technique of detailed surveying by Total Station, which to be later used in other urban areas and in the more problematic survey of the city of Kolkata itself.

In traverse survey, the main circuit covering Salt Lake City was 20.25 km long. The main circuit was divided by sub-circuits, running along the five sectors of the city. The sub-circuits were further divided by sub-traverse lines covering the respective blocks inside the sectors and the roads running inside the blocks. More than 2,500 control points have been established on the ground along the traverse survey lines with average accuracy of 1:10600. This survey was conducted conventionally by T–2 theodolite+EDM combination.

For detailed survey, the methodology followed, in short, is that the Total Station is placed on a known traverse station on the ground and the already computed coordinates of the station and the initial bearing are entered in the Total Station. Prismatic reflectors are then placed at the corners of the property boundaries successively, as far as the visibility exists from the Total Station and observations are made. This operation generates the coordinate values of the corners of a number of property boundaries from the same station in terms of its original coordinate. The Total Station is then moved to the next traverse station with known co-ordinates and the previous exercise is repeated. Apart from property boundaries, features like lamp posts, telegraph poles, sewerage man-holes and other physical features available on the ground are also con-nected and coordinated. These coordinates are plotted on the traverse plot sheet in the field for detailed plotting. Because of the limited number of observations by the Total Station at a time, high accuracy factor equiva-lent to that of the traverse survey can also be maintained in the detailed surveying. As a result, all points plotted in such cadastral maps have co-ordinate values of high accuracy. It also facilitates computerisation of such cadastral maps. The survey is continuing.

The Total Station survey is definitely proving to be much superior in respect of speed and accuracy to that of conventional methods.

## USE OF GPS AND ITS UTILITY

The Global Positioning System (GPS) is a state-of-the-art equipment for providing ground control with the help of a system of 24 satellites called

Navstar, of which at least four should be available for tracking to give better results. The accuracy factor has greatly increased in the last couple of years with the introduction of Differential GPS (DGPS), which is a combination of one static receiver with a precisely known location and another as a rover, and which should operate within a radius of 10 km of the static receiver. The control may be extended by Total Station in combination with the GPS, which is sometimes constrained by the non-availability of the required radius of the horizon in some places. However, the equipment will be very useful for survey of the following areas of the state.

- Certain parts of the hilly and forest regions of Darjeeling and in Dooars in the north, where human habitation has come up recently but which has remained un-surveyed due to physical and topographical reasons, are required to be mapped for cadastral and developmental purposes in 1: 4000 scale. The area involved is approximately 17,000 sq. km.
- A part of the forest regions of the Sunderbans and also a few adjoining estuarial islands in the south, which could not be properly mapped earlier due to inaccessibility, require to be mapped now because of extending human habitation and agricultural activities. The area involved will be around 950 sq. km.
- Large-scale town surveys are required for Kolkata, Siliguri and other urban areas of suburbs of Kolkata.

The methodology to be followed is, briefly, as follows:

- The control for detailed survey in the forest and hilly regions in north Bengal and in the forest zone of Sunderbans and estuarial islands in south Bengal will be provided by Differential Global Positioning System (DGPS), which is much faster and less laborious than theodolite traverse.
- The survey of the field details will be conducted with Total Station, based on the coordinates of the control points provided by the GPS survey. Total Station will provide coordinates of each bend and corner of the fields and plots.
- The coordinates provided by the GPS and Total Station will be fed into the computer, with the necessary software, which will generate the cadastral maps and the plotted cadastral sheets will be produced through A0 size plotter.

- Similar methodology will be followed for large-scale urban surveys too; only the system of providing ground control will be a combination of both DGPS and theodolite for greater accuracy.
- Since the ground controls and all details will be coordinated, the maps will be generated through computers.

DGPS offered by reputed foreign manufacturers have been tested by us in the field during actual survey and have been found suitable for our purpose. It has been found that a system of three DGPS, that is one static receiver and two rovers, will provide more sound ground control than by two.

A scheme has been drawn up and submitted to the government for procurement of necessary equipment.

## TOOLS REQUIRED FOR IMPLEMENTING THE NEW SCHEME

For implementing the scheme of DGPS-aided computer-generated cadastral mapping the following equipments (see Table 17.1) are to be procured:

1. three dual frequency GPS receivers with post-processing facilities with 3 mm+0.5 ppm accuracy for accurate control work, one acting as the static unit and the other two as kinematics rovers for triangular observations for greater accuracy and stability;
2. five Total Station electronic theodolites with accuracy and S/d of 1"; and
3. computer software and hardware (workstations, plotter, etc.).

**Table 17.1**

*Cost Involved in the DGPS Scheme*

| Items | Quantity | Cost |
|---|---|---|
| Dual frequency DGPS of 3 mm+0.5 ppm accuracy with one base station and two rovers | 2 sets | Rs 5,000,000 |
| Total station electronic theodolite of 1" accuracy @ Rs 1,050,000 including training | 5 nos. | Rs 5,250,000 |
| Computer software for surveying and map generation | | Rs 1,000,000 |
| **Total** | | **Rs 11,250,000** |

264 • C.R. DAS

.There will be no expense on computer hardware for this scheme as the computer installation for the pilot project for digitisation of cadastral maps (scheme already approved), will be used for the generation of new cadastral maps, as it is an extension of the map digitisation project. The total cost for this scheme of computer-generated cadastral mapping in urban and remote areas is covered under the central sector scheme of 100 per cent financial assistance from the Government of India.

The above proposal is in full conformity with the Vision Document issued by the Department of Land Resources, Ministry of Rural Development, Government of India, regarding the CoLR and SRA & ULR schemes.


## PILOT PROJECT FOR CADASTRAL MAPPING BY AERIAL PHOTOGRAPHY IN PURULIA


In the course of modernisation in survey and settlement work in West Bengal, a pilot project for preparation of latest cadastral maps by aerial photography was undertaken for the first time in the district of Purulia in West Bengal.

- In the first stage, current aerial photographs in 1:10000 scale were obtained from the Survey of India to prepare cadastral maps in 1:3960 scale.
- In the second stage of the work, theodolite traverse survey of a very high degree of accuracy (1:20000) for providing ground control for rectification and enlargement of the aerial photographs to 1:3960 scale of mauza maps, which is normally done by Survey of India, was undertaken by the Directorate of Land Records and Surveys, West Bengal successfully in all the 20 police stations covering 2,600 square miles in Purulia district in four field seasons. The field season for theodolite traverse survey is restricted to only four months (December to March) in Purulia due to extreme hot weather. It was a remarkable achievement on the part of the surveyors of the directorate in view of the toughness of the job in an inhospitable terrain, as they completed the ground control survey of 2,600 square miles in 16 working months.

- In the third stage, the accurate coordinates generated at the Directorate from the ground control survey, have been provided for the whole district to the Survey of India for preparation of the enlarged and rectified prints of the aerial photographs, which are photomaps in accurate scale showing the latest ground configuration in the mauzas.

- In the final stage, Survey of India is steadily supplying enlarged and rectified prints of the aerial photographs, which are now being used after rigorous accuracy check, for preparation of cadastral mauza maps in the present Survey and Settlement Operation in Purulia district.

# 18

# Computerisation and Digitisation of Survey and Land Records in Andhra Pradesh

### T. RADHA

## INTRODUCTION

The state of Andhra Pradesh was formed on 1 November 1956. At that time two different systems of survey[1] and settlement[2] were in existence and practice. The 12 districts of former Andhra state followed the system in vogue in the erstwhile Madras Province. Nine districts of the Telengana region of the former Hyderabad state followed the system in the former Hyderabad state. Naturally, preparation and maintenance of land records was also different. Besides this, practices and procedures of survey and settlements in the Andhra region were governed by Survey Manuals, I, II, and III, Chain Survey Manual, Board's Standing Orders 34 A, B and D and Settlement Manual. On the other hand, in the Telengana region, the procedures laid down in the Hyderabad Survey and Settlement Manual were followed.

This chapter is divided into nine sections. The first section discusses different systems of survey in Andhra Pradesh state. This is followed by

---

For all figures in lakhs and crores, please note that 1 lakh = 100,000 and 1 crore = 10,000,000.

an analysis of the physical condition of survey and land records[3] (SLRs) in the state of Andhra Pradesh. The next section discusses the necessity for computerisation/digitisation of survey and land records in general, with special reference to the state of Andhra Pradesh. The focus then shifts to analyse certain experimental projects of digitisation of survey and land records in Kuppam assembly constituency of Chittoor district of Andhra Pradesh. The section that follows discusses progress report prepared for digitisation of survey and land records and submitted to Government of India for 100 per cent assistance in August 2001. The next section deals with Dynamic Command Area Crop Monitoring System (D-CACS) in two major irrigation projects of Andhra Pradesh comprising Nagarjuna Sagar and Sriram Sagar covering about 20,000 sq. km. to be implemented through private agencies by inviting tenders.[4] This is followed by a discussion on experimental re-survey through modern technology such as Global Positioning System, Total Stations, etc,. The next section deals with practical problems encountered in the computerisation of survey and land records. The last section offers some suggestions and conclusions.

## DIFFERENT SYSTEMS OF SURVEY
## IN ANDHRA REGION[5]

In this section it is proposed to discuss different systems of survey which were adopted in Andhra region, during the initial surveys, such as (*a*) *paimaish*; (*b*) *khasra*; (*c*) simple triangulation; (*d*) triangles with offsets; (*e*) plane table; (*f*) block map; (*g*) Punganur system; and (*h*) diagonal and offset system. The diagonal and offset method is the latest.

### Paimaish[6]

The first revenue survey of which we possess some records is the paimash which was conducted in several districts of the composite Madras state during the first quarter of the 19th century. In this survey, each holding (plot) was numbered and its name, measurement from north to south and east to west, areas and boundaries were recorded on cadjan leaves or on flimsy paper. The method of measurement of individual properties and holdings underwent several changes as the survey progressed.

## The Khasra Method

As per this method, if the field was quadrilateral, four sides were measured and all irregular fields were divided into quadrilateral or triangular portions called *taks* and the field itself could be plotted only by piecing together these taks. Measurement sketches—not to scale—were prepared in some cases but these were subsequently destroyed.

## Simple Triangulation Method

Under this system a sketch of each field showing measurement of all triangles was prepared. Sometimes, the sketch book would show several fields on one page. These sketches are known as amin sketches, so named because the surveyor was called the Amin.

## Triangles with Offsets

In or about 1877, surveyors were allowed, when bends on the field boundaries were numerous, to fix by offsets the positions of all marks less than 50 links from a direct line between adjoining survey stones.

## Plane Table System

Under this system, the maximum area of survey fields was raised to 6 acres in wetland and 12 acres in dry land and work relating to measurement of sub-divisions was transferred from settlement department to survey department. The object of this system was to reduce cost of survey. The plane table is an instrument used for filling in the interior details of a survey, when traverse stations fixed by a theodolite survey have been previously projected on the map. This method was based on inter-section method. The cost of survey in this method is comparatively little as a lot of measurement work is reduced.

## Block Map System

The theodolite framework was introduced in 1892 and this change combined with plane table method of survey produced block map method. The block was divided into large triangles and all survey fields and sub-divisions are correctly plotted by offsets from the sides of these triangles. The areas of fields were then taken with area square paper. Only a few of the stations of these triangles were theodolite stations, the rest being fieldstones or even peg stations. This method was extremely cheap, but results were inaccurate and the system was not suited for maintenance.

## Punganur System

The system was first adopted in the Punganur *zamindari* of Chittoor district and then followed in Repalli *taluk* of Guntur district and Venkatagiri zamindari of Nellore district. Under this system, all points on the boundary of a field are offset from G-Line. Under this system, field boundaries are not measured but computed. The advantages of this system are saving in linear measurement and consequently in cost, accuracy and speed.

## Diagonal and Offset System[7]

This is the latest method and is presently in use. The main processes in a cadastral survey[8] are location, demarcation, measurement, mapping and computation of areas of the holdings and preparation of a field register or land register furnishing the relevant details of these holdings for taking up settlement work. An idea of the whole operation can be gathered from a description of the various steps, as listed below:

- Boundary demarcation (village as well as *khandam*s or sub-circuits)
- Traverse survey of village and khandam boundaries
- Traverse computation
- Traverse plotting
- Field demarcation
- Field measurement
- Plotting village map
- Finishing village map and area computation

**Table 18.1**

*Andhra Pradesh at a Glance, 1999–2000*[9]

| Category | Specification |
| --- | --- |
| Area | 275,045 sq. km. |
| Districts | 23 |
| Revenue divisions | 79 |
| *Mandal*s | 1,125 |
| Villages | 26,586 |
| Towns | 264 |

**Table 18.2**

*Evolution and Growth of Survey Systems in Andhra Pradesh*

| Method/System | Period |
|---|---|
| Khasra method | 1858–65 |
| Simple triangulation method | 1866–77 |
| Triangles with offsets | 1878–86 |
| Plane table system | 1887–91 |
| Block map system | 1892–96 |
| Punganur system | 1918–20 |
| Diagonal and offsets system | Since 1900 |

## PHYSICAL CONDITION OF SURVEY AND LAND RECORDS IN ANDHRA PRADESH

In this section it is proposed to discuss types of land records maintained in Andhra Pradesh and their physical condition.

### Telengana Region

The basic graphic land records maintained in Telengana region are:

1. village maps[10]
2. tippons[11]

An analysis of Table 18.3 reveals that in Telengana region maps for only 81.75 per cent of the villages (or 9,114 village maps as against 11,148 villages), are physically available with the collector (S&LR) for public use. For about 2,034 villages there are no village maps. Further, even out of these 9,114 village maps, only 88.56 per cent are in good condition, which means in respect of about 3,076 villages (11,148–8,072) or 28 per cent of the total villages in Telengana region literally do not have village maps. That means in Telengana region village maps in good condition are available only for 72 per cent of the villages.

**Table 18.3**

*Telengana Region (Availability of Village Maps)*

| Name of the district | Total villages | Total available maps | Good | Brittle | Faded | Torn | Missing |
|---|---|---|---|---|---|---|---|
| Adilabad | 1,750 | 1,554 | 1,360 | 87 | 58 | 49 | 196 |
| Karimnagar | 1,103 | 943 | 942 | – | – | 1 | 160 |
| Khammam | 1,241 | 656 | 656 | – | – | – | 585 |
| Warangal | 1,098 | 906 | 906 | – | – | – | 192 |
| Mahaboobnagar | 1,557 | 1,240 | 890 | – | – | 350 | 317 |
| Medak | 1,265 | 1,038 | 891 | – | – | 147 | 227 |
| Nalgonda | 1,158 | 978 | 760 | – | – | 218 | 180 |
| Nizamabad | 921 | 848 | 809 | 1 | – | 38 | 73 |
| Ranga Reddy | 1,055 | 951 | 858 | – | – | 93 | 104 |
| **Total** | **11,148** | **9,114** | **8,072** | **88** | **58** | **896** | **2,034** |

An analysis of Table 18.4 reveals that in Telengana region only 68.60 per cent of the total number of tippons are physically available with the collector (S&LRs), and that for about 11,67,254 (37,17,726–25,50,472) survey fields there are no tippons. Further, even out of the 25,50,472 survey field tippons only 72 per cent are in good condition. For 50.61 per cent of 18,81,685 (37,17,726–18,36,041) survey fields in Telengana region there are literally no tippons. This means in Telengana region tippons in good condition are available only for 49.39 per cent survey fields. Hence there is a need to preserve these records in electronic mode.

## Andhra Region

The basic graphic land records maintained in the Andhra region are:

1. village maps
2. field measurement book[12] (FMB)

**Table 18.4**

**Telengana Region (Availability of Tippons)**

| Name of the district | Total villages | No. of tippons available | Good | Brittle | Faded | Torn | Missing | Total nos. |
|---|---|---|---|---|---|---|---|---|
| Adilabad | 1,750 | 61,652 | 61,652 | – | – | – | 2,94,230 | 3,55,882 |
| Karimnagar | 1,103 | 4,77,765 | 1,06,957 | – | – | 3,70,808 | 1,13,681 | 5,91,446 |
| Khammam | 1,241 | 2,18,171 | 1,02,093 | 44,230 | – | 71,848 | 8,524 | 2,26,695 |
| Warangal | 1,098 | 2,59,427 | 2,59,427 | – | – | – | 1,92,432 | 4,51,859 |
| Mahboobnagar | 1,557 | 3,07,141 | 3,07,141 | – | – | – | 1,96,183 | 5,03,324 |
| Medak | 1,265 | 4,04,438 | 3,17,818 | – | – | 86,620 | 80,395 | 4,84,833 |
| Nalgonda | 1,158 | 3,39,897 | 2,52,939 | 9,583 | 2,006 | 75,369 | 1,08,668 | 4,48,565 |
| Nizamabad | 921 | 3,08,718 | 2,91,419 | 693 | – | 16,606 | 1,08,407 | 4,17,125 |
| Ranga Reddy | 1,055 | 1,73,263 | 1,36,595 | – | – | 36,668 | 64,734 | 2,37,997 |
| **Total** | **11,148** | **25,50,472** | **18,36,041** | **54,506** | **2,006** | **6,57,919** | **11,67,254** | **37,17,726** |

**Table 18.5**

*Andhra Region (Availability of Village Maps)*

| Name of the district | Total villages | Total maps available | Good | Brittle | Faded | Torn | Missing |
|---|---|---|---|---|---|---|---|
| Srikakulam | 2,088 | 1,236 | 937 | 125 | 14 | 160 | 852 |
| Vizianagaram | 1,551 | 910 | 797 | 20 | 21 | 72 | 641 |
| Visakhapatnam | 2,816 | 1,704 | 1,676 | 16 | 2 | 10 | 1,112 |
| E. Godavari | 1,412 | 1,353 | 1,353 | – | – | – | 59 |
| W. Godavari | 901 | 741 | 633 | 40 | – | 68 | 160 |
| Krishna | 1,005 | 768 | 579 | 84 | 5 | 100 | 237 |
| Guntur | 733 | 394 | 320 | 38 | 11 | 25 | 339 |
| Prakasam | 1,103 | 552 | 428 | 98 | 3 | 23 | 551 |
| Nellore | 1,207 | 1,133 | 1,133 | – | – | – | 74 |
| Cuddapah | 980 | 311 | 311 | – | – | – | 669 |
| Kurnool | 990 | 545 | 492 | 53 | – | – | 445 |
| Ananthapur | 965 | 793 | 286 | 198 | 110 | 199 | 172 |
| Chittoor | 1,550 | 676 | 676 | – | – | – | 874 |
| **Total** | **17,301** | **11,116** | **9,621** | **672** | **166** | **657** | **6,185** |

An analysis of Table 18.5 reveals that in Andhra region maps for only 64.25 per cent of the villages are physically available with the collector (S&LR), thereby implying that about 6,185 villages (17,301–11,116) do not have village maps. Further, even out of these 11,116 available village maps, only 86.55 per cent village maps are in good condition; in respect of about 7,680 (or 44.4 per cent) villages (17,301–9,621) in Andhra region there are literally no village maps. That means in Andhra region village maps in good condition are available only for 55.60 per cent of villages. Thus, there is a need to preserve these records through computerisation to prevent further damage.

An analysis of Table 18.6 reveals that in Andhra region FMBs for only 87.23 per cent of the survey fields are physically available with the collector (S&LRs), and for 608,418 survey fields (4,767,512–4,159,094) there are no FMBs. Further, even out of the 4,159,094 FMBs, only 90.42 per cent are in good condition. So, in respect of 1,006,601 (or 21 per cent) survey fields (4,767,512–3,760,911) in Andhra region there are literally no FMBs available. That means in Andhra region FMBs in good condition are available only for 79 per cent of the survey fields.

In both Andhra and Telengana regions, the land records presently maintained were prepared nearly a century ago. Due to the age of the records the majority of survey and land records (SLRs) are in a dilapidated and brittle condition and liable to crumble to pieces. Further, due to continuous usage, the SLRs are also soiled, mutilated and mostly damaged.

Table 18.6

Andhra Region (Availability of FMBs)

| Name of the district | Total FMBs | Available | Good | Brittle | Faded | Torn | Missing |
|---|---|---|---|---|---|---|---|
| Srikakulam | 2,38,743 | 1,91,968 | 1,48,194 | 18,913 | 3,161 | 21,700 | 46,775 |
| Vizianagaram | 1,97,865 | 1,76,110 | 1,50,759 | 9,457 | 4,449 | 11,445 | 21,755 |
| Visakhapatnam | 2,25,888 | 1,86,588 | 1,66,921 | 10,795 | 4,776 | 4,096 | 39,300 |
| East Godavari | 3,01,160 | 2,97,578 | 2,84,753 | 5,181 | 3,939 | 3,705 | 3,582 |
| West Godavari | 2,92,348 | 2,73,476 | 2,54,501 | 7,596 | 2,029 | 9,350 | 18,872 |
| Krishna | 3,14,192 | 3,00,346 | 2,68,000 | 20,230 | 2,604 | 9,512 | 13,846 |
| Guntur | 3,59,629 | 2,97,022 | 2,71,698 | 15,840 | 3,132 | 6,352 | 62,607 |
| Prakasam | 5,37,180 | 3,56,789 | 3,19,308 | 36,366 | 1,115 | – | 80,391 |
| Nellore | 3,65,619 | 3,58,439 | 3,58,439 | – | – | – | 7,180 |
| Cuddapah | 5,29,795 | 4,26,290 | 4,25,592 | 339 | 244 | 115 | 1,03,505 |
| Kurnool | 4,67,342 | 3,75,025 | 3,75,025 | – | – | – | 92,317 |
| Ananthapur | 4,38,477 | 4,15,106 | 3,60,245 | 18,281 | 13,608 | 22,972 | 23,371 |
| Chittoor | 5,99,274 | 5,04,357 | 3,77,476 | 65,481 | 10 | 61,390 | 94,917 |
| **Total** | **47,67,512** | **41,59,094** | **37,60,911** | **2,08,479** | **39,067** | **1,50,637** | **6,08,418** |

# NECESSITY FOR PRESERVATION OF LAND RECORDS

Survey and land records are the only source available to furnish information on all revenue lands. They serve the interests of the public and government alike. SLRs are required for land development and land management. The entire land administration is based on SLRs. Besides this, SLRs form the basis for further surveys/re-surveys. SLRs are to be maintained till they are replaced by fresh set of records generated through re-survey.

## Need for Computerisation

Computerisation technology offers greater facility in data entry, preservation, maintenance and updating and retrieval of land records. Huge data can be stored in smaller place with easy accessibility and capability of fast retrieval. It is relatively permanent and also offers scope for online updating of land records, if necessary. Further, integration of graphic and textual data collected from the field once fed into computer in its raw form, results in generation of LIS. It ensures high accuracy, and reliability.

## EXPERIMENTAL PROJECTS ON DIGITISATION OF SURVEY AND LAND RECORDS

A pilot project has been taken up for computerisation of 92,944 FMBs covering 3,65,770 sub-divisions in 369 villages in Kuppam and three other assembly constituencies of Chittoor district at a cost of Rs 55 lakh with 100 per cent grant in aid by the Government of India. So far 22,010 FMBs, and 86,356 sub-divisions have been computerised. During the inspection of work of computerisation of basic survey and land records in Kuppam the following points were noticed:

- There were several errors in field measurement sketches with regard to conversion of FPS measurement into metric measurements.
- The initial batch of FMBs sketches supplied had 100 per cent errors and even the final printouts for 8,191 FMBs had about 20 per cent errors. The quality control work should be done in-house instead of sending sketches with innumerable errors to the department.
- Village maps of 178 villages supplied by the private agency were not generated in the manner laid down in the agreement, that is by mosaicing revenue fields and by correcting mosaiced village maps using traverse[13] data. Scanning and vectorising village maps supplied by department reportedly generated maps.

The agency on its part has clarified that:

- Finalisation of specification for the conversion of Gunter chain links to metric chain links and FPS[14] to MKS[15] is made as per a reckoner made available for the purpose. Accordingly changes were made in the software. After submission of first lot of 8,191 FMBs for quality check, the Department of Survey and Land Records noticed that after conversion to metric links sum of part measurements were not matching with total measurement. For example, if total measurement is 190 links and two part measurement are 90 links and 100 links each in FPS, after conversion, metric measurements are 91 links, 101 links and 191 links (As per the reckoner, between 86 to 256 links, one link to be added for metric conversion). Thus, total measurement did not match with the part measurements. The mistake was realised and instructions were given to match total measurements, with part measurements having more length to be corrected. Initially there was lack of information on methodology for correction, and only after submission of the first lot did information become available. Though the concerned private agency had already completed computerisation of FMBs in southern states of Tamil Nadu, Pondicherry and Kerala, where similar system of survey is in existence, the aforesaid conversion of dimensions was not done. Being a pilot work, this was a new initiative both for the private agency and for the department.

• As explained above, in every FMB the nature of error is conversion error, that is from FPS to MKS. The nature of error being only of one type it is incorrect to say that the FMBs supplied had 100 per cent errors.

Along with FMBs and village maps, traverse data were not supplied by the Department of Survey and Land Records for fear that original maps could be manipulated or misplaced. So the Department made attempts to supply photocopies to the agency. However, it was realised that it might take considerable time to photocopy. In the absence of traverse data, the private agency generated village maps by scanning and vectorisation method. Based on this, the agency completed maps for 185 villages by scanning and vectorisation process and submitted the same to the Department, in contravention of the agreement communicated to Government of India and which was agreed to by the two parties. Realising that it was very easy to supply original traverse data as was done in the case of village maps and FMBs, the Department supplied traverse data and clearly indicated that village maps are to be generated by mosaicing process strictly as per the provisions of the agreement.

278 •  T. RADHA

## DIGITISATION OF SURVEY AND LAND RECORDS
## IN 278 MANDALS IN 22 DISTRICTS
## OF ANDHRA PRADESH[16]

After studying the pros and cons of the progress of experimental project work on digitisation of village maps and FMBs, it was felt that computerisation of basic survey records was essential for all villages in the entire state and the report considered taking up one mandal[17] in each assembly constituency, that is 278 mandals in 22 districts in the state (except Hyderabad district) at an estimated cost of about Rs 14.75 crore for 100 per cent grant in aid by Government of India and the proposal was submitted by Government of Andhra Pradesh to Government of India for their sanction on 27 August 2001.

## DYNAMIC COMMAND AREA
## CROP MONITORING SYSTEM (D-CACS)

In addition to above experimental projects, Government of Andhra Pradesh sanctioned an experimental project for digitisation of village maps in respect of villages covered by command areas under major irrigation projects like Nagarjuna Sagar and Sriram Sagar with an estimated cost of Rs 10.00 lakh. The aforesaid project is named 'Dynamic Command Area Crop Monitoring System' in which about 2,700 villages out of 27,000 villages in the state, with an approximate extent of 20,000 sq. km. are to be digitised. Incidentally, it is observed that there is huge variation in area of cultivation reported by revenue department, irrigation department, agriculture and statistics department. Allotment of digitisation of work to private agencies was processed under the tender system. Allotment was finalised and work order was given on 18 September 2001 to two private agencies, namely M/s Landends Solutions Limited and Speck Systems Limited, Hyderabad. Digitisation of village maps under this project is likely to be completed soon. Thereafter, digitised data of village maps will be handed over to Andhra Pradesh Remote Sensing Agency for further processing. Satellite imagery will be superimposed on digitised village maps to study digital extraction of survey numberwise irrigated and un-irrigated cropped areas for each revenue village. This will help in collection of land revenue under various irrigation projects and also for other multiple purposes.

## SURVEY THROUGH AERIAL PHOTOGRAPHY/ PHOTOGRAMMETRY OF 1991–95

In 1991, aerial photography/photogrammetric survey (taking photographs through helicopters; enlargement of photos to convenient scales; verification of ground position; then generation of field sketches and village maps, and computation of area of fields making use of computers software) was studied. For this purpose, an experimental aerial photography/ photogrammetric survey was taken up in collaboration with National Remote Sensing Agency (NRSA) and Andhra Pradesh State Remote Sensing Application Centre (APSRAC) along with Survey and Land Records Department of Government of Andhra Pradesh in Khammam district at an estimated cost of Rs 1 lakh. Its cost was shared equally by all the three agencies.

The above experimental survey was found to be defective for the following reasons:

- There were abnormal variations between measurements computed through aerial photography/photogrammetric survey and actual measurements found on ground by conventional method after field verification.
- Boundaries of government lands such as channels, roads, tanks, etc., could not be reflected in photogrammetric survey records as there were no specific boundaries (ridges) on the ground.
- To maintain accuracy level between aerial photography/photogrammetric surveys and that of ground position, photos needed enlargement and the cost was found to be excessive.

**Table 18.7**

*Comparative Statement of Area of Survey Numbers Pertaining
to Yedulapuram Village of Khammam Mandal*

| Survey no./ Sub.no. | Area by SS&LRs in sq m | Area by NRSA in sq m | Difference (+) more than and (–) less than dept. | % Difference |
|---|---|---|---|---|
| 167/8 | 2,056.52 | 2,128.8 | (+) 72.28 | 3.515 |
| 167/10 | 5,765.72 | 4,466.6 | (–) 1299.12 | 22.532 |
| 168/4 | 3,998.56 | 4,136.1 | (+) 137.54 | 3.440 |
| 168/5 | 3,902.48 | 4,090.1 | (+) 187.62 | 4.808 |
| 168/6 | 3,786.48 | 3,763.9 | (–) 22.58 | 0.596 |
| 168/7 | 2,439.52 | 2,362.5 | (–) 77.02 | 3.157 |
| 168/12 | 7,210.24 | 8,659.8 | (+) 1449.50 | 20.103 |
| 168/13 | 5,054.40 | 4,992.7 | (–) 61.70 | 1.221 |
| 168/140 | 7,255.48 | 6,548.9 | (–) 706.58 | 9.739 |
| 168/15 | 4,004.40 | 4,216.8 | (+) 212.40 | 5.304 |
| 168/16 | 17,453.48 | 16,467.8 | (–) 985.68 | 5.648 |
| 169/1 | 23,146.10 | 23,142.2 | (–) 3.90 | 0.017 |
| 169/2 | 2,293.86 | 2,404.3 | (+) 110.44 | 4.815 |
| 169/3 | 22,720.50 | 23,559.2 | (+) 838.70 | 3.691 |
| 169/17 | 4,456.16 | 4,591.3 | (+) 135.14 | 3.033 |
| 169/18 | 3,889.56 | 3,360.3 | (–) 529.26 | 13.607 |
| 169/19 | 3,210.80 | 3,943.3 | (+) 732.50 | 22.814 |
| 169/20 | 10,586.04 | 10,405.2 | (–) 180.84 | 1.708 |
| 67/P | 21,565.02 | 21,742.712 | (+) 177.692 | 0.824 |
| 61/1 | 9,420.40 | 9,958.590 | (+) 538.19 | 5.713 |
| 61/2 | 8,155.92 | 8,428.395 | (+) 272.475 | 3.341 |
| 61/3 | 8,110.12 | 7,948.170 | (–) 161.95 | 1.997 |
| 61/4 | 8,341.26 | 8,106.041 | (–) 235.219 | 2.820 |
| 62/1,2, | 5,108.84 + | 81,099.782 | (+) 1966.362 | 2.485 |
| 62/3,4 | 19,115.72 + | | | |
| 62/5,6 | 13,030.32 + | | | |
| | 12,181.48 + | | | |
| | 13,741.42 + | | | |
| | 15,955.64 = | | | |
| | 79,133.42 | | | |
| 63/1 | 22,759.92 | 22,813.249 | (+) 53.329 | 0.234 |
| 63/2 | 29,258.98 | 28,689.595 | (–) 569.385 | 1.946 |
| 63/3 | 7,297.58 | 7,092.142 | (–) 205.438 | 2.815 |
| 71 | 81,863.50 | 30,892.382 | (–) 50971.118 | 0.989 |
| 72/1 | 2,771.38 | 2,748.928 | (–) 22.452 | 30.092 |
| 72/2 | 4,876.08 | 6,343.370 | (+) 1467.29 | 1.132 |
| 73/1 | 12,523.98 | 12,665.767 | (+) 141.787 | 0.173 |
| 73/2 | 11,125.46 | 11,144.675 | (+) 19.215 | 2.235 |
| 73/3 | 23,939.64 | 24,474.600 | (+) 534.96 | 1.883 |

*(Table 18.7 contd.)*

(*Table 18.7 contd.*)

| Survey no./ Sub.no. | Area by SS&LRs in sq m | Area by NRSA in sq m | Difference (+) more than and (–) less than dept. | % Difference |
|---|---|---|---|---|
| 73/4,5 | 3,058.48 + 3,598.44 = 6,656.92 | 6,531.543 | (–) 125.377 | 2.031 |
| 73/6 | 2,609.94 | 2,662.941 | (+) 53.001 | 7.607 |
| 73/7 | 2,853.38 | 2,636.335 | (–) 217.045 | 4.158 |
| 73/8 | 11,784.56 | 12,274.574 | (+) 490.014 | 5.921 |
| 73/9 | 3,094.28 | 2,911.058 | (–) 183.222 | 2.015 |
| 74/1 | 8,112.28 | 8,275.745 | (+) 163.465 | 1.501 |
| 74/2 | 5,352.02 | 5,432.375 | (+) 80.355 | 17.198 |
| 112/1, 2 | 9,788.64 + 9,872.64 | 33,905.483 | (+) 4,975.483 | 2.893 |
| 112/3 | 9,268.72 = 28,930.0 | | | |
| 115/4, 5 | 4,573.60 + 5,148.48 | 14,632.420 | (+) 411.34 | |
| 115/6 | + 4,499.00 = 14,221.08 | | | |

Items tallying within allowance: 29
Items showing high variance: 6
Items showing very variance: 6
Item not compared: 1
Total: 42
% of items tallying within allowance to the total number of items compared: 69.5

# EXPERIMENTAL RE-SURVEY AND DIGITISATION OF SURVEY AND LAND RECORDS IN THREE MANDALS IN THREE DISTRICTS

As the modern technology (aerial photography/photogrammetry survey) could not succeed it was felt to be neccessary to take up re-survey of villages by using both modern technology and conventional methods. Accordingly, Government of Andhra Pradesh decided to take up experimental re-survey through private agencies using modern survey equipments like GPS[18], and Electronic Total Stations[19] as a pilot project in 61 villages of three selected mandals in Guntur, Chittoor and Karimnagar districts, one from each region of the state at an estimated cost of Rs 1.02 crore. All-India tenders were invited for this purpose covering an extent of 1.11 lakh acres. Selection of agencies was completed and work orders were issued in November 2001.

## PRACTICAL PROBLEMS IN COMPUTERISATION AND RE-SURVEY OF SURVEY AND LAND RECORDS

- In Andhra Pradesh land records are different in different geographical regions. Further, some records are still in FPS system. Similarly, some village maps do not have traverse data. Due to these factors, certain problems are encountered in computerisation of land records. Need-based software is to be developed for different cases.
- In the pilot project of computerisation of land records in Kuppam Assembly Constituency of Chittoor district by Vision Labs Institute, Hyderabad, the problem of matching cropped up in the conversion of FPS measurements into metric system. In conventional method, measurements are converted into metric system with the help of a ready reckoner and also sum of part measurements are adjusted manually. In computerisation process, these adjustments do not match in several cases. The problem was discussed with Vision Labs Institute, but even after rectification of mistakes the final printout of FMB was not completely error-free.
- Government of Andhra Pradesh desired maps to be generated by mosaicing of individual survey numbers within traverse skeleton of village. However, the private agency had generated 185 maps by scanning and vectorisation method. However, when mosaicing process was taken up, it was found that problem of corner matching had arisen in some cases. Periodical interaction with agency resulted in sorting out of major problems. The project is under progress and expected to be completed soon. The evaluation of the project is likely to take a few more months. Further, computerised data is to put to use for day-to-day maintenance and only then is it possible to fully evaluate the utility of the project.
- With regard to re-survey operations conducted by private agencies, it is noticed that they have sophisticated survey instruments, which can expedite cadastral survey to a great extent. But the agencies don't have adequate experience about basic concepts of cadastral surveys. Hence, private agencies have to frequently depend on department staff for guidance and cooperation.
- Further, landholders are not fully aware of the benefits of modern techniques and they have too much faith in the traditional system of survey and land records to accept modern survey methods. So there is a need to educate rural landholders.

## SUGGESTIONS AND CONCLUSIONS

- There is a need to streamline procedure for making funds available to implementing agencies by revenue/finance departments of state governments to reduce delays in flow of funds.
- There is a need to conduct re-survey as existing SLRs date back to several decades. For example, in Telengana region, survey and land records were prepared 100 years ago. Re-surveys should now be planned to be completed within a span of five to six years.
- There is a need for standardisation of software, especially for digitisation of survey records/cadastral maps on the basis of pilot projects implemented in various states/union territories. In this connection, it is seen that SLRs were prepared in FPS system, whereas the statutes require use of metric system in the country. Hence, it is necessary to covert FPS measurements into metric system during computerisation of land records.
- There is a need to create awareness among the landholders at the national level about advantages of re-survey and computerisation of land records. The Government of India may consider appropriate strategy for the creation of awareness.
- There is a need to integrate departments dealing with lands, such as survey and land records, registration department at village/tehsil/district and state levels, which could facilitate simultaneous updating of land records caused by mutation, sale of property, conveyance, partitions, exchange, gifts, settlements, release deeds, etc. This may also help in the faster updating of land records as well as cadastral maps to reflect ground realities, which may be useful to landholders.
- There is a need to train survey and revenue officials, including village-level functionaries, in the upgradation of their skills in computerisation of land records and also in error-free and monthly updated maintenance of computerised land information, as in the case of registration of births and deaths at the village level.
- It is necessary to carry out changes in the existing Revenue Code/Survey and Land Records Acts at the national and state levels to validate the legal status of computerised data/registers.

284 • T. RADHA

# NOTES

1. Land survey indicates some processes that give us accurate maps on land. The object of all land surveying, therefore, is the determination of boundaries and the relative position of the objects on any portion of the earth's surface with a view to the production of a pictorial representation of the tract of the country on paper with all its distinguishing features. Land survey has two main divisions: topographical and cadastral survey. The Survey of India conducts the topographical survey in the country whereas the cadastral survey operations are conducted by the State Survey departments (Andhra Pradesh Survey Department 1980; Reddy and Murthy 1994:1).

2. The procedure by which the assessment is determined is styled as settlement of land revenue (Reddy and Murthy 1994: 216).

3. SLRs refer to field measurement books/*tippon*s and village maps which are maintained in graphical form. Measurement book is a sheet containing measurement details of 5 acres of wetlands and 10 acres of dry lands. However, in Telengana region, every individual holding is surveyed and given survey numbers irrespective of extent of land.

4. 1 sq km is equal to 247 acres or 100 ha.

5. These are discussed in Reddy and Murthy (1994: 9–20).

6. Paimaish is an Urdu word meaning survey of lands.

7. This is popularly known as D & O system.

8. The word 'cadastre' is derived from the Latin word *Capitastrum* which was a register of capita or units of holdings for the Roman land tax as also poll tax. So, the word 'cadasture' means a public register of the lands of a country for fiscal (taxation) purposes. The three essential elements of an efficient cadastral survey are a clear demarcation of boundaries of each parcel of land, related descriptive records, and continuous updating of the maps and land records. If the above principles are followed, then the security of lands can be assured and will also greatly reduce disputes and litigation. The object of such a survey is the determination of village and field boundaries, the preparation of village map showing such boundaries and of area lists and field registers, the former giving the area of each field and village, and the latter containing particulars as to number, tenure, ownership, extent, assessment, etc., of each field (Reddy and Murthy1994: 3).

9. Source: *Andhra Pradesh Diary* 2001: v–vi.

10. It is a key to the field atlas. It is plotted to a prescribed scale showing all field survey nos, and all important topographical details. It is intended mainly to act as an index to FMB. It gives an idea of relative position of survey fields.

11. It is a sketch showing measurement boundaries of survey no. It is a rough sketch and not to a scale. It provides a record of measurement and boundaries.

12. Field measurement book contains several field measurement sheets covering measurements of all lands in a village. It is generally drawn to a scale of 1:1000 or 1:2000 showing all field and sub-division boundaries and their measurement. It is also called atlas of field maps. A record of measurement of individuals fields and sub-division is thus provided which will enable any inspecting officer to identify the boundaries whatever it is required for investigation of disputes boundaries, for the detection of encroachments and for the measurement of further sub-division, etc.

13. Traverse: Each village is taken as the basic unit for conducting cadastral surveys. Boundaries of each village are demarcated by durable stones at the village tri-junction and bi-junction which form a closed circuit. Traditionally the village circuit is surveyed by a theodolite which provides angular data up to 20" at each station. Distances between successive stations are measured with a survey chain. The village circuit is called the traverse circuit, the demarcation points are known as traverse station and angular and linear data of each station is called traverse data (polar coordinates). This traverse data is further transformed into rectangular coordinates in office and village traverse circuit is plotted. The accuracy of traverse survey is 1/2000 and used to check accuracy and errors of detailed survey of all landholdings within that village.

14. British measurement system wherein linear measurement were recorded in gunter chains and chains links using a chain of 66 ff with 100 links 1 Gunter chain = 20.1168 m. Incidentally, Gunter is the name of the surveyor.
    FPS: Foot, Pound and Second
    MKS:Metre, Kilogram and Second

15. Metric system is legally in force in India under Standards of Weights and Measures Act, 1976.

16. Andhra Pradesh state consists of 23 districts and Hyderabad district was excluded in digitisation as town survey records were already computerised in 1996–97.

17. Mandal is equivalent to *tehsil* and is a unit of administration below district level and above *gram panchayat*, with population of about 50,000 people in the plain areas and about 35,000 people in tribal and inaccessible areas.

18. GPS (Global Positioning System) is meant for mapping. It is used to collect ground-point positions with respect to the satellites in cadastral survey. It can be used to establish accurate primary base.

19. Total Station is a combination of both electronic theodolites and electronic distance meter. It is meant for total station of whole survey activities and work. Total Station provides horizontal distance, elevation, horizontal and vertical angles of any station, bearing of any line and coordination with respect to a reference station. The built-in computer can collect field data of approximately 7,500 points electronically and preserve in memory, which renders a field notebook unnecessary. The data collected renders the mistake in the field though the use of specialised plotter or printer generates serving software maps. Accuracy of linear measurement is of the order of 1mm to 1 km distance. The advantage of this instrument is that observations of several visible stations can be made from a single reference station. Surveys are, therefore, fast.

# REFERENCES

*Andhra Pradesh Diary.* (2001). Hyderabad: Directorate of Economics and Statistics, Government of Andhra Pradesh.

**Andhra Pradesh Survey Department.** (1980). Manual of Rules, Vol I.

**Reddy, P. Kasthuri** and **P.V. Murthy.** (1994). *Handbook on Survey, Settlement and Land Records in Andhra Pradesh.* Hyderabad.

# 19

# Updation of Land Records, Computerisation and Digitisation of Cadastral Survey Maps with Reference to J&K

MOHD. AFZAL AND ISHFAQ A. KHAN

## BACKGROUND

The last regular settlement operations in Jammu and Kashmir (J&K) state were conducted during 1920–25. There was no stipulation in law to conduct these operations at regular intervals of 20 to 25 years. Over time the land records, or even the village maps, have not reflected changes taking place on the ground. There have been sub-divisions/fragmentation of land units owing to transfers of land, and revolutionary land reforms introduced in the state like Big Landed Estates Abolition Act, 1950 and Agrarian Reforms Acts of 1972 and 1976. After the Implementation of Agrarian Reforms Act of 1976, the preparation of quadrilateral *jamabandis* and *girdawaris* was suspended until 1992, and so updating came to a grinding halt. The alienation of land, be it through sale, gift, mortgage with posses-sion, etc., was forbidden under this Act but transfers of land continued to take place without the same being reflected in the revenue records. Since the concept of land to tiller was aimed at under the Agrarian

Reforms Act, tenancy was altogether abolished. This created a wedge between the records and the position obtaining on the ground. Since agrarian reforms have now been completed, the state has adopted the project of 'updation of records and computerisation' for bringing the records up-to-date to reflect the changes taking place on the ground. Having regard to the adoption of metric system in measurement of land in consonance with the decision of central government and also due to the fact that village maps, whether with the field functionaries or in the central record room, have got damaged due to excessive use, the state of J&K embarked on settlement operations since 1998–99 with the latest available technology suited to the requirements of the state. The use of satellite imagery and aerial photogrammetry could have served as better options but these were not available for this border state due to security reasons. The only alternative option available was measurement with Electronic Total Stations (ETS), which were introduced in March 1998 under the aforementioned scheme.

The following are the schemes available for generating information database and strengthening revenue administration:

1. digitisation of cadastral survey maps;
2. computerisation of land records; and
3. updating of land records/strengthening of revenue administration.

While the schemes at (1) and (2) are 100 per cent centrally sponsored, the scheme at (3) has to be shared equally between centre and the states.

# DIGITISATION

The scheme is aimed at digitising the cadastral survey maps which are in good condition, for proper maintenance and upkeep. The process is to scan, capture, store, analyse, and manage large collection of *musavis* (village maps). The process will be viable for maintaining purity of data with improved quality control. The steps involved are:

1. map preparation
2. map digitising
3. OC of digitised maps

## DIGITISING METHODOLOGY

*Base map to raster conversion:* The base map is first checked and marked for reference points. If such reference points are not present on the map, a polygon is manually drawn on the map to act as a reference for the scaling purposes in the whole digitising process.

This map is then scanned using the scanner. The scanning result in a raster file which is saved in .tif format. The .tif file is then opened in CAD overlay. The reference polygon manually drawn on the base map is measured on 1:1 and a similar polygon is drawn on CAD overlay to work as a reference. The corner points of polygon drawn on CAD overlay are matched and overlapped with the polygon in the raster file drawn on the base map. The actual digitising process can now be started using the raster image as reference and development platform.

The digitisation of cadastral survey maps has not been taken up by the state of J&K because emphasis is on completing the settlement operations with ETS which will automatically generate digitised village maps.

## COMPUTERISATION OF LAND RECORDS

The basic objective of computerisation of land records is the creation of land records information database with facilities for updating and control. Land being the key input in all developmental activities, such a database shall remove all impediments by maintaining accurate and updated records. The information linked with the land is a potential input for planning developmental strategies. The computerisation programme has been adopted by the J&K state with the provision of establishing of *tehsil*-level computer centres (construction of computer rooms and provision of computers to these centres), and training of field-level functionaries (*patwaris*) in handling computers and data punching. The tehsil computer centres are to be linked with the central computer room at settlement/ central record room. Since the computerisation in J&K was envisaged to be undertaken indigenously through patwaris, it did not take off as per projections. Only some hundred odd villages were completed, when it was felt that only records of those villages would be computerised where record of rights would be compiled in settlement operations. There were other reasons also due to which computerisation received a setback. However, with the development of latest software the programme is sure to take off.

- It was thought that computerisation should be done only for villages where settlement operations have been completed. Otherwise, such computerisation is a futile exercise.
- The customised Urdu software procured for the computerisation did not include proper security checks or linkages.
- The computerisation programme was not initially introduced as a pilot project. Entrusting the programme initially to some private agencies on turnkey basis was also not considered.
- Insufficient training was given to field staff.
- Proper service support was also lacking.
- There was lack of alternative power supply to offset regular power cuts.
- The failure of timely recruitment of patwaris resulted in a 50 per cent vacancy of patwari posts in Kashmir division, with the result that the patwaris are overburdened, and unable to take up such a programme.

## UPDATING OF RECORDS/STRENGTHENING OF REVENUE ADMINISTRATION

After adoption of metric system of measurement of land, the choice of selecting the proper technology was restricted to introducing ETS as an alternative to traditional survey equipment. Initially the settlement operations in J&K state were introduced in 20 tehsils only, with provision of two to four ETS in each tehsil. About 600 villages were completed by November 2001 in spite of the fact that the survey teams had to operate in adverse security situations and with very limited electric supply for charging the batteries, downloading the data and generating maps. The steps involved in the process are as under:

1. updating of records by incorporating all changes into quadrilateral jamabandis and pedigree table;
2. demarcating sarkar, common lands, etc., wherever necessary;
3. preparation of site plan (*khaka*) of fields/plots called *chumenda*;
4. taking up the measurements through Electronic Total Stations, downloading the data into the computer;
5. preparation of village maps with references to site plan (khaka) of the fields;
6. verification of the map generated on spot vis-à-vis records, and issuing final printouts/maps; and
7. writing and verification of *khatooni* or *khatawar*, after announcing the same before village community; preparation of record of rights on the basis of khatooni and its final attestation and subsequent computerisation.

The introduction of Electronic Total Stations as a measurement tool considerably improved the efficiency and speed, besides reducing manual labour in physical measurement and making various calculations. The standard of performance of a survey team with one ETS is measured with in survey numbers. The annual target for one survey team has been fixed as 8,800 survey numbers. Settlement operations have been completed in 1,200 odd villages out of a total of 6,801 villages in the state. The revised version of the updated customised software will further minimise the manual labour in drawing up khatauni and record of rights. The field functionary has simply to punch raw data collected while taking measurements. The progress recorded so far in settlement operations is as under.

Total number of villages : 6,801
Villages completed with traditional survey: 618
Villages completed with ETS: 601
Total survey numbers measured: 800,993

No Global Positioning System (GPS) has been provided for taking measurements on world coordinates. Instead village measurements are recorded, taking the coordinates of base point as 00. This often makes rectification of overlapping/mistakes extremely difficult. The measurement on world coordinates could have proved useful in merging the village maps into tehsil and tehsil into district maps. GPS would also be effective in measuring difficult terrain.

Initially the staff resented the use of the ETS, but with the passage of time they appreciated its benefits as it avoids duplicity of labour. The progress was also slow as the staff was being trained simultaneously which resulted in overlapping of data, missing of points, etc. The lack of service support locally and unavailability of sufficient spares have been impending the progress.

Under this scheme the state of J&K has also constructed settlement record rooms at Srinagar and Jammu on modern lines, *patwar khanas*, revenue training institutes, and office complexes for revenue officers. The state has provided vehicles to the revenue officers for ensuring maximum mobility and has arranged training programmes for revenue officers/officials.

The process of computerisation of land records can be primarily classified as follows:

1. Getting the land records up-to-date online on a digital relational database management system: Building a current database of land records involves composing a database of geometrical two-dimensional representation of the plots existing on each village area definition. A plot representation database can be generated by:

   i. fresh survey by modern equipment such as Electronic Total Station, Global Positioning System, etc.; data generated with these instruments can be customised by passing through software conversions to make a database of coordinates of plot vertices; and
   ii. digitisation of old cadastral survey maps by different processes:

      ● scanning available good quality cadastral maps and using the scanned image as a visual references for guidance to draw a map on suitable CAD software;
      ● using typical drafting tools to scale out the coordinates of the vertices of different plots from a cadastral map; and
      ● regeneration of plots by composing different geometrical shapes with reference to records available, like plot area measurement books, damaged village maps, etc. Separate customised software has to be developed for this purpose.

iii. linking the plot representation database as reflected in Figure 19.1 to the corresponding:

- title information
- owner information
- irrigation information
- revenue information
- soil types
- tiller information
- situation coordinates

**Figure 19.1**

*Flowchart of Digital Relational Database Management System*

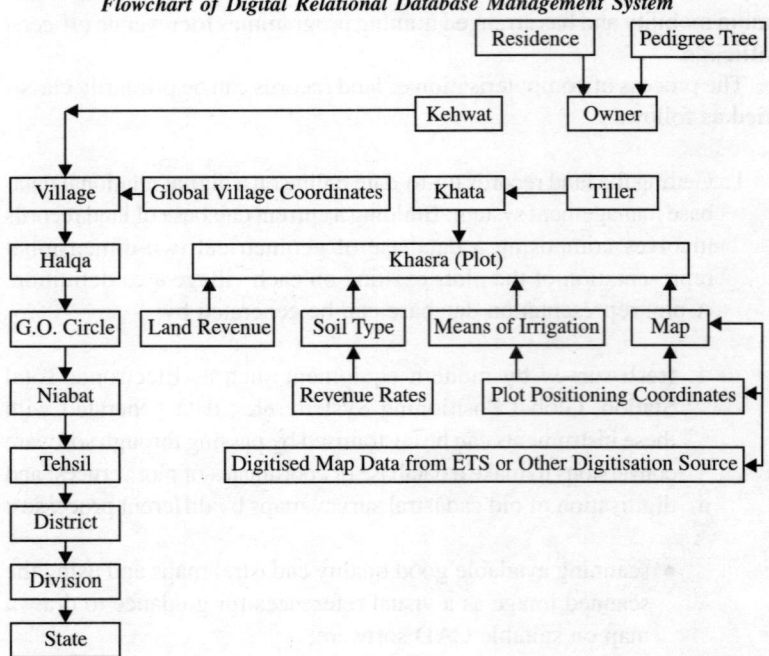

2. Regular updating of digital database records at different levels: Once a set of land records is digitised into a Relational Database Management Systems (RDBMS), the records are to be checked for correctness and locked against further editing. The reflection of day-to-day changes in the field are to be inducted into the land record database by way of appending new relational records in a

secured systematic fashion. No editing of old records should be allowed by the system.

To achieve the objective, a comprehensive secured record maintenance system is to be designed at the culmination of regular updating of the land records database. The updating of records involves the following basic activities:

   i. checking the availability legal instrument to effect any change in the land record;
  ii. keying in the relevant data from such instrument through an authorised known user of the system; and
 iii. checking/confirming the correctness of the new appended records by a responsible authorised known user of the system and subsequent locking of the new entries into the system.

The basic unit of the land record maintenance system builds up from a plot of land called *khasra*. Khasra is a single piece of land in a village associated with one ownership. Each khasra has a unique ID within a village, called khasra number. The area of land associated with a khasra number is unlimited. The land associated should be situated within the defined boundaries of the same village. A khasra number can have any number of soil types within, whether cultivable or uncultivable. The land revenue charged for each khasra number is based on its respective soil type and the respective area. The schemes of irrigation for a khasra can be more than one.

This information is split into database fields as:

   i. coordinates of the vertices of each khasra within an assumed coordinate system where the smallest easting digit is taken as origin x coordinate and smallest northing digit is taken as origin y coordinate;
  ii. the positioning coordinates of the assumed coordinate system of the respective plot. These positioning coordinates are taken within the global coordinates of a known point taken as the basic station during measurement. These coordinates are to be supplied by the Global Positioning System;
 iii. long integer data carrying the periphery;
 iv. name of the headman;
  v. unique ID generated by the system for each village; and
 vi. auto generated unique ID within the RDBMS.

## Village

Village in land records RDBMS terminology is the group of khasra composed within a common boundary. Information like the name of the village, global coordinates of a known point on the village map, measurement of the periphery of the village, name of the headman, etc., are kept at this level.
This information is split into database fields as:

- Name of the village.
- Global coordinates of a known point taken as the basic station during measurement. These coordinates are to be supplied by the Global Positioning System as per the latitude and longitude of that point.
- Long integer data carrying the length of the periphery of the village map.
- Name of the headman.
- Unique ID generated by the system for each village.

## Halqa

*Halqa* is a group of villages were the records are maintained/operated by the unit functionary of the department (patwari). This information is stored as name text field, with a unique ID generated by the system for each halqa.

## Digitisation of Damaged Maps

There are villages where the musavis in the record room and the trace copies (*lathas*) with the patwaris are either damaged or destroyed completely. In some villages these maps were destroyed deliberately with the ulterior motive of grabbing sarkar and other common lands. Therefore, the re-creation of such maps was a prerequisite to check such menace. Field book (*khasra paimaish*) prepared during the traditional survey was found useful for generating the individual plots which could subsequently be integrated on the basis of girdawari and spot position of the plots.

The khasra paimaish uses simple arithmetical methods for the calculation of area. Each plot is divided into all possible geometrical figures like right-angled triangles, triangles, trapeziums, squares, rectangles, etc. Appropriate area calculation formula for each figure separately was applied and the values for different variables of the formula were recorded in the khasra paimaish. The total area for each plot was calculated as the sum of break-up figures areas. The total area of the each khasra arrived at in this way is taken as the basic figure for building up of subsequent land records of the village.

Arithmetical area calculation formula which is used in khasra paimaish takes advantage of the known dimensions of perpendiculars and bases of respective figures. Here, it was felt that this data can also be read as casting and northing of different vertices of khasra numbers. In this way individual khasra numbers can be recreated on a graph paper or a suitable designing software. Having created the individual khasra numbers, the question of assembling different plots arises. The simple logic for putting together different polygons/khasra polygons (khasra numbers) is to look for the common sides (in terms of dimensions) and subsequent arrangement of the plots. Identifying one or more common sides and subsequent rotations, mirroring, etc., for various plots was virtually impossible in the absence of a powerful, tailored designing software. However, retrieving the village map by joining all khasra numbers can successfully be achieved with their location on spot and preparing khaka (site plan) by the field functionaries for reference.

A comprehensive system analysis in terms of software development was made for several months. Coding and on-job testing was taken up simultaneously. A successful in-house software for the purpose was developed.

This new software named as Automate Musavis is capable of generating musavi (village map) itself. The data downloaded from this software was fed into Auto Civil Software application (used for ETS data processing) for further verification and test. The working of the new system was found cent percent to its designing.

A function was developed in the system for generating the village map in GIS format, which is compatible with ETS operating system. The department is now in a position to recreate the maps from khasra paimaish and stake them out on the ground with the most modern technology.

In other words, our in-house technology can rewind the history and locate where Sir W. Lawrence had kept his flag during the settlement operations a century ago, to milimetre accuracy.

The musavis are also scanned and the output saved in *.tif format. The scanned image is super imposed into Auto CAD development platform using Auto CAD overlay. The scanned image guides the map developer to allocate coordinates to different vertices of the plots and to join the vertices. This method is used where a fairly clear musavi of a village is available.

# Part III: Land Information System

# 20

# Land Information System (LIS): The Indian Perspective

ALOK SHARMA AND LOKESH SHRIVASTAV

## WHAT IS LIS?

Land from time immemorial has been a source of pride for its owners, and means to generate revenue for the government. Land has always been considered as a status symbol deriving its strengths from area, location, fertility and other such factors attached to it. Land is also something people have emotional attachments with and hence has been a cause of jubilations and miseries, rewards and exploitations. Land has been cause of many bloody wars fought between nations and families for generations together.

India primarily being an agro-based nation has a massive assortment of land records to maintain. A greater part of the agro-based population is inadequately educated or not literate at all, and that has set off the trend of wrong practices. Boundary or ownership amendments take a long time to corroborate, because much of our land records are either untraceable or manipulated on account of the procedural red tape. All of these shortcomings in our existent system can be effectively alleviated with a little persuasion and persistence on modernisation of land information system.

Land, being such an important and critical commodity, needs proper management. Unless it is properly managed, its full potential can never be realised. Also in the absence of an efficient and up-to-date management system, land will always remain a source of grievances. In order to avoid manipulation by the rich and influential, in order to gain revenue which are just and due to the state exchequer, and in order to assess water demands for a given crop, or to identify the optimum land use for a given area, we need to have information about land.

A system which can provide such information is LIS or Land Information System. Until a few years back, land management was carried out by what can be termed as cadastre system. This system essentially involved the following:

1. a map drawn on paper and to a scale representing each parcel holding uniquely identified by a number within revenue boundary of a unit called village;
2. an ROR (record of rights), which had attributes, attached to each of the unique landholding number, showing the ownership, area, class of soil, crops grown, revenues, etc.; and
3. a village revenue officer (VRO) who was responsible for the upkeep of the two mentioned above.

The above system has many shortcomings. To list a few:

- It requires a huge manpower for the upkeep of all the historical and present maps and records.
- The system is person-dependent.
- The ownership and boundaries are a dynamic attribute requiring continuous updating. Poor upkeep of the maps and registers results in disputes between people.
- Since the VRO is concerned about his own village and the village is the unit of each cadastre, it often results in boundary disputes between the adjacent villages.
- Transfer of VRO from one village to another results in information losses, as accumulated local knowledge is lost.
- Maps are printed on paper or are cloth-bound which are subject to deterioration over a period of time.

- Since the records and maps are physical entities, they require a large space for storage.
- Each state has its land records in its own local language. The attributes maintained in each state are also not uniform.
- The upkeep of records and maps requires physical survey by the VRO. The VRO being a government employee has a retirement age of 58. The task of physical survey is a tough one requiring a sound healthy person. This often results in lethargy and unwillingness on part of the VRO.

All of the above points indicate that the age-old system that we have been following to manage our land resources is far from being efficient, and this leads us to the conclusion that we should be looking for alternatives in order to evolve a fair, user-friendly, robust and efficient land management system.

## LIS: AN ALTERNATIVE

LIS is a powerful tool that can provide an alternative to the existing cadastre-based land management system. An LIS is a digital database essentially having the same two components, that maps or the graphical/ spatial inter-phase and the spatial record attributes created in an RDBMS (Relational Database Management Systems) for each landholding. Both the components are linked together by a unique ID. The objective in creating the LIS is to provide access to the information to land managers, owners and planners.

Since the two are maintained in digital form, it is possible to edit, maintain, rectify and keep the record up-to-date with least effort. It can possibly give a reprieve to both the landowners as well as the institutions of government, which require information for planning and implementation. Whereas people will have access to the information regarding their own holdings, the institutions will be able to extract information for the entire area of their interest. It will also be able to maintain and track changes, detect errors, make online corrections, and make land management a process-dependent activity rather than a people-dependent one.

## NATIONAL LIS

A national LIS is one that caters to the need of ensuring uniformity of land attributes nationwide, as well as helps in preventing disputes over boundaries between villages, districts or states. This, though, is an ambitious proposition and would require mobilisation of vast government and private human resources as well as huge capital investments, but is worth considering. It can be equated to a hydro mega project, which may require huge investments in its inception but once completed can deliver rich dividends over a period of time. The main advantages of a national LIS can be summarised as following:

- It will ensure uniformity of attributes across the nation.
- It will ensure accuracy of calculations of revenues.
- It will ensure accuracy of forecasting crops, yields, etc., for better management.
- It will help planners to optimise the land requirements of any project.
- It will help to accurately determine land acquisition and compensation to be awarded.
- It will help to achieve land use optimisation.
- It will help to track revenue-flows arising from land-related activities.
- It will make the management, upkeep and maintenance of land records available at the click of the mouse.
- It can be used for an efficient disaster assessment and management tool in case of natural calamities.
- A national-level LIS can also help to determine the threshold limit to which each holding can be fragmented, as is evident from studies that fragmentation beyond a certain point results in diminished productivity.
- It will make the overall management of land a process-dependent rather than a people-dependent system.
- It will reduce the overall human resource and infrastructure requirements for the land management.
- Being a digital system it will be less prone to deterioration over a period of time.
- It will be more user-friendly as the information provided will be accurate, readily accessible, impartial and up-to-date.

## WHAT NEEDS TO BE DONE

In order to create LIS, the first and foremost task is to assess everything that needs to be included in the database. A consensus needs to be arrived at on the platform for generating the database (whether RDBMS or GIS platform) as well as attributes to be attached to the land parcels by the concerned authorities looking at the final objective to be achieved.

To reap all the rewards of the LIS and to generate maximum gains out of it, the database structure will have to be defined in the national context. At present different database is available in different places. There is no single source where the entire data is available as a single, cohesive whole. A national-level database can fill this vacuum. Data pertaining to irrigation, catchments, rainfall, crops, temperature, soil type, salinity, land use, revenues, can all be clubbed within the framework of a national LIS.

The exercise should take into confidence not only the settlement officers but also other public departments which can be potential users of this database, such as PWD, health services, municipal authorities, etc. This can also result in cost-sharing of generation of the LIS as these departments will also be sharing its benefits. As the cost projections of an LIS may look prohibitive, pooling of funds by other beneficiaries in the cost of development would be a good idea.

A committee of experts from relevant fields will have to be set up to define its phased implementation. Technical experts will have to decide the best methodology which should be adopted considering the existing available resources and technologies.

It is commonly said that only using DGPS and ETS technologies can help to develop an LIS. The question one has to ponder is the cost and usability of these technologies. In our opinion the process of creating an LIS has to be a combination of both conventional as well as state-of-art technologies, as this approach will provide a cost-effective solution.

Although the initiative of computerising the land records is not entirely alien to the state authorities and many states already have computerised or are in the process of computerising, different platforms/software will make the subsequent task of assimilating the land record information into a single consolidated national land record database more cumbersome. Thus, probable directives from the centre should be enforced to bring about the necessary conversions, so as to enable the development of a national LIS.

One can start with the conversion/digitisation of revenue maps and validate these on ground with total stations and/or conventional plane table surveys to ascertain the accuracy of the digital field boundaries. Once this is done the final digital spatial data can be merged together and can be integrated with the help of DGPS coordinates. Once this is achieved the strong GIS background can deliver a good LIS, as GIS will provide the necessary tools and power for LIS to become a decisive instrument. It is only within the framework of GIS that the LIS can be effectively harnessed.

All the analysis, study of evolving patterns, manipulation of resource assets, concept modelling, risk management and a throng of various activities are all promising scenarios if the LIS adjutant to GIS is used as a national land database.

## LPIS IN THE UK—A CASE STUDY

This project involved creation of a sustainable system for identification of over 500,000 agricultural land parcels to verify subsidy claims by over 18,000 farmers in the UK in view of changing parcel boundaries and ownership, and false claims.

Once such a system is in place, the agricultural council would be able to use it to:

1. develop a GIS based digital Land Parcel Information System (LPIS);
2. effectively track inflow and outflow of land related revenues;
3. reduce effort and time taken in paying and validating subsidies;
4. improve services offered to farmers;
5. take advantage of available technologies to update and amend existent record system; and
6. use remote sensing to minimise the need for inspectors to physically visit farms.

RMSI's role in this project is to develop a GIS-based land identification system. The scope of work in such a project involves capturing agricultural land parcels using the Ordinance Survey Landline and ortho-rectified photographs, and polygon data that is provided by the client, inheriting attributes from the Integrated Administration and Control System (IACS) data is also provided as an input; assigning status flags to the parcels, creation of plot files, and working tables and, finally, alteration of captured parcels as per farmers feedback (see Figure 20.1).

**Figure 20.1**

*Example of the LPIS Viewer Module*

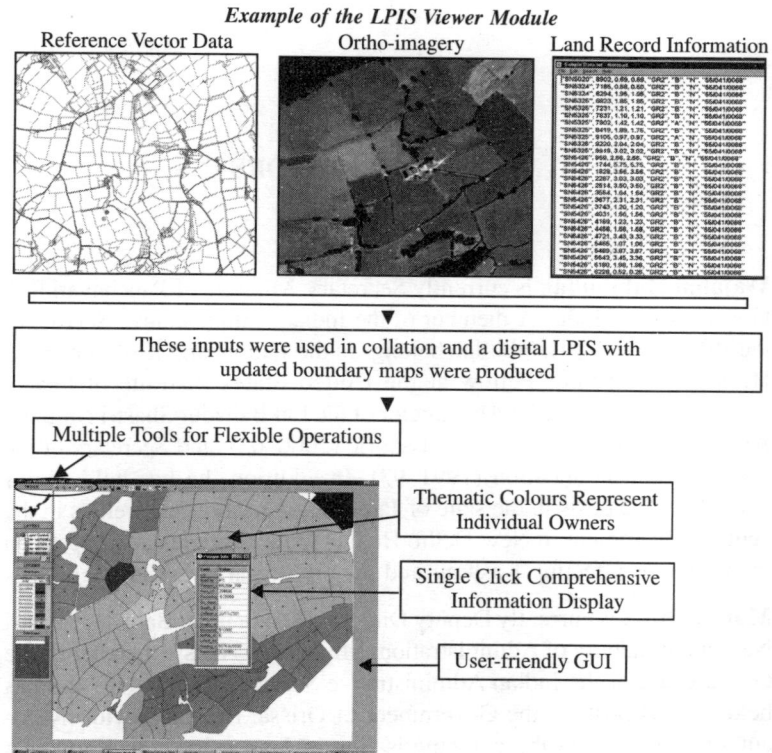

Some of the processes involved after receipt of the inputs were as follows:

1. classifying landline data;
2. grouping of landline layers and extraction of the identified layers containing the centerline of roads;
3. creation of work allocation boundary and interactive editing;
4. final quality assessment and fixing; and
5. auto creation of deliverables.

# About the Editors and Contributors

## ABOUT THE EDITORS

**Wajahat Habibullah** is currently Secretary, Ministry of Panchayati Raj, Government of India. A member of the Indian Administrative Service of the 1968 batch, Mr Habibullah belongs to the Jammu and Kashmir cadre. He has been Senior Fellow at the United States Institute of Peace, Washington, DC (2003–04); Director of the Lal Bahadur Shastri National Academy of Administration, Mussoorie (2000–03); and Secretary of the Rajiv Gandhi Foundation (1991–93). In addition, he has held senior administrative posts in the state of Jammu and Kashmir as well as in the central government in New Delhi. He has written articles and papers on the problems affecting Kashmir and the protection of human rights.

**Manoj Ahuja** is currently Deputy Director (Senior), Lal Bahadur Shastri National Academy of Administration, Mussoorie. He is a member of the Orissa cadre of the Indian Administrative Service (1990 batch) and has held various posts in the Government of Orissa. He has previously co-authored reports on the computerisation of land records in Karnataka and West Bengal. His areas of interest cover e-governance, Panchayati Raj, and computerisation of land records.

## ABOUT THE CONTRIBUTORS

**Mohd. Afzal** is Secretary, State Commission for Backward Classes, Government of Jammu and Kashmir, Srinagar.

**M.K. Agarwal** is a member of the Madhya Pradesh State Civil Services and is presently Additional Collector and ADM, Morena, Madhya Pradesh.

**N. K. Agrawal** is a retired Deputy Surveyor General and Director, Survey of India, Survey Training Institute, Hyderabad.

**P.V. Bhat** is Technical Director, National Informatics Centre (NIC), Bangalore.

**Subhash Bhatnagar** is Professor of Information Technology, Indian Institute of Management, Ahmedabad.

**Rajeev Chawla** is an IAS officer of the Karnataka cadre and is at present Special Secretary, Revenue Department (Bhoomi), Government of Karnataka, Bangalore.

**C.R. Das** is Deputy Director of Surveys, Government of West Bengal, Kolkata.

**Indu Gupta** is State Informatics Officer, NIC, Rajasthan State Unit, Jaipur.

**Ishfaq A. Khan** is Nodal Officer (Computerisation), Revenue Department, Government of Jammu and Kashmir, Srinagar.

**Rajesh Kumar** is an IAS officer of the Bihar cadre and is presently Sub-Divisional Officer, Madhpura, Bihar.

**S. Suresh Kumar** is an IAS officer of the West Bengal cadre and is presently Special Secretary, Health & Family Welfare Department, Government of West Bengal, Kolkata.

**Sunil Kumar** is Technical Director and State Informatics Officer, NIC, Punjab State Unit, Chandigarh.

**S.D. Meena** is an IAS officer of the Karnataka cadre and is presently Director, Land Reforms Division, Land Resources Department, Ministry of Rural Development, Government of India, New Delhi.

**S. K. Narula** is Assistant Commissioner, Land Reforms Division, Land Resources Department, Ministry of Rural Development, Government of India, New Delhi.

**T. Radha** is an IAS officer of the Andhra Pradesh cadre and is presently Finance Secretary, Government of Andhra Pradesh, Hyderabad.

**A. Rama Mohan Rao** is Senior Technical Director, NIC, Hyderabad.

**Alok Sharma** is Manager (GIS), RMSI Private Limited, Noida.

**Lokesh Shrivastav** is a former Senior Engineer, RMSI Private Limited, Noida, India.

**D.R. Shukla** is Technical Director, LRIS Division, NIC, New Delhi.

**A.P. Singh** is Researcher, Centre for Rural Studies, Lal Bahadur Shastri National Academy of Administration, Mussoorie.

**Maha Singh** is an IAS officer of the Haryana cadre and is presently Commissioner, Ambala division, Ambala.

**O.P. Sisodia** is retired Assistant Commissioner, Land Reforms Division, Land Resources Department, Ministry of Rural Development, Government of India, New Delhi.

**Vinay Thakur** is Technical Director, LRIS Division, NIC, New Delhi.

**R.M. Vardhan** is Director, Settlement and Land Records, Government of Goa, Panaji.

# Index

# Land Reforms in India

41 T